The

Reference Shelf®

U.S. National Debate Topic 2012–2013

Transportation Infrastructure

Edited by

Tyler Weidler

The Reference Shelf
Volume 84 • Number 3
H. W. Wilson
A Division of EBSCO Publishing, Inc.
Ipswich, Massachusetts
2012

388
U.S.

9/12

The Reference Shelf

The books in this series contain reprints of articles, excerpts from books, addresses on current issues, and studies of social trends in the United States and other countries. There are six separately bound numbers in each volume, all of which are usually published in the same calendar year. Numbers one through five are each devoted to a single subject, providing background information and discussion from various points of view and concluding with an index and comprehensive bibliography that lists books, pamphlets, and articles on the subject. The final number of each volume is a collection of recent speeches, and it contains a cumulative speaker index. Books in the series may be purchased individually or on subscription.

Library of Congress Cataloging-in-Publication Data

U.S. national debate topic 2012-2013 : transportation infrastructure / edited by Tyler Weidler.
    p. cm. — (The reference shelf ; v. 84, no. 3)
  Includes bibliographical references and index.
    ISBN 978-0-8242-1117-2 (issue 3, pbk.) — ISBN 978-0-8242-1249-0 (v. 84) 1. Transportation—United States. 2. Transportation and state—United States. 3. Infrastructure (Economics)—United States. I. Weidler, Tyler. II. Title: Transportation infrastructure.
  HE206.2.U22 2012
  388.0973--dc23

(4) Roads

2012009695

Cover: Brooklyn Bridge and Manhattan Skyline, New York City. © Paul Souders/Corbis

Visit: www.salempress.com/hwwilson

Printed in the United States of America

Contents

4

Airports and Aviation

5

Railways

6

Seaports and Waterways

7

Future of Transportation

Preface: The Federal Government and Transportation Infrastructure Spending

By Tyler Wiedler

The US transportation system is a complex national concern, closely tied to our nation's economy, defense, and national security. Paying for its construction and maintenance has become an even more complicated political issue in the early twenty-first century. Historically, the cost burden of infrastructure spending fell to private business and local governments interested in economic development. Eventually though, the federal government became more involved and financially invested as the national economy grew and issues of mobility and access became vital to the nation's interests.

In 2012, the National Forensic League resolved that its policy debate topic would be: "The United States federal government should substantially increase its transportation infrastructure investment in the United States." The policy topic implies agreement among most Americans that the nation's infrastructure needs the investment; the complication facing the country is how to pay for it.

In the nineteenth century, canal systems, water transport, and rail were the most efficient means of transporting goods to market. By the 1850s, though, rail transport was the primary means of transporting commercial products from one place to another. Railways were constructed and owned by privately held corporations, with investment from state governments seeking the economic benefits of their success. In the antebellum years, state governments financed about a quarter of all rail construction. In the 1860s, the federal government helped railroads construct lines by setting up federal land grants, which would allow the railways to sell land along the route in order to raise construction funds.

By far the biggest and most celebrated of these rail construction projects was the First Transcontinental Railroad, constructed between 1863 and 1869, connecting the east and west coasts of the United States and facilitating the flow of trade from the Atlantic to the Pacific Oceans. The transcontinental line was a significant factor in the development of the US economy, costing roughly $50 million to build—the most expensive project ever undertaken by the US government to that time. Its construction was widely hailed as an engineering and technological marvel, reducing a journey that previously took upwards of six months in a wagon to only eight days.

Throughout the latter 1800s, more extensive railways were constructed in the industrial Northeast and Midwest, until nearly all farms were within easy distance of a rail system. The South, with its economy focused heavily on agriculture, did not have a well-developed rail system, depending on short rail systems connected to water transport systems for the transport of goods. During the Civil War, the

North's extensive rail transportation system became a pivotal strategic advantage, as those materials needed for rail transport were largely produced in the North and the blockade prevented the South from accessing necessary materials. Additionally, the strategic destruction of rail lines on either side hampered the movement of necessary arms and military equipment.

While the federal government assumed the role of connecting cities on each side of the country via railroad during the mid 1800s, it left the construction of roads to the states and cities. Interest in wholesale improvements to road infrastructure began to gain widespread appeal in the late nineteenth century with the invention of the bicycle. Bicyclists began organizing into riding clubs and advocating for the improvement of rural roads. They enlisted the help of farmers interested in getting their produce to market, as well as engineers and politicians. Their combined efforts would become the Good Roads Movement, with their first success in New Jersey in 1891, when legislation at the state level supported county efforts at road construction. At the federal level, the Office of Road Inquiry was founded in 1893 to provide guidance to states and local governments on road improvement.

Between 1913 and 1914, Henry Ford made available the first mass-produced, affordable automobile, the Model T Ford, and with it, the primary means of transportation in America permanently shifted. The American public fully embraced the automobile, and the first large-scale road construction project began with the Lincoln Highway Association (LHA), a group of private individuals committed to a transcontinental highway. Beginning in 1912, the LHA worked toward funding the construction of "seedling miles," or sections of road that would stand as an example to the public of the possible future of highway construction. The leaders of the LHA thought that the construction of these seedling miles would prompt public pressure on local, state, and federal officials to consider public funding for the construction of paved roadways. In building their seedling miles, they enlisted the support of good-roads supporters and local businesses, and secured the donation of concrete from concrete manufacturers. Seedling miles were constructed in rural areas to provide a stark contrast with the existing roads.

LHA efforts were largely successful, as localities that benefited from the seedling miles sought to extend them, and those that failed to secure a seedling mile sought to remedy the situation through local efforts at road construction. The Lincoln Highway was completed in 1913, and has been in continual use ever since, connecting New York City with San Francisco, California, and covering more than 3,000 miles. The successful construction of the Lincoln Highway and the growing accessibility of automobiles to the average American brought increased attention to the state of the nation's roads. The many failed initiatives at the federal level to fund road construction began to receive increased attention, and public support for such initiatives grew.

In 1916 the US Congress passed the Federal Aid Road Act, marking the beginning of state and federal partnerships to improve infrastructure. The roads constructed under the 1916 legislation largely served local needs, focusing energy on rural areas rather than cross-state highways that would aid long-distance travel.

In the 1930s, President Franklin Delano Roosevelt made significant strides in infrastructure development through the Public Works Administration, building dams, bridges, and other public infrastructure in order to get the American public back to work during the Great Depression. He also began pushing legislation for the development and construction of a superhighway system. As was the case with earlier efforts, apportionment of funds among the states caused the most conflict, and prevented any significant action until the 1950s, when President Dwight D. Eisenhower drew attention to the national security and defense needs that a highway system would address.

In 1956, Eisenhower signed the Federal Aid Highway Act of 1956, which gave birth to our present Interstate Highway System. In 1991, it was estimated that the Interstate System cost the federal government $114.3 billion, with states covering about 10 percent of costs and the federal government bearing the rest. Eisenhower insisted that the funding of the highways would not add to the national debt, and the funding comes from user fees, which include fuel taxes, as well as taxes on tires, truck and trailer sales, and fees for heavy vehicle use.

Post-Depression and postwar infrastructure spending helped develop the national economy that we enjoy today, but what is clear to many is that our infrastructure is crumbling and cannot meet the needs of a twenty-first-century global economy. According to a 2009 assessment of US transportation infrastructure conducted by the American Society of Civil Engineers (ASCE), the country earned a cumulative D for the condition of its roads, bridges, dams, waterways, aviation facilities, transit infrastructure, and other concerns. The organization called for an investment of $2.2 trillion over five years in order to remedy the situation.

Infrastructure is directly tied to our economic competitiveness. At present, roads are overcrowded, causing traffic delays and costing the economy $78.2 billion a year. Ports are ill-equipped to handle the size of ships being constructed in anticipation of the Panama Canal expansion project slated for completion in 2014. The nation's aviation system still relies on post–World War II technology. In order for the United States to remain competitive, it has to address transportation infrastructure spending immediately. Our greatest economic competitor, China, has made significant infrastructure investments. In 2008, it committed to a $586 billion stimulus program that included infrastructure, although some question the level of debt the country has incurred in implementing the stimulus package.

The methods of funding US transportation infrastructure have not changed over the years, and because of the increased fuel efficiency of many cars, gasoline taxes are generating less revenue at the state and federal levels—so the pay-as-you-go model established by Eisenhower no longer allows for the necessary investment needed to improve the infrastructure. Lawmakers find themselves searching for other revenue streams to support much-needed construction.

The Safe, Accountable, Flexible, and Efficient Transportation Equity Act (SAFETEA) of 2005 is the most recent attempt by the federal government to improve its policy on surface transportation, including highway, transit systems, and rail operations. The bill has been renewed on several occasions, but often amid political gamesmanship. In April 2012, Congress reauthorized the transportation bill once again—its ninth reauthorization. While the measure ensures that current projects are not abandoned, it does not address the greater need for a transportation bill overhaul. The real difficulty with temporary measures is that they do not provide certainty that any future funds will be given to the states.

According to the US Government Accountability Office, the government needs to do three things: define clear national goals and interests; create a system that requires performance measures and accountability; and find a sustainable financing model. As of 2012, the system of scrambling for funding through reauthorizations and temporary measures is not sustainable and does not lend itself to a comprehensive and long-term plan.

In March of 2012, the Senate passed a transportation overhaul, hoping that the bipartisan effort would inspire the House to begin working on its own bill. The last House effort was a five-year plan that failed to gain support among the Republican majority. The Senate's bill authorized $109 billion over two years, well below suggested funding, but did present a credit assistance program that proponents say could provide $30 in private dollars for every dollar in federal aid. Unfortunately, the bill did not address the revenue concerns of the Federal Highway Trust Fund.

The nation's infrastructure is at a critical point, and in an election year, many wonder if Congress has the stomach to advance the necessary changes that will keep the country on a path of global economic competitiveness.

1
Roads and Highways

(Harrison Shull)

Aerial image of the cloverleaf interchange where highway 64 meets I-26 at Hendersonville, North Carolina.

Congressional Road Rage: How to Pay for America's Highways and Roads

By Paul McCaffrey

The backbone of the American transportation infrastructure is the Interstate Highway System. Measuring almost 50,000 miles in length, the vast network was named one of the Seven Wonders of the United States by the American Society of Civil Engineers. Though it composes slightly more than 1 percent of the nation's total public road surface, the Interstate system carries almost 25 percent of the country's passenger transport and nearly 50 percent of its motorized freight. America's highways serve as one of its main movers of people and commerce. Among the major arteries of the system are I-90, which runs from Boston to Seattle, and I-95, which extends from Maine to Miami.

Initially known as the National Defense Highway System (NDHS), the Interstate Highway System developed as part of the Federal Highway Act, which President Dwight David Eisenhower signed into law on June 29, 1956. The legislation stands as one of Eisenhower's signature achievements as president, and one he was uniquely qualified to champion and implement.

In 1919, then-Lieutenant Colonel Eisenhower took part in the First Transcontinental Motor Convoy (FTMC). Leaving from Washington, DC, the motorcade of military vehicles crossed the nation, traveling all the way to San Francisco. The purpose of the mission was informed by the armed forces' experience in World War I. Mechanization had changed the logistics of military transport. In the course of the conflict, motorized vehicles eclipsed railroads and horses as the principal means for moving men and materiel to and from the front. However, roads and bridges that could accommodate foot soldiers, horses, and even conventional automobiles could not hold up under the weight of tanks, trucks, and armored cars. In response, the American military sought to understand what infrastructure difficulties might be involved in transporting an army across a large landmass.

The convoy's roughly 3,250-mile journey took over two months to complete. The motorcade covered approximately 58 miles per day at a speed of roughly 6 miles per hour. The problems encountered along the way are almost too numerous to list. The fleet of vehicles overwhelmed the existing roadways and mostly wooden bridges along the way, and by the end of the trip, the convoy had heavily damaged or destroyed eighty-eight bridges and culverts. In many places, roads were just too narrow to accommodate the convoy's vehicles. Other bridges and stretches of roadway had been admirably designed and built, but had fallen apart due to disrepair. The Lincoln Highway, the nation's principle transcontinental motorway, was criticized as being little more than an "imaginary line."

Nine vehicles were lost in the 230 road accidents experienced along the route: some were swallowed up by quicksand or mud; others were compromised by traffic mishaps. But the toll of the journey was not limited to infrastructure and vehicles. Of the nearly 300 personnel who participated in the trek, twenty-one were listed as casualties before it was over, suffering injury or illness during the course of the mission. The underlying lesson was not lost on the military. The state of American roadways left much to be desired, and constituted a potential national security threat.

Eisenhower's experience in World War II further convinced him of the military importance of sound roadways. In the early stages of American participation in the Allied effort, Eisenhower commanded forces in the North African theatre, where long supply lines, difficult terrain, and an absence of functional roads made for nightmarish logistics.

As military leader during the Allied invasion of France, Eisenhower faced other transport challenges. Once the Nazi's Atlantic Wall protecting the Normandy coast had been breached in the D-Day assault, Allied forces advanced at a snail's pace, hampered by poor roads and Normandy's difficult topography.

When Eisenhower's army entered Germany, however, it gained access to Hitler's autobahn, a system of broad, well-maintained highways that facilitated the movement of military supplies and personnel. Referring to his experiences in later years, Eisenhower commented, "The old [FTMC] convoy had started me thinking about good, two-lane highways, but Germany had made me see the wisdom of broader ribbons across the land."

By the time Eisenhower became president in 1953, the issue of road transportation in the US had taken on increasing importance. The Cold War with the Soviet Union, and the threat of nuclear conflict, reemphasized the necessity of an efficient transportation system as part of a comprehensive national defense strategy. During the early years of his administration, Eisenhower staked much of his political capital on developing such a network. He was not the first to try. A national highway bill had been passed by Congress in the 1940s with the idea of building 40,000 miles of interstate roadways, but the programs that resulted never received the necessary funding, and the system languished. Eisenhower used all his powers of persuasion to see that his highway initiative would not suffer the same fate.

While motivated in part by military necessity, Eisenhower stressed the system's other benefits in promoting the measure. "Our unity as a nation is sustained by free communication of thought and by easy transportation of people and goods," he declared. "The ceaseless flow of information throughout the Republic is matched by individual and commercial movement over a vast system of interconnected highways crisscrossing the country and joining at our national borders with friendly neighbors to the north and south."

In 1956, The Federal-Aid Highway Act was approved by Congress, and Eisenhower signed it into law. Funding for the NHDS came from gas and highway user taxes and was dispersed according to a pay-as-you go formula. A Highway Trust Fund was established to pool the project's resources. Initial estimates pegged the total cost of Interstate construction at around $23 to $27 billion, and estimated that the system could be built within twelve years. States submitted proposed construction initiatives to the federal government. Once these plans were approved, the states would pay to build them and then be reimbursed with money from the Highway Trust Fund. Bond issues would be used on occasion to finance certain projects. Given the importance of the system to national security, the federal government took responsibility for the bulk of the funding, paying roughly 90 percent of the costs. The states covered the remaining 10 percent. According to a 1991 estimate, the final bill for the Interstate System (completed in 1992) was $128.9 billion, with the federal government supplying $114.3 billion of that money.

While the Interstate Highway System took much longer to build than initial estimates, and cost five times more to construct than first planned, it has been widely regarded as a transformative success. It is credited with helping to create the country's economic prosperity of the late twentieth and early twenty-first century. "More than any single action by the government since the end of the war, this one would change the face of America," Eisenhower presciently remarked in 1963. "Its impact on the American economy—the jobs it would produce in manufacturing and construction, the rural areas it would open up—was beyond calculation." In recognition of Eisenhower's integral role in its creation, the National System of Interstate and Defense Highways was renamed the Dwight D. Eisenhower System of Interstate and Defense Highways in 1990.

Despite the many accolades the system has received over the years, it does have its critics. The cost overruns and delays during its construction did not go unnoticed, and some detractors blame the Interstate for catalyzing suburban sprawl and the decline of inner cities, encouraging a national dependence on foreign oil, and a host of other ills. Highway aesthetics have also drawn some negative assessments. The author Charles Kuralt remarked, "It is now possible to travel from coast to coast without seeing anything. From the Interstate, America is all steel guardrails and plastic signs, and every place looks and feels and sounds and smells like every other place."

Today, the Interstate System faces immense challenges. Funding has become a fraught issue in recent years. Since 1993, 22 percent of highway revenue has been raised through a tax on gas of eighteen cents per gallon. Prior to 2000, when gas was much cheaper and cars were less fuel efficient, more gas was consumed and more taxes generated funds to construct and maintain highways. In the past decade, however, fuel-economy standards have improved while gas prices have soared. As a consequence, people are now driving less, in more fuel-efficient vehicles. This has created a shortfall in the Highway Trust Fund. From 2007 to 2010, Highway Trust Fund revenue fell by nearly 15 percent. To make up for the diminishing returns, Congress infused $34 billion in revenue from other sources into the trust fund between 2009 and 2011. Even with that outlay, funding gaps remain. In 2011, the Highway Trust Fund ran a deficit of $8 billion. That figure is expected to rise to $10 billion for 2012.

According to the Congressional Budget Office (CBO), unless other measures are instituted, the Highway Trust Fund could be tapped out by October 2012. This would mean that the states might receive delayed reimbursement—or potentially no reimbursement at all—for their highway projects. In light of the 2008 global financial crisis and the subsequent recession, many states are cash-strapped, so any delay could be painful. As Jack Basso, CFO of the American Association of State Highway and Transportation Official, comments, "This is just straight math—there is no guessing about it . . . A couple of weeks wouldn't cause any big economic disruptions, but if it goes on for a couple of months it becomes a huge cash flow problem for the states."

Meanwhile, the federal government is at an impasse as to how to address the funding deficit. The Obama administration has pledged to find additional revenue, but ruled out raising the tax on gasoline, while congressional Republicans have declared their opposition to injecting more cash into the Highway Trust Fund from other sources. They have proposed raising revenue from domestic energy production, but skeptics doubt such a plan would come close to generating the necessary funds.

The funding shortfall is not limited to the Interstate System. The United States is connected by over four million miles of roads, and many claim these are not being properly maintained. Unlike the Interstate, most of these thoroughfares are the responsibility of state and local governments, so there is no Highway Trust Fund or other federal assistance to fall back on. The scope of the revenue dilemma is a matter of some debate, but the worst-case scenarios suggest that roads are underfunded to the tune of hundreds of billions of dollars

In 2009, the ASCE issued its Report Card for American Infrastructure. American roads and highways received a D–. According to ASCE, 33 percent of major American roads are in mediocre or poor condition; 36 percent of major US highways suffer from congestion. According to the ASCE's diagnosis, American roads required $930 billion in improvements over five years to be brought up to standard. Only an estimated $380.5 billion was budgeted, indicating a shortfall of nearly $550 billion. With the uncertain economic times, a lack of revenue at the state, local, and federal levels, and a widespread aversion to tax increases, it is unlikely the roadways will receive the influx of cash necessary to meet ASCE's standards in the near future.

The consequences of underfunded roads are the same today as they were during the First Transcontinental Motor Convoy. Poorly built and maintained roadways lead to delays, accidents, injuries, and even deaths, exacting a high economic toll, as well as a steep human cost. In 2007 alone, for example, over 41,000 people were killed in automobile accidents, with nearly 2.5 million suffering injuries. Such troubling figures point to the national security dimensions of road and highway conditions. Eisenhower recognized as much more than half a century ago, but he took it one step further, seeing in a national highway network a means of not only defending the country but of unifying it. "Together, the united forces of our communication and transportation systems are dynamic elements in the very name we bear—United States," he remarked. "Without them, we would be a mere alliance of many separate parts."

For What the Tolls Pay

Fair and Efficient Highway Charges

By Rudolph G. Penner
Issues in Science and Technology, March 2006

Hydrogen cars, expensive oil, fuel efficiency standards, and inflation frighten those interested in maintaining and improving U.S. highways. All of these forces could erode the real value of fuel taxes that now are the largest single source of funding for highway programs and an important source of transit funding as well. Because of this worry, the Transportation Research Board convened a committee to carefully examine the future of the fuel tax.

The committee uncovered both good and bad news. The good news is that there is nothing structurally wrong with the fuel tax that will cause the real value of revenues to decline dramatically over the next couple of decades. The bad news is that it is a very crude way to raise revenues for our highway system. Switching to per-mile fees, the committee concluded, would be a much more efficient and equitable approach.

Looking at the good news first, worries that alternative fuels and improving fuel efficiency will undermine the finance system are definitely exaggerated. Radical improvements in efficiency will take a long time to develop and be implemented, and even less radical improvements, such as hybrid engines, affect fuel consumption very slowly because it takes so long for new models to replace old models in the U.S. car fleet. Moreover, Americans are addicted to oil partly because they are addicted to power. If you make an engine more efficient, they will want it bigger. Consequently, improving technology does not reduce real fuel tax revenues per vehicle mile nearly as much as one might think. Indeed, they have been roughly constant for a long time.

One cannot be quite as certain regarding the future price of oil. There is some possibility that demand may erode because of an upward trend in the price of gasoline. Department of Energy projections (which have been generally consistent with those from other prominent sources) are optimistic that the price of oil will not surge over the next 15 years or so. But it must be admitted that energy experts did not anticipate the recent price increase to over $60 per barrel.

However, the evidence strongly suggests that recent oil price increases are as much the result of geopolitical forces as they are the result of fundamental supply shortages. It is true that China and India are becoming major oil consumers

Reprinted with permission from ISSUES IN SCIENCE AND TECHNOLOGY, Penner, "For What the Tolls Pay: Fair and Efficient Highway Charges," Spring 2006, p. 33–35, by the University of Texas at Dallas, Richardson, TX.

as they grow rapidly, but it is also true that supplies are increasing. There may be limited supplies of the type of oil that we pump from the ground today, but as one expert puts it, the sources of oil will just become heavier and heavier. If light crude runs out, we'll turn more to heavy crude. If that becomes scarce, tar sands will be exploited more fully, and if they become expensive, we'll turn to oil shale. In the process, oil will become more expensive, but it will be a slow process. Of course, wars, boycotts, and other disturbances can cause major price spurts that make optimistic forecasts look foolish, but one has no choice but to base long-run forecasts on fundamental trends, and they are not alarming.

The imposition of severe fuel efficiency standards could upset the gasoline-powered apple cart, but new radical regulation seems politically implausible in the near future. Currently, our two political parties are so closely competitive that no one wants to ask the American people to make major sacrifices. We may be addicted to oil, as the president suggests, but as Mae West remarked, "Too much of a good thing can be wonderful."

Inflation Concerns

The possibility of accelerating inflation raises more of a political as opposed to a technical concern. The federal fuel tax is a unit tax. That is to say, it does not vary with the price of gasoline as would a percentage sales tax. Inflation therefore erodes the purchasing power value of the tax. Some, like the Chamber of Commerce (in the National Chamber Foundation's 2005 report "Future Highway and Public Transportation Finance"), have suggested indexing the tax for inflation. However, that solution may not be politically sustainable. Politicians at the state and local levels often suspend indexing if it becomes the least bit painful.

Historically, federal and state politicians have compensated for inflation by periodically raising tax rates. There is some question whether this is possible in the severe anti-tax climate in which we live today, but if this is a problem, it has nothing to do with the basic structure of the fuel tax. It is a political problem afflicting all forms of taxation.

But it should also be noted that politicians have not been strongly pressured by inflation in recent years. First, the inflation rate has been extremely low by historical standards. Second, at the federal level, the government has been able to capture additional revenues for the highway system without raising tax rates. In 1993, the federal gas tax was increased for the express purpose of reducing the deficit. The proceeds were not to be spent on highways or anything else. In 1997, those revenues were redirected into the highway trust fund and are now available to finance highway expenditures. More recently, an ethanol subsidy that was previously financed out of the highway trust fund will, in the future, be financed out of general revenues, thus releasing more resources for highways.

Congress may now have run out of such devices for increasing federal highway funding, which supports about a quarter of all highway spending. It will be interesting to see how Congress reacts in the future, especially if inflation accelerates a bit. In addition, many think that the most recent federal highway bill will more than spend the earmarked revenues that are available, although this is a controversial issue. If true, that, along with more inflation, may pressure Congress to return to its historical practice of occasionally raising the fuel tax when the federal highway program is reauthorized.

Per-Mile Fees

Although there are few reasons to fear a rapid erosion of fuel tax revenues in the near future, major revenue increases also seem unlikely. Congress and the state legislatures could raise more revenue with the gas tax if they chose to do so, but the political opposition is formidable. That makes it unlikely that enough will be spent in the near future to improve highway quality significantly, and the nation will have to continue to live with the current level of congestion. But relying solely on increased highway expenditures to reduce congestion is probably not cost-effective. Congestion must also be attacked by imposing extra costs on those who cause it.

> *Relying solely on increased highway expenditures to reduce congestion is probably not cost-effective. Congestion must also be attacked by imposing extra costs on those who cause it.*

Whether the nation just wants to maintain the quality of the current system or to improve it, there is good reason to reform our current approach to financing. In searching for alternatives, there is a strong argument for sticking with the established principle that users should pay and that the resulting revenues should be dedicated to highway expenditures. The revenues collected should be related to the costs that the vehicle imposes on the system, including congestion costs. In an extreme version of the principle, all the revenues and no more should be spent on highways, but the present practice of dedicating some revenues to mass transit certainly is defensible, because mass transit expenditures benefit highway users by reducing congestion.

The current fuel tax is only vaguely related to the amount of wear and tear that a vehicle imposes on the road, and it does not vary with the level of congestion. Per-mile fees that vary with the type of vehicle and time of day would be much more efficient and equitable.

Fifteen years ago, it was not possible to think about collecting per-mile fees efficiently. Costs included constructing tollbooths, paying toll takers, and most important, waiting in line at the tollgate. New technology holds the promise of virtually eliminating such costs.

In the immediate future, developments such as the EZpass electronic toll collection system (used on many toll roads and bridges throughout the northeastern states) and license plate imaging greatly increase the opportunities for tolling at low cost. We should exploit these opportunities to the extent possible.

In the longer run, global positioning system (GPS) technology makes it theoretically possible to charge for every road in the country, with fees varying by type of vehicle and the level of congestion. Of course, we may never wish to go that far, and much research is necessary before committing to that path. It is necessary to determine what type of technology is most efficient and to develop safeguards that will assure the public that their privacy will be protected. It is also important to resolve the many problems that will arise as we move from the current system of financing to something completely new. The necessary technology is not costless to develop, but it is very cheap. It is possible that GPS systems will be installed in almost all new cars in the near future, even if they are not required for the purpose of levying a per-mile fee.

The president's 2007 budget proposal agrees that new forms of highway funding are desirable. It requests $100 million for a pilot program to involve up to five states in evaluating more efficient pricing systems. The necessary research has already started with an experiment in Oregon, and the Germans have initiated a GPS system for levying fees on trucks on the Autobahn, the national motorway system.

An improved pricing system not only has the potential for greatly increasing the efficiency of using existing roads, it can also be helpful in guiding the allocation of new highway investment. If a certain segment of road is yielding revenues far in excess of the cost of building it, it is a pretty good indication that an expansion of capacity in the area is warranted. If, on the other hand, revenues are not sufficient to pay for costs, any request for new construction should be critically examined.

Although such a system holds the promise of implementing the economist's dream of perfectly pricing the highway system, it would be naive to believe that a perfect system could ever be implemented. The per-mile fees will be set by politicians operating in a political environment. There will be strong pressures to keep fees low just as there are pressures today to avoid fuel tax increases. In some cases, there will be legitimate arguments for subsidies. For example, the nation may choose to subsidize rural road networks much as it now subsidizes mail service to rural areas.

The Equity Argument

Many will question charging per-mile fees out of a concern that it will impose a special hardship on the poor. As the notion of charging for road use is discussed more and more, there are many derogatory comments about "Lexus lanes," as though only the rich would benefit from a reduction in congestion. It can be noted that it is frequently extremely important for poorer people to get to work on time or to pick up their kids from childcare before overtime fees are charged. But such arguments do not resolve the problem. Some people will be worse off as the result of a per-mile fee, and some of the people who are worse off will be poor.

It is not uncommon to face tradeoffs between economic efficiency and a concern for equity. But there are better ways to protect the poor than to prevent a major improvement in the efficiency of our transportation system. If it is determined that fees particularly hurt the poor—and more research on this question is probably warranted, given that the poor also pay the current fuel tax—policies that make the earned income credit or other welfare programs more generous can be considered.

If it is deemed desirable to target additional assistance more precisely on poor highway users, a toll stamp equivalent to the food stamp program might be contemplated, although administrative costs would be very high. It may not be worth it to try for very precise targeting. The basic point is that there are other ways to deal with poverty that are more efficient than not charging properly for roads.

Expanding tolling now would acquaint people with the concept. It is easier to start levying tolls on specific lanes when there are alternative lanes that are free. That will make the public aware of the benefits of congestion pricing. If there are no howls of anguish, politicians might be less inclined to oppose road pricing.

Many years ago, the economist William Vickery began extolling the virtues of per-mile fees that would vary with the level of congestion. Having been trained in engineering originally, he went so far as to provide detailed discussions of complex systems that would put wires under the street for the purpose of measuring the distance traveled by particular cars at different times of the day. He died tragically just before traveling to Stockholm to receive the Nobel Prize in economics. At the time, we were on the edge of developing new technology that could turn his dream into a practical reality at low cost. Wherever he is, he must be smiling.

❖

Rudolph G. Penner is a senior fellow and holds the Arjay and Frances Miller Chair in Public Policy at the Urban Institute in Washington, DC. He chaired the Transportation Research Board committee that produced the report "The Fuel Tax and Alternatives for Transportation Funding" (National Academy Press, 2006).

The Infrastructure Delusion

Getting Nowhere Faster

By Richard W. Fulmer
Freeman: Ideas on Liberty, November 2011

Infrastructure does not an economy make. Highways and railroads, airports and seaports, communications towers and fiber-optic cables are essential for the flow of commerce, but it is the people, goods, and information moving over and through this infrastructure that are the heart of an economy. Overinvestment in roads, bridges, and airports means underinvestment in the productive base that is an economy's life blood. Government spending means more than just an outlay of dollars; it means consuming scarce resources that cannot then be used for other things. Such spending does not increase production; it simply shifts resources into areas where they would not otherwise have gone.

As described in William J. Bernstein's book *The Birth of Plenty: How the Prosperity of the Modern World Was Created*, France's minister of finances under Louis XIV from 1665 to 1683, Jean-Baptiste Colbert, worked tirelessly to expand commerce by improving his country's roads and canals. Unfortunately, trade was hindered by more than potholes—a complex system of internal tariffs was throttling commerce. Colbert tried to dismantle the tariffs but was only partially successful. After his death, "all fiscal restraint was lost. By the end of Louis XIV's reign three decades later, the State had doubled the tolls on the roads and rivers it controlled, and the nation that had once been Europe's breadbasket . . . was bled white . . . " Bad regulations trumped good roads.

During the Great Depression Franklin Roosevelt initiated massive public-works programs to improve the nation's infrastructure in hopes of putting people back to work and jump-starting the economy. The construction efforts were staggering. According to Conrad Black:

> The government hired about 60 percent of the unemployed in public-works and conservation projects that planted a billion trees, saved the whooping crane, modernized rural America, and built such diverse projects as the Cathedral of Learning in Pittsburgh, the Montana state capitol, much of the Chicago lakefront, New York City's Lincoln Tunnel and Triborough Bridge, the Tennessee Valley Authority, and the heroic aircraft carriers Enterprise and Yorktown. They also built or renovated 2,500 hospitals, 45,000 schools, 13,000 parks and playgrounds, 7,800 bridges, 700,000 miles of roads, and a thousand airfields.

Yet these extraordinary accomplishments were not enough to pull the nation out of the Depression. Neither were the millions of jobs generated by this monumental work.

At the same time as he was directing resources away from the private sector, Roosevelt also unleashed upon it a regulatory blizzard that significantly increased the risk of doing business. Higher personal, corporate, excise, and estate taxes; wage and price controls; production restrictions; antitrust lawsuits; and constant experimentation provided few incentives for companies to expand. As in Louis XIV's France, an improved infrastructure could not revive commerce in the face of stifling government regulations.

Enough Roads; Too Many Roadblocks

Today President Barack Obama is touting high-speed rail and other infrastructure improvements as keys to economic renewal. But if massive infrastructure investments were not enough to turn the economy around in the 1930s, they are far less likely to do so today. Because Roosevelt was starting from a lower base his improvements would have had a far greater impact on the economy of his day than would similar work done now. Also, the lighter regulatory burden in the 1930s meant there were projects then that truly were "shovel-ready." Today environmental impact studies, possible archeological finds, and nuisance lawsuits may stall construction for years or halt it completely.

The real roadblock to economic growth is the burgeoning regulatory burden that President Obama, like Roosevelt before him, has placed on business. According to a study by James Gattuso and Diane Katz, "[T]he Obama Administration imposed 75 new major regulations from January 2009 to mid-FY 2011, with annual costs of $38 billion." Hundreds of additional regulations will pour forth from Obamacare, Dodd-Frank, and proposed EPA greenhouse gas restrictions. All this on top of an already monumental regulatory burden imposed by government. A Small Business Administration report estimates the cost of regulatory compliance at over $1.75 trillion in 2008 alone.

Briefly, our current economic woes were triggered by the collapse of a housing bubble, produced by loose monetary policy together with federal pressure on mortgage companies to lend to bad credit risks. When the bubble burst, housing prices fell, causing many homeowners to default on their mortgages. Investment vehicles based on those mortgages lost much of their value, leading to huge investor losses and the failure of some major financial institutions.

Lost in Transition

Absent government interference industry would retool, shifting capital and labor out of home construction and into other areas. Because neither capital nor labor is homogeneous, this shift takes time. Equipment that can be put to other uses may have to be sold or physically moved. Other equipment may have to be modified or scrapped altogether. Workers may need to increase their market value by relocating or by gaining new knowledge and skills. In a recession consumers typically reduce spending and increase savings, thus freeing up the resources needed to complete the shift.

Keynesian economists, however, see both labor and capital as homogeneous, aggregated lumps. Where Austrians see capital in transition Keynesians see "idle capital." Keynesian programs to put that capital back to work only hinder or halt the

> *Goods, people, and information will not flow freely across a nation, regardless of the quality and extent of its infrastructure, if taxes and regulations block their flow.*

needed transition, either leaving capital in its malinvested state or forcing it into the very idleness they seek to remedy. For example, expanding credit may re-inflate the collapsed bubble for a time, leading industry to continue producing unneeded goods. Stimulus spending—whether for infrastructure or other things on the government's wish list—transfers scarce resources from industry to government, further impeding the transition. New laws, enacted to prevent future recessions, make businesses reluctant to invest until the associated regulatory structures are defined—a process that can take years. Once in place the regulations may inhibit capital flow, locking inefficiencies and malinvestment in place and propping up companies that should be allowed to fail. Unemployment insurance and other such programs eliminate or at least reduce workers' incentives to move or reeducate themselves.

The country's problems are not the fault of inadequate highways. They are the result of government intervention: loose monetary policies, programs that encourage unsustainable debt, explicit and implicit guarantees to financial institutions, massive spending that crowds out private investment, oppressive regulations, higher taxes with constant threats of more to come, and political payoffs to "friendly" companies and unions. Building high-speed railroads will not stop the malignant effects of these policies; the solution is to stop the policies.

Goods, people, and information will not flow freely across a nation, regardless of the quality and extent of its infrastructure, if taxes and regulations block their flow. Trade perished in France as Colbert's improved roads and canals were made all but useless by high internal tariffs. Hundreds of thousands of miles of new and rebuilt roads were not enough to move commerce past the regulatory roadblocks that Roosevelt erected. President Obama's proposed high-speed trains—indeed, his latest nearly half-trillion-dollar jobs program—will not pull the country over the mountain of regulations that has been created in the decades since the Great Depression and that Obama has raised to new heights.

A Better New Deal

How can we get the most bang for our transportation buck?
Here are six ideas for the new president and
cash-strapped governors.

By Sam Staley and Adrian Moore
Reason, March 2009

On December 6, 2008, President-elect Barack Obama announced to a nation bat-
tered by job losses and worsening economic conditions that his administration
would make "the single largest new investment in our national infrastructure since
the creation of the federal highway system in the 1950s." The massive public works
stimulus package, estimated at $850 billion as of press time, prompted further com-
parisons to Franklin Delano Roosevelt and his Works Progress Administration. *Time*
magazine had already put Obama on the cover, superimposed over a classic image
of FDR, under the headline "The New New Deal?"; now liberal writers and activists were rubbing their hands together at the prospect of attacking the recession
through federal make-work. Obama did nothing to discourage such hopes. By repairing bridges, expanding transit, and paving roads, he claimed, "we will create
millions of jobs."

There is an important grain of truth in the new president's rhetoric. American
transportation systems are antiquated, better suited to the low-mobility days of the
19th century than the wealth-driven, movement-driven economy of today. Inadequate infrastructure contributes significantly to the burden that traffic congestion
imposes on America's urban economies—about $168 billion each year, according
to Jack Wells, chief economist for the U.S. Department of Transportation. Just
maintaining our roads, highways, and transit systems in "good repair" would mean
increasing current spending by about $36 billion a year, according to reports by
the Department of Transportation and the Transportation Research Board of the
National Academy of Sciences.

So Obama and his policy team will have to do more than think of transportation as a 1930s-style pump-priming program. Sending armies of workers out onto
the highways and byways to fill potholes won't come close to meeting the country's
urgent transport needs, nor would it be a cost-effective use of tax dollars. Rates of
return on highway investments have been falling steadily since the 1970s. Seventy-
three million Americans know this firsthand because they drive on severely congested roads almost every day. Congestion is growing so fast that 58 cities will face

chronic stop-and-go congestion during longer peak hours by 2030, according to a 2006 study by the Reason Foundation, the organization that publishes this magazine.

Instead of the old transportation hub-and-spoke system, in which towns and suburbs are tethered to big cities through straight lines made of concrete or steel, 21st-century systems should operate much more like the Internet, connecting individual nodes in a complex and dynamic web of origins and destinations, customized to the travel needs of individual residents and businesses. Just as the Internet benefits from the networked actions of millions of self-interested parties operating from the ground up, an agile, Web-like transportation network can be created only by unleashing the ideas and money of the private sector and rejecting the Rooseveltian notion that money is spent most efficiently by central planners on job-stuffing projects.

New technologies have made it possible to put the users of roads, highways, and rails in charge of decisions about what facilities get built. That, in turn, can allow future investments to be tied to steady, dependable revenue streams. Such a shift requires the still-controversial step of charging people for the roads and trains they use. With advances in electronic ticketing and boothless toll collection points (which drivers roll past without slowing down) and commuters' increasing willingness to pay their own way out of congestion, reconnecting transportation costs to use is the best method for ensuring that the government doesn't slop money onto roads and tracks that don't serve a meaningful purpose. It's also the only practical way the U.S. can tap into the available private equity—estimated by the investment analysis firm Probitas Partners to total about $90 billion—that could leverage another $200 billion to $300 billion for private infrastructure projects in 2009 alone.

With Obama promising improved infrastructure even while states and municipalities beg Washington to fill rampant budget deficits, reforming the way transport dollars are spent is a necessity, not a luxury. Obama insists that he "won't just throw money at the problem" and that he'll "measure progress by the reforms we make and the results we achieve." It's doubtful that he'll get very far with his current approach, which takes it for granted that it's Washington's responsibility to fund parking policies in Pasadena. But if we can't avoid national meddling into local problems, the feds should at least consider ways to introduce choice, competition, and sound budgeting into our subsidized and centralized transportation system. As the new Congress takes up Obama's stimulus package and weighs the six year, $500-billion-plus transportation bill reauthorization in 2009, the time has never been riper for reform.

If House Transportation and Infrastructure Committee Chairman James Oberstar (D-Minn.) has his way, we will spend about $85 billion for the infrastructure piece of the "stimulus" package. Most of that money will go to state and local governments to spend, and in theory it could do a lot to upgrade our transportation system. But Congress includes all manner of programs in its infrastructure funding, from a broadband Internet backbone to bicycle trails to bridges. Add in the amount needed just to maintain existing infrastructure, and only a fraction of that $85 billion will likely go to build new, useful projects.

A better way forward would be for Congress to a) focus the "stimulus" on crucial projects that provide measurable benefits at least commensurate with their costs, b) favor projects that draw on private investment to get more bang for the buck, and c) require that the funds be spent as advertised, with the benefits documented. Under those conditions, the spending could accomplish something useful. Of course, by the time the feds collect the money from taxpayers, pass it through the big sausage factory of Congress, then pass it again through the Vienna sausage factories of state and local governments,

> *Instead of the old transportation hub-and-spoke system, in which towns and suburbs are tethered to big cities through straight lines made of concrete or steel, 21st-century systems should operate much more like the Internet, connecting individual nodes in a complex and dynamic web of origins and destinations, customized to the travel needs of individual residents and businesses.*

there won't be much left for jobs and economic development. A one-time $85 billion tax relief package probably would stimulate a lot more job growth and consumption.

Wherever the money comes from, transportation planners should pay close attention to the innovations already taking place on the ground. As the stories below indicate, impressive projects are already coming online in places ranging from London to Anchorage to Beijing, providing lessons that the Obama administration would do well to heed.

The No-Rush Hour in Southern California

Afternoon rush hour finds thousands of cars and trucks plodding along at 15 miles per hour on the "free" lanes of Route 91 in Orange County, California. Just a few feet away, on a 10-mile stretch of median road called the 91 Express Lanes, toll-paying motorists fly by at 65 miles per hour. Pricing the roads on an hourly basis allows the 91 Express Lanes to maintain speedy traffic and carry 33 percent more cars per hour than regular lanes.

Twenty years ago, keeping rush-hour speeds at free-flow levels (i.e., 55 miles per hour or faster) in Southern California would have been unimaginable. Now advances in electronic tolling allow governments and private companies to change prices in real time based on traffic levels. Prices increase during congested times to encourage travelers to choose other routes and fall during uncongested times to encourage more use.

In 1989, after the state passed pioneering legislation crafted on ideas first proposed a year earlier by the Reason Foundation's Robert Poole, the California Private Transportation Company built and began operating the 91 Express Lanes. Unfortunately, the company's principal shareholder, Kiewit, decided to leave the toll road business, and the profitable roads were eventually sold in 2003 to the Orange

County Transportation Authority. They still turn a profit for the county and even fund public transit along the corridor.

Every three months, the transportation authority sets new prices for each hour of the day, based on the average hourly traffic volume. The price swings can be dramatic. During rush hour, lanes can cost as much as $1 per mile. At off-peak times, the price per mile can be as low as 12 cents.

Toll rates also change depending on the day of the week. On weekends the lanes are lightly traveled, so the transportation authority sets rates lower during the same period when they might be high on another day. For eastbound traffic in April 2008, a toll at 4 p.m. varied from $2.30 on Sunday for the 10-mile stretch to $8.50 on Thursday or Friday. For westbound traffic, tolls varied from $1.85 to $2.75 for the same time period on different days.

Variable rate tolling is essential because users value free-flow speeds, not the traffic volume prized by too many road planners and engineers. While maximum throughput could be achieved by allowing average speeds to fall to 45 miles per hour, the service that customers are actually willing to pay for is quick access to their jobs, homes, and appointments. Many also pay the premium for the added certainty provided by the reliable express lanes.

Variable pricing provides another increasingly important benefit: It helps identify the sections of the road network in greatest need of new capacity. In effect, it's a market test for the viability of new road investments. The more tolls can cover the costs of new facilities, the more viable the projects should be.

Swifter in San Diego

Orange County's 91 Express Lanes may be the most heralded example of variable pricing in the U.S., but it's not the most advanced. The I-15 express lanes north of San Diego were created about the same time as the ones in Orange County, under the same bill. But the I-15 project uses real time pricing to maintain free-flow speeds. Two reversible lanes in the median of the freeway allow for uninterrupted traffic along an eight-mile corridor. Southbound traffic toward San Diego begins at 5:45 a.m. At noon, the direction of the traffic flow is reversed to accommodate northbound traffic toward Riverside County. Car pools and public transit buses use the lanes for free, but solo drivers pay a toll that's billed electronically.

The I-15 Express Lanes is one of the first cases in which high-occupancy vehicle (HOV) lanes have been converted into high-occupancy toll (HOT) lanes. Minneapolis converted a section of I-394 into a privately operated HOT lane, where variable pricing maintains free-flow speeds. Denver, Salt Lake City, and Houston also have HOT lanes open and running. One of the most ambitious projects is a 56-mile HOT lane outside heavily congested Washington, D.C., on the I-95 and the I-395 beltway in Northern Virginia. Two private companies, Fluor and Transurban, combined to win the $1 billion contract from the Virginia Department of Transportation, based on toll revenues generated by solo drivers paying a premium to drive on uncongested lanes. Eighteen other cities are planning or implementing HOT lane proposals.

Public agencies simply don't have enough money to pay for many of these projects, nor can they borrow at the levels necessary to finance them. So policy makers have brought in private capital to pay for anywhere from 25 percent to 100 percent of construction costs on these projects. The tolls generate enough revenue to cover road maintenance and pay back both private investors and public bondholders.

Market-Rate Parking in Anchorage

Up to 30 percent of congestion in urban central business districts is caused by vehicles cruising around looking for curb parking, according to Donald Shoup, a professor of urban planning at the University of California at Los Angeles. In his 2005 book *The High Cost of Free Parking*, Shoup recommended that cities price parking to reflect market demand, recognizing that the best spots should cost the most. Shoup believes that only about 85 percent of curbside spaces should be filled at any given time, leaving enough spots empty that drivers can readily find parking rather than circle blocks searching and creating more congestion. As demand changes, so would prices, so that some spaces probably would always be empty. New meters would be required, but they would pay for themselves.

Anchorage, Alaska, and Portland, Oregon have adopted the 85 percent target and are using demand-driven pricing to achieve the goal. Two California municipalities, San Francisco and Redwood City, also price their parking spots according to desirability, although they have not adopted an explicit 85 percent occupancy target.

Shoup also advocates cash-out programs for employee parking. In these schemes, rather than pay for employees' parking spaces as a benefit, employers give workers a cash amount roughly equivalent to the value of the subsidy, to spend however they want. A handful of California companies who tried the system found that when employees faced an explicit cash parking cost to weigh against the benefit of driving, the number driving to work fell by 13 percent on average.

These ideas are not without problems. Drivers, who are also voters, are never happy to start paying for something they thought they were getting for free, a fact that obviously doesn't escape the elected officials who determine parking policy. Downtown merchants object because free city-provided parking helps draw business.

There are also pressures to overprice or undersupply parking. The "demand management" culture found in most transportation agencies sees parking as a problem in that it enables driving, which is the behavior planners are always trying to reduce. Parking policies often function as a tool for discouraging mobility, rather than a crucial adjunct to the road network that could be tweaked to produce significantly less congestion.

That said, market-based parking prices have worked in many places that have tried them. Such a scheme in Old Town Pasadena, California, not only reduced congestion but improved access to, and total spending in, the shopping and entertainment district.

Traffic Jumping in Manhattan

Most of the people causing gridlock in Manhattan don't even want to be on the island in the first place. Many drivers are merely passing through the borough on their way to destinations outside or on the outskirts of the world's most famous chunk of bedrock.

The local roadway network, unfortunately, does not allow them to bypass one of the country's most congested city centers. Instead, motorists are crammed together, crosstown travelers with locals. Many become box blockers, drivers who effectively close intersections when the traffic backs up, preventing cross traffic from moving through.

Few U.S. cities pose a bigger challenge to adding physical road capacity than New York City, Manhattan in particular. Many people, including elected officials and transportation planners, simply presume that the capacity cannot be increased, so they rely exclusively on transit and law enforcement approaches to manage traffic and "tame" bad driver behavior. Despite their learned pessimism, several opportunities exist to add physical road space in Manhattan and other dense urban areas where right of way is scarce and expensive.

In many cities across the world, including Beijing, Paris, and Washington, commuters can avoid stopping at intersections by either driving over or under them using "queue jumpers"—short elevated or underground roads. In New York, the Murray Hill Tunnel already serves this function, allowing express traffic to bypass the locals. The tunnel, which carries two lanes of car traffic from East 33rd Street to East 41st Street, is a great way to avoid the congestion on Park Avenue.

Queue jumpers and tunnels often make sense in dense urban spaces and neighborhoods, as well as areas constrained by environmentally sensitive surface factors, because they operate within existing rights of way. Thus the use of eminent domain is limited, which is a major benefit in streamlining construction and honoring property rights alongside major thoroughfares.

Cities such as Paris, Sydney, Melbourne, Tokyo, and even Tampa, Florida, have upgraded beyond queue jumpers to provide longer underground and above-ground motorways. While much of a metropolitan area is packed with subway and train tunnels and other utilities, elevated facilities need only airspace. Furthermore, on the western edge of Manhattan, there are no serious underground obstructions from the Battery to the George Washington Bridge that would prevent building express intersection bypasses. Various east-west streets are also free of subway tunnels. And as Frank Sinatra sang, if you can make it in New York, you can make it anywhere.

Watching Over You in London

Around 300,000 traffic signals turn red, green, and yellow every day in the United States. According to the Institute of Traffic Engineers, a leading professional association, three-quarters of these could be improved by updating equipment or improving timing. The institute surveyed 378 traffic agencies in 49 states and discovered that only a third actively monitor traffic signals for accidents, signal malfunctions, or cars having to wait more than one cycle to get through an intersection.

Traffic light optimization—timing and synchronizing lights to minimize delay at intersections—can improve traffic flow significantly, reducing stops by as much as 40 percent, gas consumption by as much as 10 percent, emissions by as much as 22 percent, and travel times by as much as 25 percent, according to the institute.

In London the regional transportation agency uses 1,200 cameras to watch over the city's streets through a Traffic Control Centre. (These cameras, unlike others found in the English capital, are used solely for traffic and safety monitoring, and do not record anything.) If there's an incident—anything from a fender bender to a celebration of England's rugby team at Trafalgar Square—staffers can reset traffic lights remotely to improve flow, sometimes varying signal lengths by just a few seconds to smooth things out further along the network. As with road pricing, technical control of signals allows real-time changes to the system to help cars and trucks move more smoothly, based on the ebb and flow of traffic.

This strategy is comparatively cheap. One billion dollars allocated to the largest cities in each of the 50 states to coordinate the timing of traffic lights at intersections could significantly improve signal operations and traffic flow on arterials and other major roads. Since the early 1980s, a statewide California program has optimized more than 3,000 signals; the state estimates that the benefits of increased circulation and traffic flow in terms of travel time, reduced delays, and reduced stops at intersections outweighed costs by 58 to 1. A 1995 study by the Texas Transportation Institute, one of the nation's leading research centers on congestion, traffic management, and transportation policy reform, looked at 26 similar projects in Texas. It found a signal optimization benefit-to-cost ratio of 38 to 1. Although Texas officials spent only $1.7 million combined on the optimization projects, they were able to cut fuel consumption by 13 percent, stops by 9 percent, and delays by 19 percent.

President Obama says he wants to reduce car emissions. Few changes could have a more immediate impact on that goal than improving traffic flow, since stop-and-go traffic requires cars and trucks to burn more fuel at inefficiently slow speeds.

Night Shift in Indiana

The average value of time for each person on the road is $14.60 per hour, according to the Texas Transportation Institute. So a repaving project that causes 40,000 people 15 minutes of delay each day for a week can impose $1 million in largely uncounted costs.

Performing road maintenance often means closing one or more lanes of a road, which can cause long delays during rush hour and other times of the day. Since construction work, which is mostly maintenance, causes between 8 percent and 27 percent of all delays in a typical large city, according to the Transportation Research Board, these costs are not uncommon.

There are a number of strategies to avoid or minimize congestion increases from maintenance work. The most effective is to do most of the work during low-traffic times such as nights and weekends. That can cost a bit more on the government balance sheet, since workers may demand higher pay to work night shifts, but the real-world benefits can be much greater.

A good way to encourage off-hour scheduling is making it an important part of maintenance contracts and having companies' bids include incentives to avoid traffic delays. According to a 1998 report in Public Roads, the Indiana Department of Transportation had bidders for an Interstate 70 rehabilitation job include in their proposals the cost of traffic delays caused by the road work. As a result, the winning contractor finished the work almost two months ahead of schedule, with one-third fewer lane closures than expected, saving travelers between $1 million and $1.5 million in fuel, time, and other user costs.

❖

Sam Staley is director of urban policy at the Reason Foundation. Adrian Moore is vice president of research at the Reason Foundation. They are co-authors of Mobility First: A New Vision for Transportation in a Globally Competitive 21st Century *(Rowman & Littlefield, 2008).*

Federal Roadblocks

A saner regulatory regime would help us update our transportation infrastructure

By Robert Verbruggen
National Review, February 9, 2009

As part of his stimulus plan—which in total adds up to nearly $1 trillion—President Obama has proposed investing $85 billion in the nation's infrastructure.

Many have asked: Why not spend more in this area? U.S. infrastructure is under severe stress, with highways congested and roads and bridges in need of repair, and Obama's planned investments will hardly make a dent in the problem. The U.S. will need to spend $225 billion annually for a half century to "upgrade our existing transportation network . . . [and build] more advanced facilities," according to the government's National Surface Transportation Policy and Revenue Study Commission.

One likely reason for Obama's modest goal: regulation. The theory behind the stimulus is that *immediately* pumping money into the economy can pull the country out of a recession—and by the time many projects jump their various regulatory hurdles, it will be too late. To the degree these hurdles are necessary, the delays they cause are acceptable. But many of the regulations burdening construction projects give no apparent benefit.

The biggest culprit is the National Environmental Policy Act (NEPA), enacted in 1970. The act seems sensible enough: It doesn't even prohibit anything. It just states that for all federally funded projects, builders must explain how the construction could harm the environment, whether there are less harmful alternatives, and what the builders plan to do to mitigate the harm. They must also allow the public to comment.

Thousands of times each year, this process takes the form of an "Environmental Assessment" document, and hundreds of times, the more detailed "Environmental Impact Statement" is needed. EAs add about 1.4 percent to a project's construction costs, and EISs add about 2.3 percent, according to a study by the National Cooperative Highway Research Program. When a project falls under a "categorical exclusion"—that is, it's a common type of project known to have no serious environmental impact, so no review is necessary—obtaining the exclusion adds only about 1.1 percent.

NEPA isn't always such a mild nuisance, however. In 1989's *Robertson v. Methow Valley Citizens Council*, the Supreme Court confirmed that the law is "procedural" rather than "substantive," mandating only that those executing federal projects document potential environmental harm. But this leaves a window open for abuse, and gives builders a big reason to worry—if an activist group can point to some flaw, real or imagined, in a builder's NEPA process, it can file a lawsuit and tie up construction.

In 2005, A. Kathleen Craft of Nevada's Frehner Construction testified about such lawsuits before the House Committee on Resources (on behalf of the American Road and Transportation Builders Association, or ARTBA, a construction-industry interest group). At the time, the committee was considering various changes to NEPA.

Craft's company had obtained a final Environmental Impact Statement and begun widening U.S. 95 (outside Las Vegas) in 1999, but in 2004, a Sierra Club lawsuit halted the process. The Sierra Club alleged that car exhaust from the highway would hurt those living nearby. Craft suggested a time limit for complaints, and a requirement that complaints deal only with issues raised during the public-comment period. A subsequent law has put a 180-day deadline in place for activists to challenge approvals, but they still aren't required to limit their suits to issues that actually came up during the NEPA-required debate time. They're free to keep silent about their grievances until after the final impact statement, and then complain that the statement doesn't address their problems.

> *Many of the regulations burdening construction projects give no apparent benefit.*

To be fair, the committee's report concluded that fewer than 1 percent of NEPA decisions produced lawsuits, and that in 93 percent of those lawsuits, judges didn't issue injunctions. But the mere threat of a lawsuit is enough to scare potential builders into bulletproofing their plans. In 2000, the average Environmental Impact Statement was 742 pages long—too long for most citizens to read, defeating the purpose of public comment, and not a good use of anyone's time.

And of course, NEPA itself is only part of the story. Projects that receive federal funding must first go through a state planning process. Then, during the NEPA process, the builders must explain how they plan to follow other regulations. "If you touch a body of water, which is pretty broadly defined, you have to get a Clean Water Act permit. If you have endangered species, you have to deal with that. If you're disrupting a historic property, there's a whole other regime for that," says Tyler Duvall, who was acting undersecretary for policy in the Department of Transportation in the Bush administration. "NEPA is kind of an umbrella for all of those."

The Endangered Species Act in particular can be a problem. Sometimes it halts construction that might harm specific types of wildlife, but more often it's the ESA *process* that presents an unnecessary burden. Until Bush changed the policy last month, federal agencies couldn't review projects themselves, but had to turn to the federal wildlife agencies, even when there was clearly no threat to any endangered species—a requirement Obama hopes to restore.

Not to mention that private environmental groups like to sue under the ESA. In December of 2008, the Center for Biological Diversity teamed up with Greenpeace and the Defenders of Wildlife to contest Bush's aforementioned change to agency-review procedures. Earlier, it had filed suit against the Department of the Interior concerning 55 species in 28 states, spread over 8.7 million acres whose protection had been removed.

Also, states have their own environmental laws. California often leads in this regard, and currently, strict emissions regulations there have made it difficult for the construction industry to use equipment and heavy machinery. In addition, local governments need to approve projects.

Funding creates still more delays, as every money source can bring with it regulatory baggage. "Federal investment is about 45 percent of transportation investment nationwide," says Jeffrey L. Solsby, director of public affairs for ARTBA, the construction industry group. "The rest comes from state and local sources, and many governments fund projects on a multi-year basis."

Thanks to NEPA and other federal regulations, many states forgo federal funding on some projects to avoid delays and other costs, according to a December 2008 report by the Government Accountability Office. In addition to complying with NEPA, projects that receive federal money must pay workers the "prevailing wage" under the Davis-Bacon Act, hire minority contractors under the Disadvantaged Business Enterprise program, and buy only American steel under the Buy America program. By the GAO's count, 39 state departments of transportation have used only non-federal money on projects that were eligible for federal programs, and 33 of them had done so because of NEPA.

For transportation projects that receive federal funding, it takes a long time to wade through all this red tape. Environmental Assessments and Environmental Impact Statements do a lot of the damage: Between 2003 and 2008, the median EA completion time fluctuated between about 20 and 30 months; the median EIS time between 50 and 70. Even if the Federal Highway Administration hit its stated targets, the median EA would take a year, the median EIS three. There is absolutely no way to stimulate the economy with new projects requiring these assessments.

All told, major highway projects take an average of 13 years, start to finish, according to the Federal Highway Administration. This doesn't have to be the case: After the I-35W bridge in Minnesota collapsed, it took about a year to rebuild, thanks to a categorical exclusion from NEPA requirements (which itself was rushed through, taking only three weeks instead of the normal three to six months). Of course, it takes time to investigate and approve new projects, as opposed to rebuilding, so not all projects can or should qualify for such exclusions. But the current delay for Environmental Assessments and Environmental Impact Statements is "simply too long," as the National Surface Transportation Policy and Revenue Study Commission has stated.

President Obama, not to mention state and local governments, could build a lot more a lot faster under a saner regulatory regime. Once he spends his trillion dollars, he might think about establishing one.

2

Bridges

The Robert F. Kennedy Bridge, which spans from the borough of Queens toward Manhattan, is seen following a ceremony renaming the bridge after the senator on November 19, 2008, in New York City. The bridge connects three of the boroughs of the city and was completed in 1936.

The Golden Gate Bridge at 75

Innovation, Economics, and the Challenges Today

By Paul McCaffrey

On May 27, 2012, San Francisco's Golden Gate Bridge turned seventy-five years old. The anniversary marked a moment worthy of celebration. Of all the bridges in the world, the Golden Gate is one of the most beautiful and iconic, standing as a signal of achievement in American engineering. The American Society of Civil Engineers (ASCE) declared the breathtaking span—which connects the city of San Francisco, California, with Marin County to the north—one of the Seven Wonders of the Modern World. Though the bridge took a mere four years to construct, the planning phase lasted well over a decade.

A bridge across the Golden Gate, the narrow strait connecting the Pacific Ocean with San Francisco Bay, had been proposed as early as the 1860s, but most dismissed the idea as a farfetched pipe dream. The bridge would have to extend over 4,000 feet and withstand gale force winds, violent ocean currents, and earthquakes. Such an engineering feat was beyond the capacity of nineteenth-century technology.

During the first two decades of the twentieth century, the need for the bridge became increasingly acute. As the population of San Francisco and the outlying area expanded, growing numbers of people needed to get back and forth across the strait, and the various ferry services struggled to keep up with demand. As a consequence, in 1916, James Wilkins, a San Francisco newspaper editor, devised and implemented an editorial campaign dedicated to promoting the construction of the bridge. Michael M. O'Shaughnessy, San Francisco's chief engineer, was paying attention and reached out to experts across the country to determine whether such a scheme was feasible.

The general consensus among the engineers of the day was that building such a span was either impossible or too expensive to be cost-effective. Estimates at the time envisioned a price tag of $100 million. But one engineer, Joseph Baermann Strauss, had a different take: not only was a bridge across the Golden Gate a realizable dream, it could be built for less than $30 million. Born in Ohio, Strauss already had an accomplished career: as an engineer, he had had a hand in designing almost 400 bridges, but the Golden Gate would be his masterpiece.

Strauss laid out his initial proposal to O'Shaughnessy in June 1921. According to his calculations, the bridge could be built for $27 million. Once his plans were submitted, Strauss shifted gears and started working to promote the project. The funding question was the major dilemma. The San Francisco–Oakland Bay Bridge connecting San Francisco and Oakland was already in the works and drawing much of the available resources of the federal and state governments. As a consequence, it would be another twelve years before ground could be broken on the Golden Gate Bridge.

To secure the necessary funding, O'Shaughnessy and other San Franciscans decided to bring in other stakeholders who stood to benefit from the bridge to help in its construction. With representatives from the northern counties that would be serviced by the span, they formed the Association for Bridging the Gate in 1923. The California legislature subsequently passed the Golden Gate Bridge and Highway District Act, which gave the association and its affiliated counties authority to issue bonds and borrow money in order to construct the bridge.

With the financial and institutional structures in place, the Association now needed the approval of the federal government. The US War Department owned the land on both ends of the proposed bridge and had authority over the shipping lanes. In order to proceed with construction, the War Department had to conclude that the financing was in place to build the bridge and that the span would not interfere with military navigation or constitute a threat to commercial sea traffic.

San Francisco and Marin County presented their bridge-building plans to the War Department in 1924. Based on the strength of the proposals and the overwhelming support they enjoyed from the affected communities, Secretary of War John W. Weeks signed off on the initiative in December 1924.

As the project moved forward, local opposition sprang up, inspired largely by the ferry companies, which stood to lose out financially if the span was completed. Bridge opponents voiced concerns about the pace of development and the impact the construction would have on the region's quality of life. These fears were soon overshadowed by increasingly packed ferries and long waits at the ferry terminals. By late 1928, the campaign to stop the bridge had lost its momentum, and on December 4, 1928, representatives from San Francisco, Marin County, and several other Northern California counties formed the Golden Gate Bridge and Highway District. This new body was tasked with raising the money, devising the plans, and finally constructing the bridge.

Chosen as the project's chief engineer, Strauss worked with several other experts to fine tune his earlier designs. Strauss's initial schematic envisioned a hybrid construction, but the design team soon concluded that a long suspension bridge, the longest in the world, would better serve the purpose. Additional engineers were brought in and the final plan was submitted to the District in August 1930.

With permission from the Department of War and the final plans approved, the next step was getting the financing in place. Complicating matters was the onset, in 1929, of the Great Depression. No public money was forthcoming; the bridge had to be built with private funds. To raise the $35 million necessary to construct the span, a bond election was held in 1930. Voters from the Golden Gate Bridge and Highway District approved the bond issue by a roughly three-to-one margin. Those who bought the bonds earned an interest rate of 4.75 percent with the principal to be paid back over the next forty years.

During the next two years, the bond issue secured the necessary financing, and on January 5, 1933, workers broke ground on the Golden Gate Bridge. A marvel of engineering, the span was equally renowned during its construction for the innovative safety measures put in place by it planners. The bridge was among the first construction projects to require that all workers wear hard hats while on the job. Crews also had to pass sobriety tests to ensure that nobody worked while under the influence. A massive safety net was installed across the length of the span to catch any workers that lost their footing and fell. Nineteen men were saved by the net and became members of the so-called "Half Way to Hell Club." Despite such measures, eleven men did lose their lives during the construction of the bridge. Though tragic, the number of deaths was lower than anticipated. At the time, a fatality was expected for every million dollars spent on bridge construction. With a final price tag of $35.5 million, the Golden Gate Bridge set a new standard in safety.

On May 27, 1937, the Golden Gate Bridge was opened to pedestrians for the first time and over 200,000 people showed up to mark the occasion. The next day, on a telegraph signal from President Franklin Delano Roosevelt in the White House, the bridge was opened to vehicular traffic.

In total, the bridge is composed of 83,000 tons of steel. It is 90-feet wide and measures 8,981 feet from one side to the other, with its suspension span running 6,450 feet. The roadway is supported by two 746-foot tall towers spaced 4,200 feet apart and equipped with two primary suspension cables running 7,650 feet long and measuring nearly one meter in diameter. During the bridge's first full year of operation, approximately 3.3 million total crossings were registered; by 2011, that number had increased to over 40 million annually.

Thanks to toll collection, the debts incurred in the bridge's construction were paid off by 1971. Despite the intense weather, ocean currents, and seismic activity, service across the bridge has only been suspended on a handful of occasions. Until 1964, when the Verrazano-Narrows Bridge connecting the New York City boroughs of Brooklyn and Staten Island was completed, the Golden Gate Bridge was the longest suspension bridge in the world. In 2012 it stands as the ninth longest. The bridge's unique color, international orange, was chosen by one of the span's leading architects, Irving Foster Morrow, who felt the tint would blend nicely with the surrounding scenery.

In March 1999, ASCE ranked the bridge second on its list of the twentieth century's top ten construction achievements. While it may not hold the length record anymore, the Golden Gate remains one of the most awe-inspiring bridges ever constructed. But the job was not finished when the bridge opened for business. Maintaining the structure for over seventy-five years has required a great deal of work. The span is currently in the care of a permanent staff of around fifty painters and ironworkers.

Though the Golden Gate Bridge stands among the greatest feats of American engineering, the condition of American bridges in general does not offer the same cause for celebration. The tragic collapse of the I-35W Mississippi River Bridge in Minneapolis, Minnesota, on August 1, 2007, is the most vivid example of the deteriorating state of many American bridges. According to the United States Department of Transportation, in December 2008, over 12 percent of the 600,905 bridges in the

United States were declared structurally deficient, while nearly 15 percent were labeled functionally obsolete. A structurally deficient bridge is one with weight limits and other restrictions that may inhibit the flow of traffic; a functionally obsolete span, on the other hand, is one that is technologically outdated and unable to handle the volume of traffic it is required to accommodate. An additional problem was that these troubled bridges were found predominantly in high-traffic urban areas.

By virtue of these shortcomings, the 2009 ASCE Report Card on American Infrastructure awarded American bridges a grade of C. Most bridges, ASCE pointed out, are designed to work for half a century before they need to be replaced. In the United States, the average age of a bridge in 2009 was forty-three years old, suggesting that the average bridge needed to be replaced sometime within the following seven years. Rolling bridge funding in with the funding of roads and highways, ASCE proposed that a five-year investment of $930 billion was required to bring American bridges, roads, and highways up to code. According to ASCE estimates, funding fell short of that figure by a projected $549.5 billion.

All bridges over twenty feet in length must meet safety standards instituted by the Federal Highway Administration's Office of Bridge Technology. Funding for repairs comes from a variety of state, local, and federal sources. The national government distributes construction and repair funds through its Highway Bridge Replacement and Rehabilitation Program. How much the national government pays out is based on how much the individual states have allotted to bridge construction and repair.

Due to the difficult economic circumstances between 2008 and 2012, funding for bridges has been declining across the board, as federal, state, and local governments have trimmed their budgets to make up for falling tax revenue. Since ASCE issued its 2009 report, most experts believe that bridge conditions have worsened. According to a 2011 study released by the coalition Transportation for America, 11.5 percent of US bridges—69,000 in all—need to be fixed or replaced. The problem was most severe in Pennsylvania, where 5,906 of the state's 22,271 bridges were deemed structurally deficient. Transportation for America declared, "The nation's bridges are aging and traffic demands are increasing, even as state and local revenues are shrinking." The group called for the federal government to step in and increase its share of the funding.

Viewed through the prism of such troubling conditions, the Golden Gate Bridge's 75th anniversary stands out as an even more remarkable occasion. At every stage—whether in its planning, funding, or construction—the bridge's architects embraced innovation and in doing so, achieved historic results, creating one of the world's most memorable structures. Properly applied, the lessons of such an accomplishment might inform efforts to address the current state of American bridges.

Bad Vibrations

By Mason Inman
Science News, November 24, 2007

The ancient craft of bridge design still holds surprises.

In the middle of rush hour on Aug. 1, at 6:04 p.m., traffic zoomed across the westbound span of the I-35 Mississippi River bridge in Minneapolis. By 6:05, the 40-year-old structure had buckled and broken, dumping most of the bridge into the river and killing 13 people. Though it came as a shock, this was in retrospect an accident waiting to happen, experts say. The Minneapolis bridge had been poorly maintained, with cracks in its iron arches that had been patched up over the years. And the bridge's design lacked redundancy.

London's Millennium Bridge swayed alarmingly as soon as the first pedestrians started walking across in 2000, and had to be closed until a fix was devised. Novel bridge designs have surprised engineers with a variety of unexpected behaviors.

"This is a classic example of how . . . a single failure can lead to a collapse," says Spiro Pollalis, a bridge designer who teaches at Harvard University. "At the time [the bridge was built], it was considered an acceptable risk," he adds. "Now we try to be more careful."

Whether because of obsolete design or disrepair, thousands more U.S. bridges are similarly at risk, according to the American Society of Civil Engineers' 2005 "Report Card for America's Infrastructure." Yet the majority of bridges built in the 1950s and 1960s are still holding up, even though they typically carry much more traffic than they were designed to handle.

With increasingly sophisticated computer tools and wind tunnel tests, and more-detailed understanding of steel, concrete, and other materials, engineers have a better grasp than ever of how bridges work. But some recently built bridges have surprised their designers by showing disturbing and unexpected vibrations.

Every new bridge that's different from those that have been built before—with a longer span, say, or a novel design—represents a leap into the unknown. "Until you build structures, they really are like scientific hypotheses," says Henry Petroski, a civil engineer and historian at Duke University in Durham, N.C. "If it's never been done before, no matter how many theoretical supports you have, the proof is only in building it."

Lessons Learned

The most famous bridge collapse in history—caught on film and burned into engineers' memories—was the 1940 failure of the Tacoma Narrows suspension bridge, south of Seattle. Nicknamed "Galloping Gertie" because of the way its roadway wriggled in the wind, the bridge failed spectacularly after being open just 4 months. High winds induced the bridge's extraordinarily slender deck—the horizontal span that carried the roadway—to twist back and forth, wrenching the structure past its breaking point. "That was obviously an inferior design," says Khaled Mahmoud, president of Bridge Technology Consulting in New York City. "It did not provide enough stiffness for the bridge."

The disaster impressed on engineers the need to understand bridges' aerodynamics—that is, the way they respond to wind-generated forces. Today, engineers typically conduct wind tunnel tests of full-scale sections of a bridge's decks and sometimes also of a scale model of the entire bridge, occasionally set in a mock-up of the surrounding landscape. Computer modeling can complement such empirical tests, and allow engineers to factor in the inevitable imperfections in steel beams and other parts, says David Goodyear of the San Francisco engineering firm T.Y. Lin International.

Such methods have not only made traditional bridge designs safer but have allowed architects and engineers to try innovative designs that may be more cost-effective but are also more difficult to analyze.

These trends are behind the increasing popularity of so-called cable-stayed bridges, which typically sport towers of solid concrete that anchor high-tension cables running in straight lines down to the deck, either splayed like the ribs of a handheld fan or parallel to each other like harp strings. Usually the cables run from both sides of the tower down to the roadway in a symmetrical pattern, so the forces pulling on the tower from each side are in balance.

But that general form allows a wide variety of designs. Some cable-stayed bridges have separate spires on either side of the roadway; others have a single tower in the center of the bridge, with cables running to both sides of the roadway. Some have a triangular arch over the roadway. And some even have a leaning tower that balances the tension in the cables with its own weight. Compared with suspension bridges, cable-stayed bridges give engineers much more "freedom of expression," Petroski says.

They're also typically cheaper. A suspension bridge needs large anchors sunk into the ground at both ends to support the tension of the cables. In a cable-stayed bridge, by contrast, tension is balanced where the cables meet at the central tower, and no external anchoring is needed. Such bridges must have taller, thicker towers and stiffer decks than suspension bridges do, but can use thinner, shorter cables.

A recent innovation could make cable-stayed bridges even more attractive. Figg Engineering Group in Tallahassee, Fla., has pioneered a "cradle" in which cables are routed through a curved tube set inside the central tower rather than being anchored to the tower. This seemingly subtle change has big repercussions. It makes the bridge simpler and allows individual strands of a multistrand cable to be pulled out and inspected while the bridge is in use.

With this system "you can test new kinds of cables in the context of a new bridge, and if they fail, you can replace them," says Petroski. On the Penobscot Narrows

Bridge, between Bangor and Brewer, Maine, one of two bridges in the United States that use the cradle system, engineers have installed test strands of carbon-fiber composite in a few of the cables.

Shimmies and Shakes

Although the calamity that befell the Tacoma Narrows bridge has not been repeated, some cable-stayed bridges have suffered wind-induced trouble of a novel kind. In the mid-1980s, reports came in that moderate winds of about 20 to 50 kilometers per hour could set these bridges' cables fluttering. The phenomenon usually happened only during light or moderate rain—something that puzzled engineers for years.

These vibrations can make cables sway by more than a meter at their midpoints—not enough to bring a bridge crashing down, most experts say, but potentially enough to shorten a bridge's life span through wear and tear on the cables and their anchors.

In the early 1990s, a combination of lab tests and field measurements suggested that moderate winds can cause rain to trickle in rivulets down the cables, which typically have a smooth plastic coating. The resulting change in the cable's profile can affect the way it reacts to wind, creating an aerodynamic instability that sets the cable vibrating at some resonant frequency, somewhat like a guitar string. "While the cause is known, it still remains impossible to predict the cable-excitation process from first principles," says Anton Petersen of COWI, an engineering firm in Kongens Lyngby, Denmark, that consults on many of the world's biggest bridges. "The physical mechanism responsible . . . is still an active area of research," he says.

A team led by Emmanuel de Langre at the École Polytechnique in Paris recently developed the first mathematical model to predict how the rivulets will run on a cable vibrating in the wind. Their model, described in the October *Journal of Wind Engineering and Industrial Aerodynamics*, supports earlier ideas that wind pressure, along with friction between the water and the cable, causes the rivulets to form.

Engineers have been installing retrofits to deal with vibrating cables. "We don't have any cases where the problems were not corrected," Harvard's Pollalis says.

One solution has been to add cables that run between the main stay cables. Tying the cables together creates a more complex aerodynamic response and removes the simple resonance that can lead to vibration.

More popular now are dampers, like shock absorbers, that attach to the stay cables near where they connect to the deck. China's Dongting Lake Bridge, a midsize cable-stayed bridge in northeast Hunan Province, was the first to employ a new kind of sophisticated damper incorporating a magnetorheological fluid. When the cables start to vibrate, it triggers the damper to turn on a magnetic field. This causes the fluid—which has iron nanoparticles suspended in it—to stiffen, putting resistance on the cable. Tests show that it works better than earlier dampers, according to a study by Jan-ming Ko and his colleagues at the Hong Kong Polytechnic University in the April 2006 *Journal of Intelligent Material Systems and Structures*. Other researchers are working on subtler ways of fixing these vibrations, using bumps,

> **Hundreds of people surged across, but within minutes, many of them were hugging the handrails as the bridge slithered back and forth like a snake.**

wires, or flanges that wrap in a helix around the cables to break up the flow of water.

Another kind of vibration, familiar but still capable of causing surprises, can afflict pedestrian bridges. Engineers know to design bridges so that they don't have a natural vibration frequency close to 2 Hertz, because that's the frequency that an average person's footsteps hit the ground. Soldiers have long been ordered to break step when crossing a bridge so as not to set it oscillating. Failure to take that precaution seems to have contributed to the collapse of at least two suspension bridges. One in Manchester, England, collapsed in 1831 with 60 soldiers on it, and in 1850 the Dordogne Bridge in France fell, killing more than 220.

A variant of this old problem resurfaced when London's Millennium Bridge opened to fanfare in 2000. Hundreds of people surged across, but within minutes, many of them were hugging the handrails as the bridge slithered back and forth like a snake. After only a couple of days, officials shut the bridge.

The bridge's engineers at the London-based firm Arup studied the bridge, checked the literature, and found that the same thing had happened before on at least a few other pedestrian bridges. However, as they said in a report about the Millennium Bridge, "these cases have not been widely published and as a result the phenomenon has not become known to practicing bridge engineers."

Even after Arup retrofitted the bridge with dampers that prevented the swaying, the reason for it was obscure. Researchers surmised that the instability might begin because of people's tendency to push sideways a little with each step as they walk. In the Nov. 3, 2005 *Nature*, a team led by applied mathematician Steven Strogatz of Cornell University showed how feedback between pedestrians and the bridge could turn this effect into wholesale swaying. A few people falling into step by chance could make the bridge sway a little. Then other people would tend to fall into step because synchronizing one's pace with the bridge is more comfortable than fighting the sway—except that this positive feedback would only make the bridge sway more.

These problems with swaying footbridges and vibrating cables are more of a nuisance than a real danger, most experts say. But it's hard to know what would happen if they weren't dealt with. "Swaying could have led to failure of Millennium Bridge," Petroski says.

Going Further

Despite computer modeling and wind tunnel tests, vibrations in new bridges caused by pedestrians, wind, and rain came as a surprise to engineers. "There's always a question whether scale models really reflect the full bridge," Petroski says. The models are typically built of wood, fishing line, and other materials totally different from steel and concrete, but they are tuned to have stiffness and elasticity similar to what's predicted for the real bridge, says Guy Ferguson of RWDI, a wind-engineering firm in Guelph, Ontario.

Whether computers can supplant empirical models remains debatable. With improvements in computational fluid dynamics to describe wind flows, "maybe in 10 years, [computer simulations] may take over from wind tunnel tests," Goodyear says. But others disagree. "We're still a long way away from that," Ferguson says. "There's so much going on in a wind tunnel—to model it accurately [on a computer] is next to impossible."

Even as computer simulations improve, more surprises could spring up as engineers push bridges to longer spans, and try out simpler, cheaper, or more daring designs. One idea that's been floating around for a few decades is for a buoyant tunnel that sits just under the surface of the water. A team of Italian and Chinese engineers is aiming to build such a tunnel to span the 3-km Jintang Strait on the coast of Zhejiang Province, China. The engineers call it an Archimedes bridge, after the ancient Greek mathematician who first understood the principle of buoyancy.

The Archimedes bridge would stay in place through buoyancy, counteracted by cables tethering it to the floor of whatever body of water it crosses. Such a bridge would be much cheaper than a suspension bridge, and might be the only way to cross spans longer than a few kilometers, argues Federico Mazzolani of the University of Naples in Italy. "In principle, we can cross a span of 20–30 km without any difficulties."

"But nobody wants to be the first one to build it," he adds. For now, Mazzolani and his colleagues are aiming to build a much smaller prototype, a pedestrian bridge in a lake in China, just 100 m long and a couple of meters underwater. "We will use it as a full-scale laboratory," Mazzolani says, to try out the manufacturing and see how the tunnel reacts to vibrations. But he has his sights on distant shores. "After the prototype is built, it will be a revolution in bridge design."

For modest-size bridges, engineers are confident they understand the mechanics well enough to take more liberty with the designs, blurring the line between architecture and engineering, Pollalis argues. "You can take this in two directions," he says. "You can make things cheaper and more efficient, or you can make them more appealing. But people aren't so interested in having things cheaper." The growing popularity of cable-stayed bridges, Petroski argues, is in part because communities want distinctive, signature bridges.

As the recent collapse of the bridge in Minneapolis showed, it's not just the design of a bridge that gives it a long life but also how it's maintained. But the two may be tightly intertwined. "My old adviser . . . used to say, if you want a bridge to last, make it beautiful, because people will want to preserve it," Goodyear says. "If it's ugly, people will want to tear it down."

Whitewashing the I-35W Bridge Collapse

By Barry B. LePatner
USA Today Magazine, May 2011

On Aug. 1, 2007, the I-35W Bridge collapsed during rush hour, killing 13 people, injuring 145, and bringing massive economic disruption to the Twin Cities area. The November 2008 National Transportation Safety Board (NTSB) report, which followed 15 months of investigation, advised the public and transportation officials around the country that the bridge collapse was a one-time occurrence, caused by a design error that had gone undetected at the time of construction. In short, the collapse was a one-off from which no lessons could be learned to avoid future failures. That simply is not the case, as there is a desperate need for reform in the way we fund and maintain the nation's infrastructure.

NTSB tellingly ignored a host of critical factors that were not disclosed to the public or other state bridge operators, thus delegitimizing the efficacy of the report, which masked far more than it revealed about how the bridge was maintained, funded, and operated. NTSB claims that the bridge's collapse was the result of the underdesign of certain gusset plates (metal plates used to connect structural members of a truss and hold them in position at a joint) at six nodes of the deck truss. These should have been an inch thick but, instead, were only half that.

Adding to the stresses on the too-thin gusset plates, the report states, were increases to the bridge's load. According to the NTSB, had all the gusset plates met design standards at the time of construction, then—even with the increased weight from the bridge's additions, the increase in traffic, and the weight of the construction materials and machinery—the collapse would not have occurred.

The reality is that the NTSB's findings virtually ignored 16 years of inspections by the Minnesota Department of Transportation that reflected the steady decline of the bridge. Widespread evidence of corrosion for critical steel members, frozen bearings that locked the structure in place, and cracks throughout the bridge and approach spans rendered its condition "poor," requiring that some of its traffic lanes be closed.

All of these critical factors were highlighted in several outside engineering reports commissioned by the Minnesota DOT. These reports, which detailed the frailties of this fracture-critical bridge—meaning the failure of one structural member would trigger the collapse of the bridge—made a series of recommendations, which went completely unheeded, for addressing the problems resulting from neglected maintenance.

The NTSB report wrongly exonerates the Minnesota DOT. Based on the maintenance history of the I-35W Bridge's extensive wear and tear, corrosion, and signs of incipient failure for many years prior to its collapse, dismissing the DOT of any responsibility for its collapse is inexcusable. Inspections dating back to 2001 identified widespread corrosion and fatigue caused by weather and traffic volume. Recognizing the fragility of the bridge's original fracture-critical design, engineering firm consultants stressed the need for added redundancy to strengthen the bridge. A June 2006 inspection—the last one before the collapse—found cracking and fatigue problems and gave the structure a sufficiency rating of 50%. A rating of 50% or lower pursuant to Federal standards is interpreted to mean that the bridge should be considered for replacement.

The NTSB reported none of these facts. It dismissed any connection between the bridge's collapse and the DOT's maintenance, or its poor condition for a decade and a half prior to its failure. The report said nothing about the DOT's decisionmaking process or whether it had acted prudently in light of the engineering consultants' recommendations to protect the well-documented fragility of the bridge.

> *The reality is that there has been a mass exodus of engineers out of the public sector. It is likely that the lack of engineers, not the decades-old design of the bridge, contributed to its collapse.*

The NTSB's findings were subjected to criticism even before they were published. After Chairman Mark Rosenker made a preliminary announcement concerning the design of the gusset plates, Rep. James Oberstar (D.-Minn.)—chairman of the House Committee on Transportation and Infrastructure, who promptly had introduced a bill to overhaul national bridge inspection procedures following the I-35W disaster—angrily accused the NTSB of rushing to judgment. Right after that in the *Minneapolis-St. Paul Star Tribune*, Jim Carlson, a member of the Minnesota legislature's joint committee on the I-35W Bridge collapse, wrote, "The collapse was not an act of God; it was an error of oversight. Something was missed."

The NTSB report obviously was influenced by politics. On Aug. 14, 2007, the Minnesota legislature appointed a joint committee to investigate the bridge collapse, which hired the law firm Gray Plant Mooty to produce its own report.

Months later, Rosenker appeared at a press conference. Although in his opening statement he was careful to say that "We have not yet determined the probable cause of the accident," he went on to call 16 underdesigned gusset plates the "critical factor that began the process of this collapse." This statement earned him a sharp rebuke from Oberstar, who wrote in a letter to Rosenker that, "Such announcements undermine the process and create the potential for committing the Board to conclusions which will be difficult to change if subsequent investigation suggests other possible conclusions."

Rosenker retracted his statements, but found himself at loggerheads with Oberstar again after the NTSB announced that it would not hold an interim public hearing on the collapse. The three NTSB members—all Republicans—who voted against holding an interim public hearing explained their decision by stating that the NTSB staff feared that, by doing so, time and resources would be taken away from their investigation. Oberstar and the two Democratic members of the NTSB (who issued a dissent from the majority's decision) replied by arguing that performing a thorough and trustworthy investigation was more important than speed. It was no small matter that the head of the Minnesota DOT was Gov. Tim Pawlenty's lieutenant governor, Carol Molnau, who herself was not an engineer experienced in infrastructure management.

The politics surrounding the NTSB investigation certainly provide much fodder for speculation as to the possible motivation of the board's leadership and findings, but it does not require a political orientation to observe that the NTSB report has significant flaws, including errors of apparent neglect or omission as well as of technical understanding.

The NTSB report wrongly places blame on the engineers. The reality is that there has been a mass exodus of engineers out of the public sector. It is likely that the lack of engineers, not the decades-old design of the bridge, contributed to its collapse. The Gray Plant Mooty report pointed to various organizational weaknesses within the DOT that compromised the safety of the bridge: a poor flow of information; bad use of expert advice; and an organizational structure that impeded the maintenance process.

The inadequate flow of information within the DOT was related to the loss of engineering personnel. Placing the primary blame for a failure of this magnitude on engineers was an attack on the profession as a whole. Yet the American Society of Civil Engineers, the largest professional engineering association in the country, has marshaled no protests and has conducted no investigations of its own to challenge this indictment of individual engineers who no longer are around to defend themselves.

The NTSB report does not mention the bridge's rusted bearings. A June 2006 Minnesota DOT inspection noted surface rust corrosion and pack rust connected with the unsound condition of 15% of the paint; numerous problems with the main truss members, including poor weld details, section loss, and flaking rust; and a variety of problems with the floor beam trusses, stringers, truss bearing assemblies, and other components.

While the NTSB findings on the cause of the collapse made no reference to the condition of the bridge bearings, frozen by years of rust, they may have played a contributory role in the collapse. The DOT's inspection reports acknowledge that the I-35W Bridge's members were bent or misaligned, and that critical bearings had been rusted and frozen in place, preventing movement. All of these signs of deterioration should have required close scrutiny, but that never happened.

In reality, the likely cause of the collapse was triggered by a weakness in one of the bottom chords of the design trusses, a finding that appears to have been identified separately by the structural engineering specialists retained by the attorneys for many of the plaintiffs in the civil action against the bridge's contractors and engineers.

What is most important to note about the role of the NTSB is that it failed to serve as a clearinghouse to alert all other state bridge operators about the lessons that should have been learned from this collapse. There still are 7,980 bridges in the nation that are structurally deficient and fracture-critical, each of which is in danger of suffering the same fate as the I-35W span.

To have failed to identify the true causes of the collapse is one notable failure of this governmental agency, but to have ignored the lessons that should be alerting the other 49 states that their citizens, too, are in jeopardy of suffering the same tragic fate is inexcusable. The risks of continuing to pay no heed to our ill-maintained national infrastructure are almost unimaginable. This discussion must turn into a dialogue at every level of government and policymaking. No less than our future national security and ability to retain our global leadership status are at stake.

❖

Barry B. LePatner, founder of the New York based law firm LePatner & Associates LLP, is the author of Too Big to Fall: America's Failing Infrastructure and the Way Forward *and* Broken Buildings, Busted Budgets: How to Fix America's Trillion-Dollar Construction Industry, *as well as the coauthor of* Structural and Foundation Failures.

A Bridge to Somewhere

By Terence P. Jeffrey
Human Events, September 10, 2007

A magnificent ongoing act of defiance of the forces of nature, the Golden Gate Bridge symbolizes the scope and fragility of American greatness.

I grew up near the bridge, commuting across it every day when I was in high school. My father, who drove me, called it the most spectacular commute in the world. I once suspected him of hyperbole, but passing years and travels taught me otherwise.

No bridge is as elegant as the deep red Golden Gate. None matches its splendid setting. With the precipitous Marin Headlands on one side and the craggy face of San Francisco on the other, it is a perfectly cut ruby set in gold.

From this bridge, sublime vistas shimmer across the water at every compass point: the tree-studded peninsulas of Marin; the prison island of Alcatraz; the high hills of Alameda; and the skyscrapers of San Francisco. On clear days, the distant Farrallons loom above the Pacific like mirages on the horizon.

The most commanding sight, however, is the bridge itself. It is a ribbon of concrete suspended by threads of steel, hanging down from parallel cables that are three-feet wide and nearly 8,000 feet long. These cables ascend from building-sized concrete piers at either end of the bridge, and then form matching upside down arches strung between twin towers rising 750 feet above the sea.

Almost two miles from end to end, the roadway sits 220 feet above the water. The foundation of the South tower lurks 110 feet in a murky deep churned by ceaseless tides. No wonder many engineers said a bridge could not be built here.

According to a history of its construction on the website of the transportation district that runs the facility, the bridge was championed, starting in 1916, by a now-defunct newspaper, the San Francisco *Call Bulletin*, and, later, by an indefatigable engineer named Joseph Strauss, who wanted to build it himself.

Even in the boom times of the 1920s, however, neither the federal nor the state government would finance it. A rival project had already monopolized the government money. "There was no federal or state funding to build the Golden Gate Bridge because the San Francisco–Oakland Bay Bridge, which was being promoted during the same time period, had already received the limited funds available," says the bridge website.

The lack of state and federal funding did not stop the bridge builders, however. They formed a special transportation district—comprising all of four Northern

> *It is a ribbon of concrete suspended by threads of steel, hanging down from parallel cables that are three-feet wide and nearly 8,000 feet long . . . No wonder many engineers said a bridge could not be built here.*

California counties and parts of two others—to move the project forward. They planned to fund the bridge by selling bonds to be paid off by toll proceeds.

Their opponents planned litigation.

"More than 2,000 lawsuits were filed to stop the project," says a monument on the San Francisco side of the bridge. "Strauss persevered and in 1930 at last won approval for a bond issue."

With the Great Depression on, however, the initial $6 million in bonds could not be sold. "Finally, Strauss went to A. P. Giannini, founder of Bank of America," says the monument. "Giannini also had a vision—of serving fully California's growth. Giannini asked one question: 'How long will this bridge last?' Strauss replied: 'Forever. If cared for, it should have life without end.'" Giannini bought the bonds.

Construction began in 1933 and was completed in 1937. The bonds were paid off in 1971—entirely by bridge tolls.

Eleven men fell to their death building the bridge, but 19 more were saved by netting Strauss built from one end to the other. They called themselves the "Halfway to Hell Club."

In 1989, when a 7.1 earthquake hit, the badly damaged federal-and-state-funded Bay Bridge shut for repairs. The undamaged Golden Gate handled record traffic.

The Bay Bridge closed again for three days over the Labor Day weekend so 350 feet of new roadway could be installed.

In seven decades, by contrast, the Golden Gate Bridge has never closed for more than a few hours. Steelworkers and painters labor constantly to preserve it against corrosion caused by fog and salty air, and a major retrofitting is underway to ensure it can survive an 8.3 earthquake, the magnitude that struck in 1906.

Looking back through history at the Golden Gate Bridge, it can be seen as a monumental marker demonstratively placed at the far edge of a continent by an energetic people who had turned a wilderness into a wonderland. When engineer Strauss told banker Giannini the bridge would last forever, he was not putting his faith in perishable concrete and steel, but in the imperishable spirit of the people who built it.

So far, Americans have proved Strauss right.

Where Might a Needed Economic Stimulus Come From? A Private Infrastructure Initiative

By Michael Silverstein
The Moderate Voice, August 20, 2011

One of the save-the-economy notions floating around Washington these days is something called the American Infrastructure Financing Authority. It's a public-private approach to refurbishing and modernizing our roads, bridges, public transit, schools, and other infrastructure.

In its current proposal form, it would have the government front $10 billion in start up capital for infrastructure projects that would pay for themselves over time (e.g. through tolls), with private parties providing the bulk of the capital needed to fully fund these projects. The incentive for these private parties is government guarantees to protect their investments.

Not a bad idea. It's pathetically small in terms of the badly aging infrastructure it hopes to improve and the jobs it seeks to create. But in the context of present-day Washington, surprisingly commonsensical.

Only there's a better way. One that could generate far, far more capital toward infrastructure improvement and create far, far more jobs. It's a private sector–only approach to these challenges.

Here's the idea:

Corporate America has an estimated $1.5 trillion in house it isn't using to expand because demand (at least in this country) doesn't warrant investing this vast sum in expansion. This money is now also being seen by CFOs as necessary reserves in case the economy tanks still further. This $1.5 trillion is therefore not likely to go into a private infrastructure initiative.

Large corporations, however, have one other major asset that might be applied to this purpose: Their ability to borrow at the exceptionally low rates being held down by the Fed. While small businesses can't tap this cheap money because banks and investors shy away from lending to them, large corporations with good looking balance sheets and the implied backing of the Fed can tap this well easily. Thus a great deal of cheap borrowed money could potentially go into a large corporations–only private infrastructure initiative.

What would it cost an individual company to be part of such an initiative? Not much on a yearly basis. Borrowing rates (from banks or via bonds) for highly rated corporations are piddling today. A $10 million or $20 million project to improve schools, roads, public transit, bridge repair, or other infrastructure could be funded for a few hundred thousand in interest payments annually—and the principal easily rolled over years down the road.

Multiply that one private company–funded project by thousands of projects, you get big bucks flowing into infrastructure improvement and big number job creation. The source of funding here is banks or the market, with no government participation. The cost guarantor is not one government but many large corporate entities.

Now, one might ask, why should companies do this? One answer comes from not viewing large corporations as inherently evil entities and their top management as mindless parasites. These people know the consequences of deficient infrastructure better than most Americans, and the consequences of excessive long-term unemployment for company bottom lines. They're also, by and large, decent people who don't wish to watch their country's economy going down the drain and their fellow Americans suffering.

In purely business terms, a company leveraging annual outlays of a few hundred thousand dollars in interest payments to put hundreds of people to work on worthwhile infrastructure projects is great public relations, and could almost certainly be written off as such or otherwise handled in a tax-friendly way via a corporate-related foundation.

Only there's a better way. One that could generate far, far more capital toward infrastructure improvement and create far, far more jobs.

Infrastructure that benefits everyone might also be especially beneficial to companies funding it. Roads on which company trucks run, public transit and highways bringing company employees to work, clean water needed in huge qualities by many companies for their own operations, might be a special focus of any given company's own initiative. And if this spending relieves a local government from a project's cost, would that government object? A silly question. That government would simply have more money to spend on other infrastructure needs.

It's obvious to anyone who knows how large corporations actually operate that the basic idea here is anything but new. Some computer companies have long supplied schools with their products to promote computer literacy and product identification that will help their sales in the future. Some financial service giants have long promoted financial education in schools because they want to gain cred with tomorrow's investors. Big companies have been gifting public infrastructure in all sorts of ways over the years.

What's new here is the scope of the proposal, its systematic and far more expansive nature. And most important, the funding mechanism—tapping the huge pool of capital in banks and in the market that is currently not going to where it should be going (infrastructure improvement and jobs creation) at a time when a

Washington train wrecked government can't (for fiscal reasons) or won't (for political reasons) provide the capital to do what has to be done in this realm.

So Corporate America has to step up and do the job. Corporate America, which for sound business reasons won't tap its $1.5 trillion in stockpiled wealth to reanimate the economy, must use its good credit borrowing status to unlock the unused (or misused) capital in banks and markets to repair America and put it back to work.

There are many vital things at stake here. One of them is the salvation of the kind of capitalism this country has long known and whose fruits we've long enjoyed.

3

Mass Transportation

(Dan Bannister)

Traffic on Interstate 405 in Los Angeles, California. In 2008, a segment of the interstate was traveled by an average of 374,000 vehicles each day.

The Evolution of American Mass Transit

By Paul McCaffrey

The era of public transportation in what is now the United States is thought to have begun in Boston in 1631. Founded the previous year, the young town possessed a deep and protected harbor that made it an ideal port for ships sailing up and down the coast, and back and forth across the Atlantic. It was well on its way to becoming one of the principal cities of North America, but the colonial legislature was concerned about the town's tenuous connection to the mainland. Geographically, Boston was a peninsula joined to the rest of the colony by a narrow isthmus. For those transporting goods overland from nearby settlements or the surrounding countryside, this meant long and expensive roundabout routes. For residents of Boston proper, this meant there was little opportunity to venture outside the settlement. Taking up the issue in 1630, the colonial legislature of Massachusetts extended a charter to anyone who would set up regular ferryboat service between the city and the community of Charlestown to the north. The following year, Thomas Williams took advantage of the offer and started up a ferry operation in Boston Harbor, sailing passengers and their cargo from the town of Chelsea—then known as Winnisimmet—to Charlestown, on to Boston, and back.

In mass transit or public transportation systems, a shared vehicle—be it a ferry, bus, trolley, or train—is employed to move people across a metropolitan region on a particular route and schedule. The goal is to increase efficiency and lower costs by pooling resources and building the necessary infrastructure.

The "public" in public transportation can be misleading. Public transportation systems serve the public but are not necessarily owned by the public. Williams's ferry service, for example, was a private, family-run operation, albeit with the backing of the colonial government. Though the majority of public transportation systems started out as private, for-profit enterprises, most of the major mass transit systems in the United States today are owned in whole or in part either by the localities they serve or by public-private partnerships.

In the modern era, there are three predominant modes of mass transit: buses, heavy rail, and light rail, with ferries composing a distinct and enduring subgroup. Other forms of public transportation have come and gone since Williams first ferried customers across Boston Harbor. The evolution of these systems is based largely on economic and technological factors. As Boston grew in both population and (thanks to land-filling projects) geographic area, traversing the city on foot grew impractical. As a consequence, omnibuses were introduced starting in the 1820s. These immense horse-drawn wagons were the forerunners of today's buses, transporting a number of people to stops along a designated route.

The invention of the steam-powered railroad in 1825 opened up numerous possibilities for mass transit. In 1838, the first steam-powered commuter trains started transporting workers into Boston from the outlying suburbs. Though it would be some time before local motorized rail systems were deployed in Boston proper, rail lines were laid on the city's streets and the first tram, or horsecar, debuted in 1856. Like the omnibus, the tram was horse-drawn, but since it was rail-based it avoided the ruts and bumps of the roads of the era, making for a smoother and quicker ride and enabling the horses to pull more weight.

But any mass transit system that depended on horses dealt with certain inconveniences. Horses had to be fed and stabled and were prone to disease and injury. On average, they had a working life of five years. Electrification soon offered an alternative power source. Impressed by the electrified streetcars of Richmond, Virginia, Boston city planners decided to follow suit. In 1888, Boston rolled out its first electric cable car, or trolley, and the city's first electric trolley line commenced service on January 1, 1889.

Electric streetcars grew in popularity in Boston and across the nation, spreading to just about every city with 10,000 or more inhabitants. With their increased use, traffic problems developed, as streets became crammed with pedestrians and all manner of vehicles, from electric trolleys to horse-drawn carriages and trams. To ease the congestion, the Massachusetts legislature sponsored the creation of the Boston Elevated Railway Company (BERY) in 1894, and over the next forty years, heavy and light rail construction boomed. Along with elevated trains, subways began travelling through underground tunnels dug beneath downtown Boston.

Along with railroads, automobile use expanded as well. The city's first municipal bus line was established in 1922 and other routes soon followed. Unable to compete with trains, buses, and eventually passenger cars, trolleys fell out of favor during the ensuing decades and much of their infrastructure was dismantled. Nationwide, streetcar ridership peaked in the 1920s at around 12 or 13 billion trips per year; this number had plummeted to several hundred thousand by the early 1960s. As cars grew more affordable, people started to drive in greater numbers and took fewer trips on mass transit. BERY's financial situation deteriorated and the state soon stepped in, absorbing BERY into the newly formed Metropolitan Transit Authority in 1947.

As the car came to dominate transportation in the United States, highway construction spiked, and public transportation and mass transit in Boston fell further behind. Government subsidies were required to keep Boston's passenger rail systems running. But the reliance on the automobile had its downsides, among them traffic congestion, sprawl, and pollution.

To better address the region's complex mass transit needs, the Metropolitan Transit Authority was reorganized and its purview expanded when the Massachusetts Bay Transit Authority (MBTA) was established in 1964. The T, as it came to be known, sought to integrate Boston's mass transit systems with those of the outlying communities, including the commuter rail, vastly expanding the reach of the network. In 2011, on the average weekday, passengers took nearly 1.3 million trips on the MBTA. Today, the MBTA is the fifth largest mass transit system in the United States, coordinating a system of twelve commuter rail lines, five light rail lines, four heavy rail lines, 183 bus routes, four trolley bus lines, and four ferryboat services. Of those four ferry services, one still carries passengers from Boston to Charlestown, as Thomas Williams did some 380 years ago.

On different timetables and with varying combinations of shared vehicles, Philadelphia, New York, and Chicago's mass transit networks experienced evolutions similar to Boston's. They transitioned in whole or in part from ferries to omnibuses, horsecars to streetcars, to heavy and light rail. Though the systems were at first privately owned and operated, the government, in varying capacities, eventually stepped in to save them from bankruptcy and obsolescence. Aside from their large populations and comparatively long histories, what distinguishes these American cities from most others is that they have invested in municipal rail lines—specifically heavy rail like subways and elevated trains—for over one hundred years. Elevated trains were constructed in New York in the 1800s, and its first subway opened in 1904. Much of the mass transit infrastructure of these municipalities thus predates the automobile and the car culture, with its sprawling settlement patterns, that came to dominate American life. Perhaps not coincidentally, these cities have some of the most well-used and well-integrated public transportation systems in the country.

Though both are powered by electricity, heavy rail is distinguished from light rail by its speed and carrying capacity. In general, heavy rail can transport more people at higher rates of speed. Heavy rail systems were constructed throughout the twentieth century in a number of American cities. Three of the most successful municipal heavy rail networks were built in the 1970s: San Francisco's Bay Area Rapid Transit (BART) commenced operations in 1972; the Metro of Washington, DC, opened in 1976 and today is the second busiest heavy rail system in the country after the New York City Subway; and Metropolitan Atlanta Rapid Transit Authority (MARTA) started running trains in 1979.

Of course, constructing heavy rail networks is a massive and expensive undertaking, with costs running well into the billions, and while subways and elevated trains may make sense for densely populated, pedestrian friendly cities like San Francisco and Washington, DC, other municipalities have different mass transit needs. Over the past several decades, many of these cities have turned to a less expensive alternative—light rail. There is a certain déjà vu quality to the light rail renaissance, recalling the days of trolleys and streetcars in the late nineteenth and early twentieth centuries. Thankfully, unlike the trolley-congested streets of 1890s Boston, most new light rail systems have exclusive rights-of-way and don't have to compete with other traffic. San Diego, California, and Portland, Oregon, led the charge, opening light rail lines in the 1980s. Los Angeles, St. Louis, Denver, Dallas, and Salt Lake City followed in the 1990s, and the trend has continued up to the present, with Phoenix, Houston, Seattle, and Charlotte, among other municipalities, opening up new light rail networks in recent years. Though cheaper than heavy rail, light rail still requires a sizeable investment and many critics wonder if they are worth the cost.

Even with all the heavy and light rail construction of the past decades, buses still take up the majority of the mass-transit burden. In 2011, buses supplied over 50 percent of all public transportation trips in the United States, down from 61 percent in 1998. Though they showed marked increases over 2010, heavy rail accounted for 35 percent and light rail a mere 5 percent of mass transit trips in the first six months of 2011. Buses have certain key advantages over rail systems: they require little in the way of infrastructure investment and are exceedingly flexible, relying on the existing road system.

According to a report by the American Public Transportation Association (APTA), people took approximately 10.4 billion total trips on mass transit systems in the United States in 2011. This marked the second highest total since records began being kept in 1957 and the sixth year in a row that mass transit ridership exceeded 10 billion. The all-time high, achieved in 2008, was 10.7 billion trips, but many analysts expect that ceiling to be cracked in 2012, as high gas prices coupled with increasing employment rates propel growing numbers of people onto public transportation.

Extrapolating from these statistics, many believe that mass transit is poised to take on an expanding share of the transit load in the years ahead. Whether and to what extent such a scenario comes to pass will depend on a number of factors—the price of gasoline as well as congestion and environmental concerns among them. Current conditions will play a role as well. Despite the older established networks in places like Boston and New York, at the moment only a handful of metropolitan areas have mass transit systems that offer viable alternatives to the automobile. Indeed, of the 10.4 billion public transportation trips taken in 2011, more than a third occurred in New York City alone, while according to estimates by the American Public Transportation Association (APTA), about half of US households do not have any access to dependable mass transit systems. Consequently, reliable public transportation is unlikely to be available nationwide any time soon.

But there are impediments to even modest expansion. Some object to mass transit on ideological grounds, doubting the cost-effectiveness and environmental benefits of public transport systems, especially rail-based ones, and seeing in government-sponsored mass transit a disruptive intrusion by the state into the free market.

Cash-strapped states and municipalities, meanwhile, are looking to trim outlays rather than expand them and lack the money to invest in ambitious and expensive rail projects. The federal government finances mass transit through its Highway Trust Fund and New Starts program. The former generates revenue in part via a tax on gasoline of 18.6 cents per gallon. Twenty percent of the trust fund is reserved for mass transit, but due to the high price of gasoline and increased fuel economy of automobiles, less tax money is being collected. New Starts funding is also limited by budgetary constraints.

Beyond the financial dilemma is the logistical one. Effective public transportation networks like those in Boston extend over multiple jurisdictions and require a degree of coordination and cooperation that can take decades to achieve. If this coordination and cooperation falls short, the developing system may as well. For example, Norfolk, Virginia, introduced the Tide, a light rail system, in 2011. The network was supposed to have been regional in scope, extending into nearby Virginia Beach. But Virginia Beach voters decided not to participate, limiting the Tide's overall impact.

Of course, rail systems are not the only alternatives to passenger cars, traffic congestion, and high gas prices. Many municipalities are expanding their bike lanes, commuter lanes, and bus services. With a nod to both fuel costs and environmental concerns, the nation's bus fleets are going green, employing vehicles in ever-larger numbers that rely on hybrid engines or run on alternative fuel. Such measures may lack the glamour of a new rail network, but they offer a more economical approach to the same set of problems. As Boston's nearly four centuries of experience demonstrate, developing mass transit infrastructure involves both small adaptations and bold transformations.

Engine of Prosperity

By Christopher B. Leinberger
The American Conservative, August 1, 2010

Real estate has caused two of the last three recessions. That is because real estate and the infrastructure that supports it—transportation, sewer, broadband, etc.—represent 35 percent of the asset base of the economy. When real estate crashes, the economy goes into a tailspin.

To speed up the recovery now slowly underway, the real estate sector must get back into the game. If over a third of our asset base is not engaged, the U.S. will be condemned to high unemployment and sluggish growth.

But the real estate recovery will not just be a continuation of the type of development of the past two generations—low density, drivable development. The Great Recession highlighted that there has been a structural shift in what the market wants. The bulk of the collapse in the housing market has been on the metropolitan fringe, exactly where the focus of drivable suburban housing growth has been. Fringe housing in most metro areas has lost twice the value the metro area as a whole has shed from the mid-decade peak. But the value of the opposite type of housing, known as "walkable urban," where most daily needs can be met by walking or public transit, only experienced about half the decline from the housing peak.

In fact, some metro areas have seen the highest housing values per square foot shift from drivable suburban neighborhoods in 2000, like Great Falls in the Washington suburbs or Highland Ranch south of Denver, to walkable urban neighborhoods, like Dupont Circle in Washington or LODO in downtown Denver, in 2010. The lines crossed in the decade. The last time the lines crossed was in the 1960s, and they were heading the opposite direction.

But housing may not play the same catalytic role during this recovery unless fundamental changes in transportation policy are adopted.

Most observers recognize that drivable suburban infrastructure has been massively subsidized. Some studies show that a drivable suburban home would have to pay 22 times what it currently pays for publicly and government-regulated private infrastructure. Suppose a city government, in its infinite wisdom, mandated that all restaurants must charge the same price for whatever customers ate or drank. That would mean patrons on a diet who do not drink alcohol would be massively subsidizing people who are stuffing themselves and getting drunk. This is not a free market at work.

This subsidized system has resulted in an oversupply of the wrong kind of house in the wrong location for what the market now wants. Federal, state, and local governments subsidize this type of product by building roads to nowhere while existing roads are left to deteriorate. The American Association of Civil Engineers recently gave American roads a near failing D– grade. Meanwhile, the Federal Highway Trust Fund is bankrupt, getting continuous federal cash infusions to subsidize the system.

The market wants the walkable urban alternative, which explains the 40–200 percent per-square-foot price premiums this type of housing commands and the hue and cry (or shouts of joy) about gentrification in urban neighborhoods. What is missing is an adjustment to this new market reality by investing in infrastructure, particularly transportation infrastructure, which will spark the type of housing and development the market wants.

Why transportation infrastructure? Because transportation drives development. For the 6,000 years that we have been building cities, the transportation system a society chose dictated what real estate developers could build. Starting in Sumer (present-day Iraq) through Pompeii, from Pepys's London to Franklin's Philadelphia, and from Henry Ford's Detroit to the Beach Boys' Los Angeles, the transportation system is the rudder that steers the investment of a large portion of a society's wealth.

So how do we pay for the transit, especially rail transit, that will allow developers to give the market what it wants: walkable urban development? The answer can be found in the past. In the early 20th century, every American town over 5,000 people was served by a streetcar system—this at a time when the real per capita household income was one-third what it is today. By 1945, metropolitan Los Angeles had the longest passenger rail system in the world. Atlanta's rail system was accessible to nearly all residents. Until 1950, our grandparents did not need cars to get around because they could rely upon various forms of rail transit. The average household only spent 5 percent of its income on transportation 100 years ago, versus 24 percent for drivable households today.

How did the country afford that extensive rail system? Real estate developers, sometimes aided by electric utilities, not only built the systems but paid rent to cities for right of way. Henry Huntington built the Pacific Electric in Los Angeles; Robert Lowry in Minneapolis built the Twin City Rapid Transit; and Sen. Francis Newlands in Washington built the Rock Creek Railway going up Connecticut Avenue from Dupont Circle in the 1890s. Newlands did not get into the rail transit business because of the profit potential of streetcars. He was a real estate developer, buying 1,700 acres between Dupont Circle and suburban Chevy Chase, Maryland, served by his streetcar line. The Rock Creek Railway did not make any money, but it was essential to getting homebuyers to Newlands's developments. So he subsidized the railway out of the profits. Most other streetcar/development entrepreneurs did the same thing. They understood that transportation drives development and that development had to subsidize the transportation.

After World War II, the wealth of the country was so vast that the federal government, along with the states, disconnected transportation and development. We decided that "your tax dollars at work," as every highway construction sign would proclaim, did not require a financial payback. One Polish refugee turned real estate developer, Nathan Shapell, who owned a large tract of land outside Los Angeles, was approached in the 1960s by the California highway department about building a freeway through his property. His first reaction was to of-

> *For the 6,000 years that we have been building cities, the transportation system a society chose dictated what real estate developers could build.*

fer for free as much land as needed for the road and to pay for the interchange to get customers to his land. The state official said that would not be necessary; the state would buy his land for the road and completely pay for the interchange. His reaction was, "What a wonderful country!"

But now, our transportation funding system is clearly broke. As transportation specialist Rob Puentes, senior fellow at the Brookings Institution, has said, "We've run out of money. It's time to start thinking."

It is time to go back to the future and redirect some of the property appreciation caused by rail transit to fund its expansion. This approach, called "value capture," is best known in this country by its public version, tax-increment financing, which uses increased future tax revenues expected from an investment in public infrastructure to pay off the debt incurred to build it. It has been used extensively in Chicago by Mayor Daley to fund that city's remarkable turnaround.

At present, only a fraction of the value added to private property by public transportation is tapped to support infrastructure. Property taxes are around 1 percent per year in many parts of the country, so only 1 percent of the upside can be captured. Yet the increase in private property values could yield much more, and there are many methods by which support for transportation can be linked to rising land values. Property owners along a proposed rail corridor could vote in a special election, for example, to decide whether they want to fund the project.

In a Brookings Institution analysis of a proposed $140 million streetcar line, just 17 percent of the increase in private property values would pay the effort's entire capital costs. This is what Senator Newlands found out over a century ago: development can help pay for transportation improvements. Using value capture to pay for rail transit and highways is charging those who benefit the most from these public investments, the property owners, for at least some of the cost of transportation improvements.

There is no reason all transportation project costs, not just those for rail, should not be paid for in part by the property owners who profit from the improvement. If property owners would benefit from any transportation project, rail or road, and they are willing to help pay for it, that is the market speaking and we should listen—and benefit by their financial contribution. Levy exemptions could be made for existing communities that are too poor to pay if the project's main purpose is to provide existing residents transit to work, though even road or rail projects to parts of a metropolitan area that are underserved may spark economic growth that could then be used as value-capture revenue.

A few metro areas are experimenting with how these value-capture mechanisms would be structured. A developer, along with his adjacent property owners, funded a third of a new $100 million Metrorail station in Washington, D.C., that serves their projects. He felt he got a 10–20 times return on his investment by bringing rail transit to his front door. And it is important to note that this is only partially about the redevelopment of American cities. My research shows the majority of the market demand will probably be satisfied by transforming suburbs into walkable urban places.

Investment in rail transit is essential if we want to get the 35 percent of the economy in real estate growing more substantially. No economic recovery will be sustainable without the growth of the largest asset class in the economy. And looking to the past to understand how to pay for that rail transit is not only good policy, it is one of the only options we have left.

❖

Christopher B. Leinberger is visiting fellow at the Brookings Institution, a real estate developer, author, and professor at the University of Michigan. His most recent book is The Option of Urbanism.

Easy Rider

My Revolutionary Folding Bike

By Judith Shulevitz
New Republic, July 8, 2010

I bought a folding bicycle earlier this year in the hope that it would help me solve an embarrassing personal problem. I live in New York City, but, though I love the people I live among, I just don't like the place. I'm loath to move out, because I only recently moved in. I left a house and a yard in Westchester for an apartment in Morningside Heights, near Columbia University, where my husband works and where life seemed likely to be more lively. But then, I got here and realized that I hated the noise and the filth and the smell. Worse, I felt trapped, unable to move around except by means of slow or unreliable public transportation. I wanted to hop in my car and go wherever I wanted at the speed to which I had become accustomed, but my car lived at a garage seven blocks away, and it would be impossible to park once I got where I was going anyway.

My folding bicycle, made by a British company called Brompton, is odd-looking enough that people stop me on the street and ask about it. It's robin's-egg blue and looks like a swan that stretched out its neck and stuck it into a wheel. The first time I tried out my Brompton, I refused to get off. I pretended to be oblivious to the looks I was getting from the pedestrians I was weaving around, illegally though adroitly (because the wheels are small), on one of the most crowded sidewalks in Manhattan (East 14th Street). I refused to think about the stepson I left at the store, who was imagining me lying under a truck. My bike has a steel frame and a good shock absorber and felt much sturdier than expected. I glided past East Village landmarks I hadn't seen in years, because they weren't close to any subway stops: Avenue D and 9th Street, where David Schearl lived in *Call It Sleep*; Tompkins Square Park, historic parade ground for anarchists and other radicals. For the first time in a long time, I glimpsed freedom. No longer would my way be blocked by gridlock, overly complicated subway connections, and inchworm-like buses. Now, I could scoot around everybody and everything and go where I wanted, when I wanted, faster than everything else on the road aside from other bicycles, and then, I could fold up my bicycle and hoist it onto whichever mode of public transportation I chose to further my escape.

I now know enough about the history of the bicycle to know that bypassing dead ends is what bicycles do. The very first bicycle-like vehicle, the velocipede, was invented in 1817, a year when there was a severe shortage of horses due to a volcanic eruption that spewed ash into the air and created weather that destroyed the oats that fed the horses. Bicycles invariably make a comeback during oil shortages and other energy crises, as happened during World War II and in the 1970s, and as some energy activists are hoping will happen now, in the wake of the oil spill and the moratorium on new drilling in the Gulf. But bicycles help people circumnavigate social barriers, too. In the mid-1890s, bicycle manufacturers improved on the "high wheeler," which had one huge front wheel, and came up with the "safety bicycle," which looked much as bicycles do today. This turned bicycles into an affordable form of mass transit, at which point it became acceptable for women to travel farther, unchaperoned, than ever before. They also began to wear bloomers, the first version of women's pants.

The folding bicycle has been around as long as the safety bicycle, but only recently has it been marketed to the general consumer, along with an array of other bikes that challenge the supremacy of the purely recreational bike: cargo bicycles and tricycles, which haul stuff; recumbent and semi-recumbent bikes, which go faster and farther with less effort than upright bikes; even electric bikes, which supplement leg power with motor power and can be especially useful in hill country. To my mind, though, the folding bicycle is the most revolutionary of them all. Here's what it does that no other kind of bike does: It obviates the waiting game. Right now, in New York City and other cities around the country, urban planners and transportation officials are trying to undo the damage done by twentieth-century visionary planners, such as Robert Moses, who bet, incorrectly, on automobiles. Cars turn out to be a terrible technology for cities, too big and dirty for crowded, narrow streets and unnecessarily powerful for the short trips that city dwellers make. And, though it's hard to get people to abandon their cars for bicycles in an environment that cars make unsafe, studies have shown that, when cities signal their willingness to accommodate bicycles, people become more willing to risk riding them, and that, when more people ride, fewer of them get into accidents, because motorists are forced to pay closer attention to the cyclists in their midst.

Bicycles invariably make a comeback during oil shortages and other energy crises, as happened during World War II and in the 1970s, and as some energy activists are hoping will happen now. . . .

This is why, if you pedal around a U.S. city, you will encounter more bicycle lanes than you used to, both the kind painted right onto the street and the kind protected by median strips. You will discover new bicycle parking spots; bicycle-oriented signage and traffic lights; even bike-sharing programs, in which you borrow a bicycle from one of several bike stands around the city and return it to any of those stands. (Washington, D.C., just announced an expansion of its bike-sharing program, from 120 to 1,100 bikes; Boston, Denver, and Minneapolis have such programs in the works.) What you're less likely to find are buses and trains that let you board with your bicycle, especially during rush hour, since most of them were designed before it occurred to anyone that the real secret to urban mobility isn't the ferrying of people but the ferrying of people plus their human-powered vehicles.

But now, if your city can't make itself bike-friendly fast enough to suit you, with a few turns of a screw and a kick to knock your wheels in place, you can make your bike city-friendly instead. (It still takes me close to a minute to collapse my Brompton, but my stepson, who has owned his for more than a year, can do it in under 20 seconds.) You can forego parking, because you can take your bike with you; you can stop worrying about theft, for the same reason; and you can get your bicycle home by subway or taxi or commuter train if you need to.

My Brompton has made New York City feel both bigger and smaller than it used to. It feels smaller because I move faster. I spend up to 30 minutes taking my children 24 blocks to school on a public bus, then ride home along the Hudson River in under 10 minutes. I can get to Greenwich Village for lunch with my downtown friends in much less than the 40 minutes I previously allotted for the trip by subway—and I can shove my bicycle under the table in the restaurant before the waiter quite realizes what I'm doing.

But the city feels bigger because I see much more of it, and I see that it really is changing. There's a glorious new skate park along the Hudson River, right next to the extraordinary new bike path; there are bike lanes downtown nearly everywhere you look; and there are cyclists to fill them. (The bicycle activists at Transportation Alternatives say that there are roughly 200,000 cyclists in New York City every day. New York City does not conduct a rigorous survey, as other cities do.) My fellow riders aren't just the grim speed freaks in Lycra who race past me on their Trek bicycles, muttering about people who clog the lane. They're people like me in civilian clothes, commuting to work, carting purchases home, marshalling broods of children on scooters, tricycles, and princess bicycles. We're a tiny army of unwitting urban reformers, making the city safe for cyclists by making cycling a part of our everyday lives, rather than a sport we have to set aside time for.

Which reminds me: I've also stopped going to the gym, which has always struck me as a Dickensian place, a factory of the urban body, all wheels and gears and the urgent expenditure of energy on nothing. This policy may backfire; as a writer who works at home, I don't have enough of a commute to gin up much exercise when I make my daily rounds. But I can always veer off to Fort Tryon Park, which has one of the most beautiful gardens and the single best view of the Hudson in the tri-state area; or loop around Central Park; or bundle my bike onto the subway and get off at South Ferry and take the greenway back uptown. I couldn't do that in the suburbs. Now that I'm finding ways to get around, I'm starting to think that there may be a point to New York City after all.

Unblocking the Box

Congestion relief may be coming soon to a city near you

By Robert W. Poole Jr.
Reason, March 1, 2012

Twenty years ago, high-occupancy vehicle (HOV) lanes were virtually the only politically acceptable way to add freeway capacity. But now it is becoming politically
palatable to add capacity with high occupancy toll (HOT) or express toll lanes,
which are open to toll-paying vehicles and usually some form of high-occupancy
vehicle—bus, vanpool, or carpool. The success of HOV-to-HOT conversions, and
the demonstrated ability of private firms to raise large sums based on projected revenues from such projects, has stimulated activity in several of the most congested
metro areas. Here is a sampling of the projects:

Atlanta. After several years of study, the Georgia Department of Transportation
in December 2009 adopted a $16 billion plan to add express toll lanes to nearly all
the metro area's freeways. The first project, built by a public-private partnership
similar to those adding capacity on the Capital Beltway and in Dallas/Fort Worth,
will be on the I-75 and I-575, just outside the I-285 ring road (known locally as the
Perimeter). Separately, the local toll agency is converting HOV lanes into HOT
lanes on a 15-mile stretch of I-85.

Miami. The Florida Department of Transportation (FDOT) added one lane
each way when it converted HOV lanes into HOT lanes on I-95 in 2008. Where
there was previously a single congested HOV lane in each direction, there are now
two variably priced express lanes, which have brought major congestion relief (as
well as faster and more reliable express bus service). FDOT has embraced a public-
private partnership to rebuild I-595 in Fort Lauderdale, adding three reversible express toll lanes to this congested east-west commuter route. FDOT is also studying
a complete network of such lanes for the three-county metro area.

Houston. The local toll agency financed the addition of two HOT lanes each
way as part of the complete reconstruction of the Katy Freeway, which opened to
traffic in 2008. Houston Metro, the local transit agency, is in the process of converting HOVS into HOTS on five freeways. Texas DOT is considering a public-private
partnership for much of a planned outer beltway, the Grand Parkway.

Phoenix. The Arizona legislature passed public-private partnership legislation
for transportation in 2009. The Arizona Department of Transportation and the
metropolitan planning organization for greater Phoenix are developing plans for a

> *Where there was previously a single congested HOV lane in each direction, there are now two variably priced express lanes, which have brought major congestion relief (as well as faster and more reliable express bus service).*

number of HOT lanes in the region, most of which are expected to be privately financed and developed.

Los Angeles. Southern California, the longtime congestion capital of the United States, until recently had only one express toll project, the landmark 10-mile 91 Express Lanes in Orange County. But Los Angeles County is now converting HOV lanes on the Harbor and San Bernardino freeways into HOT lanes. The metropolitan planning agency is considering plans for a region-wide network of such lanes. Projects are in the planning or development stages in Orange, Riverside, and San Bernardino counties. Current plans call for using public-private partnerships to add several missing links to the region's freeway system, including a five-mile toll tunnel on I-710 (beneath South Pasadena) and the planned 63-mile High Desert Corridor in northern Los Angeles County.

San Francisco. Although no public-private partnership proposals have yet surfaced, the Bay Area has opened two HOT lanes in the East Bay and has several more under development in Silicon Valley. Its metropolitan planning organization was one of the first in the nation to include a region-wide network of HOT lanes in its long-term transportation plan.

Seattle. The Washington State Department of Transportation (WSDOT) reintroduced toll financing in the Puget Sound region a decade ago for the second span of the Tacoma Narrows Bridge. Two other major projects—a toll tunnel to replace the structurally unsound Alaskan Way Viaduct and a new toll bridge to replace the SR 520 floating bridge—are underway. The legislature may allow a long-term public-private concession for WSDOT's $2 billion project to add express toll lanes to about 40 miles of I-405 in Renton, Bellevue, and Redmond.

Of the 18 most congested metro areas, whose 2009 congestion costs totaled $72 billion (out of the national total of $115 billion), the only ones thus far largely ignoring these trends are New York, Philadelphia, Boston, and Detroit.

Urban Outfitters

By John Norquist
The American Conservative, August 1, 2010

Why are so many on the Right hostile to rail transit? When I was mayor of Milwaukee from 1988 to 2004, I wanted to restore some of the streetcar system that had been removed back in the fifties. Republicans, fueled by talk radio personalities, attacked the idea as if I'd proposed Sovietizing the bratwurst industry. This attitude plays out across the United States, in any state that has a city big enough to have or desire a transit system.

Conservatives in Europe, Canada, and Japan aren't so resistant. In Switzerland, arguably Europe's most politically conservative nation, streetcars and commuter trains run almost everywhere people live. Is the reaction so different here because American conservatives oppose all government spending? No, the Republican Party, home to most conservatives in Congress, has supported comparatively large increases in spending when it has held power, most recently under George W. Bush. But enthusiasm for spending on the Right seems to focus on war, highways, and prisons. Prisons and war I understand, as the modern Republican Party openly promotes itself as uniquely patriotic and aggressively devoted to law and order. But why support spending lots of tax money on highways?

The reasons are highly situational. Republican support tends to be strongest in middle- and outer-ring suburbs developed in the second half of the 20th century when transportation and zoning standards yielded cul-de-sac subdivisions, malls, and business parks, all requiring cars to navigate. The Republican base spends a lot of time in automobiles, so their representatives feed them more and wider lanes of concrete. There are always other issues on which to take principled anti-spending stands, even as highway expansion projects soar in cost and leave regions just as congested as before.

Highway contractors are also an easy touch for campaign donations. As with military contractors, nearly all of their revenue is derived from government funds. As described by Robert Caro in *The Path to Power*, Lyndon Johnson learned this early in his political career, raising funds from Texas-based Brown and Root to help elect Democrats. It didn't take Republicans long to line up at the same counter. For the road-building industry, trading relatively small amounts of campaign cash for billions in government contracts is an easy decision.

But this politically motivated interference has negative side effects. In Canada, where there is no national highway or transit program, cities and provinces fund their own mix of roads and transit. And all Canadian large cities have good transit and street networks. Conversely, in the U.S., declining core cities like Detroit and Buffalo have been covered with federally subsidized highways. Rather than profiting from the investment, Detroit is sinking and the greater region ranks as a leader in traffic congestion along with Atlanta, Houston, Los Angeles, and other areas with massive highway systems. Results like that shouldn't please a movement that insists on efficient use of government funds.

> *The avenues and boulevards of our nation have not been a priority for federal funding even though they host much of America's social capital and commerce.*

One oft-repeated critique of conservatives is that they are stuck in the past. When contemplating transportation policy, I wish that were true. After all, it was my fellow Democrats, with some unenthusiastic help from President Dwight Eisenhower, who performed the *coup de grace*, driving a dagger into the faltering private, but still taxpaying, passenger rail and streetcar transit industries. In 1956, the Interstate Highway Act, sponsored by Sen. Albert Gore Sr., passed through a Democratic Congress. Senate Majority Leader Lyndon Johnson played a key role, pushing escalating subsidies for federal highways from a 40/60 fed/state match when he arrived in Washington to 90/10 in the interstate bill. Federal capital for trains and rail transit was zero. Railroads got the message and dumped passenger service; private transit companies shut down.

Meanwhile, the Right has become dysfunctionally attached to a transportation system that violates its principles. Highways appropriate private property. In greater Milwaukee, systemwide highway widening is on track to cost taxpayers nearly $7 billion, while resulting in the seizing and demolition of nearly $200 million worth of private property. Even where construction doesn't always require outright confiscation, wider highways drain the value from neighboring private property and have corrosive effects on compact central cities.

Before the recent push by the state to expand highways in Milwaukee, we took the opportunity to remove an aging elevated freeway that was causing blocks and blocks of blight along riverfront land. Occupying property next to the freeway was like living next to the Berlin Wall. Removing the freeway has helped downtown grow as young people and retirees choose the convenience and excitement of urban living. Where before the freeway repelled high-value, jobs-producing uses, a new boulevard is home to a boutique hotel and serves as the gateway to the new headquarters of Fortune 500 Manpower Inc.

Throughout much of the history of human civilization, transportation infrastructure supported a fully functioning *civitas*—something the Right should care to conserve. Streets served three purposes: movement of goods and people, economic or market functions, and social functions. But for decades, federal policy has mandated that only movement be considered in allocating federal tax dollars. Streets that serve as a setting for people to walk, shop, and engage in civic life are not part of the Department of Transportation playbook. Instead, the federal and state DOTs push big grade-separated roads that focus only on vehicle throughput and not on markets that flourish on streets like Michigan Avenue in Chicago, Broadway in New York City, or Main Street in Hometown, America. The avenues and boulevards of our nation have not been a priority for federal funding even though they host much of America's social capital and commerce.

Like urban boulevards, transit systems tend to fit comfortably in urbanized metropolitan areas. Thriving in tight spaces, transit systems involve far less seizing of property, and they attract development, boosting the value of neighboring property. Unlike highways, they generally function better as they attract more users. It's no surprise that cities with good transit have high concentrations of jobs and real estate value while places dominated by highways and without transit have faltered economically. Forcing road expansion on cities that don't want it while blocking investment in value-adding transit improvements seems imprudent and even punitive. Throughout history, cities—created by market forces and the complex interactions of the people drawn to them—have been a setting for the growth of individual liberties, property rights chief among them. The city states of Renaissance Italy and the North European Hanseatic League flourished as trade and private ownership expanded and declined only when large nation-states taxed them to wage wars. Today, conservatives still claim to value personal freedom and cherish markets, but they are alienated from the cities that nourish both. Instead, they are committed to a central state more interested in crusading abroad than building community at home.

The billions we devote to war would be better spent renewing America's own cities. Not blindly paving to satisfy federal mandates but prudently planning and efficiently constructing infrastructure to serve local needs. What could be more conservative than that?

❖

John Norquist, who served as Democratic mayor of Milwaukee from 1988 to 2004, is president of the Congress for the New Urbanism.

How Traffic Jams Are Made in City Hall

By Sam Staley and Ted Balaker
Reason, April 2007

If you want to know why so few people use mass transit, meet Sue, a college administrator in Minneapolis. If anyone would use transit, Sue would. She's single, she lives in a condominium, and she can afford any additional out-of-pocket expense. She could use her city's Hiawatha Line, a light rail route newly completed at a cost of $715 million. But she doesn't, although she feels guilty about it. That's because her car gets her where she needs to go. Faster.

According to the U.S. Census Bureau, the typical driver in America's metropolitan areas takes 21 minutes to get from home to work. If you take public transit, the average commute stretches to 36 minutes. That's 71 percent longer. Workers in the New York metropolitan area have the longest commute: There it takes an average of 52 minutes to get to work, even though the New York-New Jersey-Connecticut mass transit systems are among the most extensive in the nation.

Minneapolis-St. Paul is about average. The typical commuter takes 21 minutes to get to work by car or 32 minutes by public transit. Congestion can be pretty bad: The average driver in the Twin Cities spends 43 hours—more than an entire work week—stuck in traffic every year. According to the Texas Transportation Institute at Texas A&M University, that costs Twin Cities drivers almost $1 billion in wasted time and fuel. But mass transit takes even longer, and it isn't as flexible as a car when it comes to picking where and when you'd like to go. Is it any wonder Sue drives to work rather than taking the bus or train?

The U.S. Department of Transportation puts the yearly cost of congestion at $168 billion. But the planning gurus who are supposed to solve our transportation problems are in the grip of transitphilia and autophobia; their beliefs about how cities and transportation work are grounded more in nostalgia than in a realistic view of the world we live in now. The public policies they design and try to enforce make it harder for us to get to work, pick up our kids from school, or go shopping. They are *deliberately* fostering congestion. In the words of David Solow, head of the Metrolink commuter rail in Southern California, congestion is "actually good" because "it drives people out of their cars."

Keeping Minneapolis Congested

Every major urban area in the country has an official bureaucracy responsible for planning roads, highways, and mass transit. It has to; it's required by federal law.

Minneapolis has one of the more competent planning agencies. The Metropolitan Council—or Met Council, as locals call it—has at least acknowledged the importance of congestion and has tried a few innovative ways to address it. Unfortunately, its solutions will have minimal impact on the problem. It provides an instructive example of how poorly even our better regional planning agencies are addressing one of the most important policy problems they face.

The Met Council has some extraordinary powers. Established by the Minnesota legislature in 1967, it has legal responsibility for managing the Twin Cities' sewers, parks, transportation, aviation, and land use planning. But the primary focus of its huge organizational bureaucracy is transportation. Of its 3,718 employees, 73 percent do transportation-related work, spending three-quarters of the agency's annual budget.

The council says it aims to enhance "transportation choices" and to "improve the ability of Minnesotans to travel safely and efficiently through the region." So far, so good. The council goes even further: "To a growing number of metro area residents, traffic congestion ranks as the No. 1 livability issue. It affects the length of their daily commute, the times of day they choose to make trips, and the amount of time they sit in traffic, even where they choose to live and work."

But is the Met Council really focused on reducing congestion? Its stated goal isn't to solve the problem; it merely calls for "slowing the *growth* in traffic congestion and improving mobility" (emphasis added). In other words, traffic will continue to get worse, just not as much worse as it would if the council did nothing. The Met Council also has priorities besides congestion: reducing the number of people living in single-family homes, preserving open space, limiting sprawl—and increasing transit use.

During the next 10 years, the Met Council is planning to invest $4.2 billion in the highway system and $1.4 billion in transit facilities. In other words, the region's primary transportation planning agency has decided to spend 25 percent of its budget on mass transit. But transit accounts for just 2.5 percent of all trips in the region, whether they're for pleasure, taking kids to school, going to the supermarket, or commuting to the office. Less than 5 percent of the Minneapolis-St. Paul region's population uses public transit to get to work, and that share is declining: According to U.S. Census statistics, the number of passengers using mass transit increased slightly in absolute terms between 1990 and 2000, but its market share fell by 12 percent.

The Met Council hopes to double bus capacity by 2030 and greatly expand its light rail line and commuter train system. It also intends to boost transit use from 74.9 million passenger trips per year to 150 million by 2030, even though the current trend projects virtually no growth in use and even though transit lost market share from 1990 to 2000, according to the Census Bureau's decennial data. The Met Council expects 574,625 new jobs to be created in the area by 2030. But even though the vast majority of Minneapolis-St. Paul's population travels to work by car, the planners improbably expect per capita road use to *decline*.

The council does plan to expand the road system. It will add 300 additional lane-miles of freeway, or about 12 lane-miles per year. That works out to about three miles of a two-lane (in each direction) freeway each year. That's well below the expected growth in travel demand.

The net result? Without road improvements, highway congestion is expected to increase from 28 hours annually per traveler in 2001 to 40 hours in 2030. With the improvements, congestion should "moderate" to 37 hours in 2030. Congestion would be 32 percent higher than in 2001, rather than 42 percent higher without the improvements. "Just to keep pace with these [highway] needs," the council's *2030 Regional Development Framework* says, "would add $4.7 billion to current plans for the next decade" above the currently planned spending.

For most regional planning agencies, automobility and congestion relief simply are not high on the priority list. Sometimes they aren't on the list at all. Portland, Oregon, distinguished itself among its peers when it made a conscious decision in the mid-1990s to let congestion approach gridlock because it feared that otherwise fewer people would use the transit system. The drive to reduce sprawl creates a conflict of interest, too, since congestion relief makes it easier to commute long distances.

To make "more effective use" of the road system, the Met Council believes it has to get people out of their cars. That's unfortunate, especially since the agency admits congestion is many residents' "No. 1 livability issue." The council is spending 25 percent of its transportation funds on a solution that, at most, might improve the quality of life for 5 percent of the population, and it will do nothing for people like Sue. Even transit users might not be better off, since they will be spending more time commuting than if they used a car. Drivers will definitely be worse off. They will be spending *much* more time stuck in traffic in 2030 than they did in 2006.

If Minneapolis has one of the best planning agencies, what are the others like?

Fiddling While Atlanta Burns Gas

According to the Texas Transportation Institute, Atlanta is the nation's fourth most traffic-clogged metropolitan area, measured by the amount of time stuck in traffic. Its residents crawl and wind through more than 5,000 congested lane-miles each day. Most of these congested roads are arterials and collectors—local roads that let residents navigate short trips around town or their neighborhood or that take them to major highway interchanges. An analysis by the Atlanta Regional Commission of 75 intersections found that 60 were "deficient"—that is, they performed below engineered standards—during the morning rush hour and 68 were deficient during the afternoon rush. The freeways are even worse off: Almost 60 percent of Atlanta's interstates are congested, twice the incidence for local roads.

The South isn't normally seen as a hotbed of progressive government, but the Atlanta Regional Commission was the nation's first government-supported multi-county planning commission. The Atlanta Chamber of Commerce hatched the idea in 1938, and it became official with an act of the Georgia General Assembly in 1947.

As clogged roads slowly choke Atlanta's economy and its quality of life, traffic reduction should be the commission's No. 1 priority. And the commission appears to take its role seriously. During the next 25 years, it plans to spend $57 billion on transportation projects even if the federal, state, or local governments don't cough up more money. (Presumably the funds would come from tolls or other user fees.) Its plan, however, assumes that vehicle miles traveled per person—a common measure of travel demand—will fall by 5 percent and that average travel time won't change. The plan anticipates "significant improvement in congestion and travel times" along the corridors targeted for investment, saving billions of dollars through improved efficiency and productivity.

The commission has some reason for optimism. Travel demand appears to have fallen in Atlanta from a peak of 35 vehicle miles traveled per person each day in 1998 to 31 vehicle miles in 2002. Total demand has increased—from 109 million vehicle miles traveled in 1998 to 113 million in 2002—but that's because population has grown so much. (The number of people living in the Atlanta area increased by more than 200,000 during the same four years.) Each person is driving slightly less, but since there are so many more people, the roads are getting more use than ever.

The freeways are even worse off: Almost 60 percent of Atlanta's interstates are congested, twice the incidence for local roads.

Naturally, congestion increased during this period too, reflecting the increase in travel demand without a similar investment in roadway capacity. Travel times to work also increased, according to the U.S. Census Bureau, rising 24 percent during the 1990s to 30 minutes in 2000. The commission reports that this was the largest increase in the nation.

So congestion is increasing, even though demand seems to be moderating. And local policy makers aren't expecting much more help from the federal, state, or local governments.

What's Atlanta's plan? Roadway expansion will get $8 billion. Car pool lanes will get another $5 billion, bringing the total pavement capacity building budget to $13 billion. The commission has slotted another $14 billion for nontransit operations and maintenance. These efforts will add 2,000 additional miles of arterial and collector roads and 300 miles of new freeway lanes. Another $3 billion is slated for improving the management of the road system.

Atlanta also believes that improving traffic signal timing to smooth out traffic flows, using meters on entrance ramps to prevent too many cars from entering the freeway at the same time, and similar measures that "manage" travel demand will reduce delays on local roads by 25 percent and increase freeway speeds by a similar magnitude. If those plans are implemented comprehensively and efficiently, that estimate may be plausible.

Meanwhile, $5 billion will be used to expand public transit, while $15 billion more will go toward maintenance and operations. A program expanding options for bicyclists, walkers, and others not using cars will get $2 billion. All in all, 38 percent of the regional planning budget is devoted to getting people out of their cars and onto buses and trains. Transit ridership, the commission boldly asserts, will increase "72 percent between now and 2030."

That conclusion is hard to swallow. Transit isn't fulfilling its promise in Atlanta now, and the trends in the city's census data aren't much different from what's happening in Minneapolis. Atlanta's regional work force is 2 million. Transit ridership increased to 75,272 workers in 2000 (an 8 percent increase), hardly making a dent in general commute patterns. And despite that modest uptick in absolute numbers, transit's market share fell from 4.7 percent of all commuting trips in 1990 to 3.7 percent in 2000.

Almost 2 million jobs will be added to the regional economy during the next 30 years. If Atlanta achieves its transit ridership goal, 129,467 people will be using mass transit in 2030. And even then, transit's commute share would fall. Put another way, Atlanta is investing almost 40 percent of its transportation budget on less than 4 percent of the market, and the latter number is shrinking.

This might be a worthy investment if the main beneficiaries were people too poor to afford cars or otherwise restricted from getting around. But the commission wants to compete with the automobile—to get working-class and middle-income commuters out of their cars and onto buses and trains.

Even our more skeptical analysis of the city's transit trends might be overly optimistic. According to the U.S. Department of Transportation's National Transit Database, Atlanta's bus transit system logged 235 million passenger miles in 2003. That's down from 273 million miles reported in 2000. Atlanta's subway system reported 487 million passenger miles in 2003, down from 504 million reported in 2000. So transit use is falling even in absolute terms. For transit to turn around and increase market share would be unprecedented.

Atlanta's policy makers can still shift course. Traffic in the city has become so bad that in 2004 Gov. Sonny Perdue convened a task force that called for making congestion reduction the top priority for regional transportation planners. The Atlanta Regional Commission, along with the Georgia Department of Transportation and other agencies, recently agreed to set specific targets for reducing congestion in absolute terms, as measured by travel delay in peak periods, by 2030. Local officials appear receptive, but have not yet revealed how and to what extent they will follow the recommendations.

We'll see if the follow-through lives up to the promises. If it does, we can only hope the rest of the country's urban planners are paying attention. The myths that have held Atlanta back are hardly unique to that city.

City House, Country House

In 2005 the *Urban Transportation Monitor*, a biweekly industry newsletter, surveyed more than 600 transportation professionals to find out their thoughts on traffic congestion. About 19 percent responded. Of those, 45 percent thought the profession was "doing all it can do" to stop congestion. Half thought congestion was the result of too many people using their cars, and 45 percent attributed it primarily to the desire to live in low-density suburbs.

The preferred solutions were predictable: 51 percent thought mass transit should be improved or expanded, and 50 percent thought the government should manage demand better by getting people to telecommute or carpool. Only 29 percent believed increased highway capacity could be a cost-effective way to reduce congestion significantly. (The survey did not ask whether new capacity should be provided if it were privately funded.)

Many believed the problem is simply too many cars. Fifty-one percent said one of "the main reasons for the high level of congestion in many metropolitan areas" is the desire "of many to use cars for all their trips." Indeed, of the 11 options offered by the survey, that was the biggest vote getter. For traffic engineers, planners, and other transportation professionals, the solution to traffic jam is to keep us from using our automobiles.

The planning profession clings tenaciously to its foundational myths. Even as overwhelming evidence to the contrary piles up, planners keep claiming that cars are inefficient and socially destructive; that expanding road capacity isn't practical; and, most fundamentally, that the government can determine how we choose to travel by planning where and how we live.

That last assumption is the logical conclusion of a rather sophisticated (if largely incorrect) way of looking at human behavior. It's rooted in a common-sense observation: How we live influences how we travel. If we live on a farm, we are going to travel by car. Buses simply don't go out to farms to pick people up and take them into town for work or to buy groceries. Trains don't either. A neighbor might, but she would probably be driving a car and doing this as a service because you don't have a car. School buses are the exception that proves the rule. They pick up a large number of kids, but only because they're being delivered to one destination, the school building.

The flip side is the experience of the Manhattanite. If someone lives in the densest neighborhood of an American city, cars are costly, frustrating, and inefficient. Most Manhattan residents can get to their destination far more efficiently using the subway, taking a bus, or walking. Because parking is so costly, they also can get around fairly efficiently using taxis.

So people in dense urban areas have more choices, and personal automobiles are inefficient ways to get around town. Congestion, in fact, leads people to use alternative modes of transportation. Many regional planners, like those in Atlanta, conclude that the way a region develops dictates how people are likely to travel and what transportation strategies are most feasible. And the way to influence development patterns, they believe, is to carefully plan where and how much to invest in the transportation system. But proximity to work is only one of many factors people consider when finding a home; other criteria, such as price, neighborhood safety, and proximity to good schools, are often deemed more important than living close to the office.

Of course, Atlanta is not Manhattan. In fact, it's virtually the opposite. At 1,783 people per square mile, Atlanta is the poster child for low-density residential development. The New York metropolitan area is three times as dense, with 5,309 people per square mile. Manhattan's density is even higher: more than 50,000 people per square mile.

According to the Atlanta commission, "Land use is an important determinant of how people choose to travel. No other variable impacts [mobility] to a greater extent. The Regional Development Plan policies help shape future growth and protect existing stable areas by encouraging appropriate land use, transportation, and environmental decisions."

To say this is an exaggeration would be charitable. While land use can influence travel behavior in small and crude ways, to claim that it is the biggest factor distorts the mainstream research on the subject. A 2004 study sponsored by the Federal Transit Administration (FTA) cautioned against the tendency to "overemphasize vertically mixed uses such as ground-floor retail and upper-level residential." In particular, it noted that "outside of dense urban locations, building mixed-use products in today's marketplace can be a complex and risky proposition; few believe that being near a train station fundamentally changes this market reality."

This isn't to say that these developments can't generate more transit riders. The FTA study found that those living near rail stations were five to six times more likely to commute using transit than other residents. While those seem like dramatic effects, the majority of commuters near transit stations (often two-thirds or more) still use cars to get to work. Moreover, many of the people living in these transit areas were transit users already. They just moved so they could be closer to transit.

Put differently, if 5 percent of a region commutes using transit—about the national average—then 25 or 30 percent of those living in a transit-oriented development will commute using transit. This is consistent with case studies of transit use in San Francisco and Chicago. (Incidentally, those results invariably come from studies of predominantly *heavy rail* commuter systems, such as subways. Light rail and buses are more fashionable in planning circles these days, but they're also slower and carry fewer riders.)

To get such high use rates, densities have to be very high. The traditional American home with a private yard doesn't fit this model. The typical new house in the United States is built on about one-fifth of an acre. A study in San Francisco found that doubling densities from 10 units per acre to 20 units per acre would increase transit's commute share from 20 percent to 24 percent.

In short, even cramming four times more people into the typical U.S. subdivision of 4–5 units per acre would produce only a modest uptick in transit use. And it isn't an uptick for the region. It's an uptick for the neighborhood—those living within a quarter mile of a transit stop. There is virtually no effect beyond the immediate vicinity of the transit stop, regardless of density.

At these densities, Americans would literally have to give up any hope of having a decent-sized yard and most would have to live in townhouses. The land use pattern would have to fundamentally change, resembling the landscape more common in the carless 19th century than in the highly mobile and adaptable 21st century.

Forget, at least for the moment, whether the government *should* effect such a sweeping change. It almost certainly *can't*. In a forthcoming report, Adrian Moore of the Reason Foundation (the nonprofit organization that publishes this magazine) and Randal O'Toole of the Thoreau Institute examine data from the National Personal Transportation Survey and find that doubling an urban area's density would, at most, reduce the total number of car trips by 10 percent to 20 percent. No U.S. urban area has managed to double its density or to reduce car travel by such magnitudes.

Real Solutions

Believe it or not, there *are* ways to reduce traffic congestion, even if most politicians and planners haven't been eager to adopt them. Here are five potent suggestions, ideally done not alone but in conjunction with one another:

Creative construction. Expanding capacity doesn't always mean adding lanes to congested roads, although that's often a good idea as well. In densely populated Southern California, portions of the highway network are elevated well above the ground, including the Harbor Transitway approaching downtown Los Angeles. In Texas, San Antonio and Austin have double-decker freeways as well. In 2006 Tampa opened its cross-town expressway, an elevated road built in the median of an existing four-lane highway.

If going up is a problem, you can also go down. Australia has done an effective job of using tunnels to connect highways while preserving neighborhoods, an excellent alternative to destroying businesses and homes.

Smarter management. Building new capacity can get you only so far. The Federal Highway Administration estimates that half of all congestion could be eliminated simply through better management of the existing road network. Among other approaches, this could mean metering freeway ramps, turning two-way streets into one-way streets, and improving traffic light coordination. According to the Institute of Transportation Engineers, better-coordinated lights can reduce stops by as much as 40 percent, thereby cutting gas consumption, emissions, and travel times.

Market pricing for roads. One especially fruitful idea is high-occupancy toll (HOT) lanes, which allow drivers who put the highest priority on quick commutes to pay a premium for uncongested lanes. These have been built in Denver, Houston, and—yes—Minneapolis, among other cities. In Atlanta several private companies have submitted plans to build new HOT lanes on their own dime. During rush hour, the congestion difference between the special lanes and the regular lanes can be the difference between going 15 miles per hour and doing 65.

Areas with lots of car pool lanes could convert those to HOT lanes, add some connectors, and create a congestion-free HOT network. Transit boosters, take note: It would be easy to tweak the arrangement to guarantee bus riders a speedy trip too.

Market pricing for parking. On 99 percent of our trips we park for free, thanks largely to the minimum parking requirements embedded in our zoning codes. Eliminating those requirements would allow market forces to reflect the true cost of parking. Instead of adhering to arbitrary regulations that often order more spaces than necessary, developers would have greater flexibility to build only the number of spaces that is needed. Workplaces would be more likely to adopt parking cash-out programs, which give employees who do not drive to work a share of the money that otherwise would have gone toward parking costs. Employees would be more likely to work from home.

Market pricing for parking would reduce traffic too. If drivers had to pay the full cost of parking, they might be less inclined to take certain trips, thus putting a dent in congestion. More important, when parking is scarce but free (or underpriced), drivers have an incentive to keep the spots as long as possible. When it is scarce but costs money, drivers are less likely to dally. One additional result: Other drivers have less need to circle around and around, hoping eventually to spot an empty space.

Traditional parking meters can be notoriously inconvenient, but they aren't the only way to pay for parking. Aspen, Colorado, uses a variety of new technologies, including personal in-vehicle meters. The town determines its parking rates by zones; prices are highest in the city center and drop the further you are from the core. Motorists simply park, type in the number of their parking zone, turn on the meter, and hang it from the rearview meter. A timer deducts the prepaid amount until the driver returns. No one has to hunt for loose change.

Privatization. We're much more likely to adopt ideas like the above when roads are built and managed by companies responding to market incentives, not by government officials responding to planning fads and political clout. Private companies can create and operate highways using toll revenues as a funding source. The government can also convert existing roads to privately managed systems to allow improvements and expansions of the existing network.

For a spectacularly successful example, consider the 407 Electronic Tollway outside Toronto. This innovative road isn't fully private, but it was built by a private company (the Canadian Highways International Corporation) and is now managed by another private company (407 International) that bought a 99-year lease from the government of Ontario. Yet another company, Hughes Electronics, equipped it with an electronic toll-collecting system that eliminates toll booths and the congestion they can cause.

Baby, You Can Drive Your Car

There is a fundamental disconnect between transportation planners and the typical American commuter. Most travelers believe the car is a good thing, a source of freedom and mobility. Giving up the flexibility of the private automobile reduces our quality of life; it's a step back, not a step forward. That's the main reason the use of mass transit is declining in the U.S., despite the billions of dollars poured annually into such systems.

Yet transportation planners believe public transit and sharing rides with strangers increases the typical American's quality of life. It doesn't, and our behavior reflects this. That's why the vast majority of us choose not to use public transit.

Back in Minneapolis, Sue may hop aboard the Hiawatha Line from time to time. But when even well-off, condo-dwelling rail fans like her continue to rely on their cars, the currently dominant school of transportation policy seems destined to create many more traffic jams than transit users.

❖

Sam Staley is director of urban growth and land use policy at the Reason Foundation. Ted Balaker is the Jacobs Fellow at the Reason Foundation. They are the authors of The Road More Traveled *(Rowman & Littlefield), from which this article is adapted.*

4

Airports and Aviation

(AFP/Getty Images)

The 747-8 Intercontinental, Boeing's largest-ever passenger airplane, takes off for the first time from Paine Field in Everett, Washington State, on March 20, 2011.

What Ails the Air Transportation System?

By Paul McCaffrey

America's air transportation infrastructure is a complicated system composed of many different elements. First, there is the physical framework, consisting of airports: runways, terminals, hangars, and control towers, as well as the transit networks that connect them to their outlying communities and the larger transportation grid. Secondly, there are the planes themselves, and the human infrastructure: the mechanics, air traffic controllers, pilots, and other personnel who work to convey passengers and cargo through the system and onto their destinations. Contained within the larger whole are smaller networks governing security, communications, and other operations, ensuring that airplanes take off and land in a safe and timely manner. Given the sheer size and complexity of all these diverse components, broad generalizations about air transportation infrastructure can be problematic. Nevertheless, analysis tends to focus on technology and labor issues, as well as the largely negative assessments of the US aviation system.

In general, the consensus is that the American air transportation infrastructure is deeply flawed, and in dire need of increased investment and fundamental reform. In its 2009 Report Card on American Infrastructure, the American Society of Civil Engineers (ASCE) found much to malign, giving the aviation system an overall grade of D.

The worst performing airports—those with the most delayed and cancelled flights—tend also to be the busiest. Those serving New York City, Chicago, and other major metropolitan areas usually top the list in each category. On the whole, weather is the principal cause of delays and cancellations, accounting for roughly 68 percent of the total. Approximately 23 percent of delays and cancellations are the avoidable result of excess volume—more flights than the air traffic control system and the airport facilities can handle. Crowded runways and crowded skies, in turn, create traffic jams that send reverberations throughout the entire system.

Although delays and cancellations related to weather are largely beyond human control, volume delays are seen as a result of human and technological factors that defy easy and immediate solution. Some have suggested building additional runways to accommodate the higher number of flights. But the nation's busiest airports, located in densely populated urban environments, do not have access to the additional land necessary to construct more runways. Moreover, each airport has a limited amount of airspace and flight paths through which planes can be routed, so even if more runways could be constructed, they wouldn't necessarily relieve the glut.

Some critics lay the blame for volume delays, especially in the major cities, on a shortage of qualified air traffic controllers. A notoriously stressful profession, air traffic control requires a great deal from its operatives. In the more well-traveled hubs, the demands are particularly intense. According to a 2012 US Department of Transportation report, 40 percent of air traffic controller trainees at the busiest facilities do not complete their training and end up leaving the industry. In places like New York and Los Angeles, attrition rates are even worse. The average attrition rate nationwide is 24 percent.

Meanwhile, of the air traffic controllers now on the job, nearly one in three is eligible for retirement. At the Dallas-Fort Worth facility of the Federal Aviation Administration (FAA), almost two-thirds of the air traffic controllers now qualify for retirement benefits. Some fear that mass retirements, coupled with high trainee attrition, could create a potentially critical shortage. Despite the Department of Transportation's findings, the FAA, the government agency responsible for monitoring and policing aviation in the United States, insists that it is meeting its hiring goals, and that enough qualified personnel are entering the ranks to ensure the system's integrity.

Rather than a lack of seasoned air traffic controllers, certain analysts (ASCE among them) attribute volume delays to outdated equipment. Despite over a half-century of modern air travel, the national air traffic control system continues to depend on radar-based technology from the World War II era.

Efforts to devise a new air traffic control system over the past decade have met with mixed results, and have demonstrated how air transportation infrastructure—air traffic control, in particular—often serves as a political battleground in the conflict between organized labor and its opponents. For the most part, these disagreements have had an entirely negative impact on air transport institutions.

In 2003, the FAA began developing a new air traffic control framework—NextGen—that relies on a satellite-based global positioning system (GPS) rather than radar. This technology is expensive, will take decades to implement, and requires a steady influx of funds to plan, build, and refine it. In 2007, the FAA's congressional authorization expired, and over the next five years, the agency received only incremental stopgap funding from the federal government, slowing NextGen's progress. The major impediment to a comprehensive agreement was a dispute between Democrats and Republicans over the collective bargaining rights of airline and railroad workers. Before approving an extended funding measure, Republicans in Congress wanted to include a provision in the bill that critics claimed made it more difficult for workers to unionize. Specifically, according to a 2010 ruling of the federal National Mediation Board (NMB), employees could form a union after securing a simple majority vote. This altered an earlier statute that held that nonvotes in union elections had to be counted as no votes. Republicans wanted to restore that system.

The disputes in Congress, and the growing concern about the FAA's funding had other side effects beyond just limiting the progress of NextGen. Uncertain whether the FAA would ever acquire the money to complete NextGen, the airlines held off on investing their own resources to equip their planes with the new technology.

In Washington, DC, meanwhile, the imbroglio came to a head in the summer of 2011. Without any appropriations from Congress, the FAA was forced to place nearly 4,000 workers on furlough. The agency also instructed its contractors to cease work on a number of construction projects. Following two weeks of a partial FAA shutdown, which resulted in the loss of millions in revenue, Congress put in place yet another temporary funding measure.

Finally, in February 2012, after twenty-three short-term appropriations since 2007, Congress passed a $63.6 billion bill to finance the FAA for the next four years, which US President Barack Obama signed into law. On the labor front, the measure altered the Railway Labor Act. Previously, in order to hold a union election, at least 35 percent of a company's labor force had to sanction a vote. As a result of the 2012 legislation, 50 percent is now required. Included in the measure was extensive financing for the NextGen system. With its funding secured until 2016, the FAA moved forward with the new air traffic control system, which is expected to cost $22 billion to implement through 2025.

Air traffic control has a history of labor disputes. Indeed, a 1981 strike by nearly 12,000 members of the Professional Air Traffic Controllers Organization (PATCO), a public-employee union, continues to influence both the state of air traffic control and organized labor in the United States. PATCO represented American air traffic controllers starting in 1968, and has demonstrated throughout its history a certain confrontational streak when dealing with the FAA in contract negotiations. To gain leverage, PATCO has, on occasion, encouraged work slowdowns and mass "sickouts." At the time, such measures were not unusual in conflicts between labor and management. Though among public-employee unions strikes were technically illegal, as was bargaining over wages. Nevertheless, that did not stop some organizations from employing the tactic and with some success.

Then, as now, air traffic control was a high-pressure career involving enormous responsibilities, and PATCO insisted that this be reflected in the working conditions of its members. Contract negotiations with the FAA went poorly throughout the 1970s, but during that time PATCO built itself into one of the best-organized unions in the country. Disappointed with its treatment by the FAA under President Jimmy Carter, PATCO endorsed his opponent, Ronald Reagan, in the 1980 elections.

With Reagan's victory, PATCO expected its concerns would be addressed. Though a Republican, Reagan was a former union leader himself, and offered considerable concessions to PATCO. However, they were not enough for the union's increasingly agitated membership, and were rejected. As PATCO geared up for a strike, Reagan vowed to fire any controller who walked off the job. On August 3, 1981, around 13,000 PATCO members went on strike. Reagan issued an ultimatum: return to work within 48 hours or lose your jobs. Two days later, Reagan fired those that remained on the picket lines—about 11,345 in total—and banned them all from ever working for the federal government again (President Bill Clinton rescinded the federal employment ban on striking PATCO workers in 1993). As air transport in the United States ground to a halt, replacement workers—some of them air traffic control supervisors, others military personnel—were brought in. Two weeks later, the FAA started hiring new air traffic controllers. By October, PATCO was decertified. It would take about a decade and billions of dollars before the air traffic control system returned to its pre-strike capacity.

In the three decades since the showdown, the PATCO strike has come to be seen as a seminal moment in modern American labor relations. For organized labor, the 1981 strike was a critical defeat from which it has never fully recovered. Up until that time, employers could legally replace striking workers on a permanent basis, but avoided doing so as a matter of course. Thereafter, taking a cue from the White House, private companies embraced the strategy and jettisoned striking employees. Chastened by the setback, unions were put on the defensive, and strikes and other hard-edged maneuvers fell out of favor. Indeed, rather than exacting better pay and benefits from management, unions, both public and private, started making concessions. Among conservatives, this sea change was a long time coming, and a welcome correction to what they perceive as a bloated and inefficient labor movement that inhibited the free market. Many on the left, meanwhile, continue to draw a direct line between the 1981 strike and three decades of stagnant and declining wages among blue-collar and middle-class workers. The PATCO strike casts a long shadow for both organized labor and labor skeptics, and as the FAA funding dispute demonstrates, air traffic control has yet to emerge from it.

Beyond air traffic control and air traffic controller–related concerns, the air transportation infrastructure is also threatened by a potential shortage of seasoned pilots, one that is only expected to grow more severe in the years ahead. Worry over inexperience in the cockpit was exacerbated in 2009, following the fatal crash of Colgan Air Flight 3407 in Buffalo, New York, on February 12. The crash occurred after the pilot, attempting to land the plane in wintry conditions, responded incorrectly to a stall warning. The tragedy struck a powerful contrast with an event that occurred in the previous month. On January 15, Captain Chesley Sullenberger III guided US Airways Flight 1549, its engine crippled by birds, to a miraculous landing on the Hudson River. Though both the pilot and copilot of Flight 3407 had each logged in excess of 2,000 hours in the cockpit, Congress passed a measure to increase pilot-training requirements over the course of two years. Before they can steer a commercial airplane, pilots must log 1500 hours in the air. Prior to the measure, the requirement was 250 hours.

However, new training standards only emphasized a larger dilemma. Flight training is expensive, costing in excess of $50,000, and due to the high rate of defaults, lenders are disinclined to advance the money to aspiring pilots. Entry-level pilots at regional airlines, the minor leagues of the industry, tend to earn yearly salaries in the low $20,000s. Senior pilots for the major airlines can take in close to $200,000, but those positions are hard to come by, requiring decades of service to obtain. The airline industry is also a tumultuous one. Bankruptcies are not uncommon, and pilots regularly endure furloughs, benefit concessions, and other difficulties.

Such circumstances dissuade many potential pilots from entering the field. As a consequence, airline pilots tend to be older, with an average age of 48.9 in 2009, an increase of over five years since 1990. Due to fears of a shortage, the FAA raised the mandatory retirement age of airline pilots from sixty to sixty-five in 2007. According to estimates, nearly 100,000 new pilots will be needed in North America by 2029. Where they will come from is as yet unclear. Nevertheless, the sense of worry is not universal. Robert Sumwalt, a member of the National Transportation Safey Board (NTSB), observed, "I've been hearing about a pilot shortage now for about the last 30 years, and I have yet to see it." In testimony before Congress, however, Sullenberger spoke for many in the airline industry when he observed, "My pay has been cut 40 percent. My pension, like most airline pensions, has been terminated and replaced by a [pension] guarantee worth only pennies on the dollar. . . . While I love my profession, I do not love what has happened to it."

Smart—and Fair—Skies

A Blueprint for the Future

By James C. May
Vital Speeches of the Day, August 2006

Delivered to the International Aviation Club of Washington, D.C., April 18, 2006

Hello. I'm delighted to be here. This is the second time that I've had the honor of addressing the International Aviation Club of Washington, D.C. In addition to the long history of your club, one of the beauties of this venue is the fact that the club is open to and attracts people from all parts of the world of aviation.

Let me begin, then, by recalling a bit of history that reminds us of our common heritage and—even more importantly—our common destiny. The year 2007 is notable for something more than the FAA reauthorization. It will also mark the 80th anniversary of Charles Lindbergh's historic flight across the Atlantic. I would like to dwell for a moment on the multiple accomplishments of Charles Lindbergh in bridging the two worlds of general and commercial aviation.

Like most amateur pilots, Lindbergh flew for the sheer joy of flight. He wrote: "I owned the world that hour as I rode over it—free of the earth, free of the mountains, free of the clouds, but how inseparably I was bound to them."

Lindbergh frankly admitted that he tackled the New York-to-Paris challenge out of a sheer love of adventure. He wanted to be the first. Beyond that, however, he was also powerfully motivated by another objective. As he said, he wanted to "establish aviation as a common means of transport." That is why he moved from stunt flying to airmail, before his historic flight. And that is why he went on a 48-state tour following his return—landing at 2 p.m. at 81 airports. Now, people might write off the transatlantic flight as nothing more than a daring adventure, like being the first to climb Mount Everest—but 2 p.m. at 81 airports that was solid proof of the idea that aviation had arrived as a reliable means of transportation.

I'd like to quote a few words out of Lindbergh's book, *The Spirit of St. Louis.* They show us how strongly he felt about having the right equipment and infrastructure in place, to turn what was eminently possible into a practical reality. This is Lindbergh in his own words:

"Businessmen think of aviation in terms of barnstorming, flying circuses, crashes, and high costs per flying hour. Somehow they must be made to understand the possibilities of flight. If they could see the real picture, it wouldn't be difficult to

---

finance an airline between St. Louis and New York, even at the price of three Bel-lancas (the most advanced new monoplane of the day). Then commercial pilots wouldn't have to fly old army warplanes and make night landings with flares instead of floodlights. If only I had the Bellanca, I'd show these businessmen what modern aircraft could do; I'd take them to New York in eight or nine hours. They'd see how swiftly and safely passengers could fly."

Lindbergh lived long enough to see the first American land on the moon. In fact, he and Neil Armstrong were close friends. There is a revealing quote from Armstrong in the Leonard Mosley biography of Lindbergh. As Armstrong and the other astronauts were going through various tests to prepare them for their trip to the moon, they were surprised to discover how much Lindbergh knew about space medicine. As Armstrong recalled—"He talked to us about things like air stresses, acceleration tolerance, the so-called Oxygen Paradox, as if the guy had spent hours in air pressure chambers himself—turns out he had, too. He knew more about some of the problems than the doctors did."

Everything I've told you indicates how passionately Lindbergh felt about using the latest and best technology to advance human flight in all its dimensions—from the exploration of space, to recreational flight, to the movement of people and goods.

Now let's imagine that Lindbergh had lived for another 30-plus years and were with us today. What would he think of our air transportation system? Well, even though we've advanced from flares to floodlights, and from beaten-up old warplanes to modern jets, there's one thing I think we can all agree on. Lindbergh—who was always so precise and meticulous in planning his own journeys—would be shocked and appalled at our lack of progress in some areas. More than three and a half de-cades after landing on the moon, it would strike him as very strange to see that we were still using a WWII era ATC architecture and communications.

While it is true that system components have vastly improved over the past 60 years, Lindbergh would find it hard to believe that we still rely on old technology that forces aircraft to fly inefficient, less direct routes, with unnecessarily inefficient separation requirements. That means more fuel and emissions, and wasted time and money for everyone—the military, business travelers, weekend fliers, and the airlines and their passengers. We're all paying the price.

So let me start by telling you about Smart Skies—ATA's blueprint for modern-izing and streamlining our air traffic control system, and finding a fair and equitable way of dividing the cost between users. Make no mistake: Fundamental reform in the way the current air traffic system operates is necessary because the current system is nearing overload. Looking out over the next 10 years, the FAA's work-load—according to its own numbers—is projected to rise 36 percent, from 45,100 flights per day to 61,400 flights per day. And that's even before completely factoring in the potential for an additional 20,000 VLJ flights. Before you take comfort in the thought that these VLJs won't be using major commercial airports, be warned that experts at MIT have concluded that 50 percent of future VLJ flights will begin or end in the same markets as those big commercial airports. That means that busi-ness aviation jets departing from Teterboro, and commercial flights departing from

Newark, will consume the same ATC resources. Remember—the dilemma facing us concerns the airspace—not airports.

Now if Lindbergh—having awakened from a long snooze, like Rip Van Winkle—decided to visit different segments of the aviation community and find out who was lobbying for the preservation of the antiquated and inefficient system that we now have, he would get a second surprise. Everywhere he went, he would find genuine and even passionate agreement on the need for change—but surprisingly little progress.

If he went to the National Business Aviation Association, he would hear that the first of the NBAA's five guiding principles was "Modernize with Satellite Communications." What's more, he would hear that the second principle was "Invest in the National Air Transportation System."

If he went to General Aviation Manufacturers Association, he would hear the exact same thing. And ditto with the National Air Transportation Association. Recently, the three organizations—NBAA, GAMA and NATA—joined together in enunciating those "principles" as their navigational beacons for aviation policy reform.

Lindbergh would also find that the FAA administrator is working hard to reform the FAA and accelerate the transition from a ground-based to a satellite-based system.

And if Lindbergh came to the Air Transport Association—or to any of the leading airlines that we represent—he would find four-square, enthusiastic support for modernization and reform along the same lines.

So why in the world are we having such a difficult time moving forward?

Well, it has something to do with money—who pays and how we divvy up the cost between different users. It also has to do with group dynamics. To quote the writer Warren Bennis, "We all see and understand the need for change, and instinctively avoid it at all costs."

So, let's be smart about figuring out how to manage our resources and build a system that accommodates all users and transforms our current inefficient, constrained framework into a modern, top-notch air traffic control system. First, FAA must reduce current costs by consolidating unnecessary facilities, managing airspace system wide, minimizing reliance on ground-based equipment, decommissioning obsolete equipment and procedures, and rationalizing the workforce. With a $14 billion budget, nearly 41,000 national airspace operational facilities, FAA-operated or contract towers at 489 air-

Looking out over the next 10 years, the FAA's workload—according to its own numbers—is projected to rise 36 percent, from 45,100 flights per day to 61,400 flights per day.

ports, and over 45,000 employees, this won't be easy—to say the least. And while streamlining its operations, FAA must retain responsibility for the inspection and certification of over 220,000 aircraft and 620,000 pilots.

Administrator Blakey's progressive, performance-based approach to management and Russ Chew's Air Traffic Organization, or ATO, are making headway, but it's going to be a long, hard fight. FAA needs to apply the valuable lessons it's learned from previous ATC system development and rely on the invaluable expertise of aviation experts who know what works and what doesn't. I cannot emphasize enough how FAA is going to need the industry's full support as it tackles fundamental, systemic challenges. Even with our support, this transition won't happen overnight . . . so let's get moving.

Aligning the infrastructure and workforce around the workload will enable FAA to utilize all of its resources more productively. Inevitably, politics will rear its ugly head, and there will be trade-offs that not everyone will like (including, undoubtedly, some ATA member carriers). Congress will not hesitate to insert itself into the political mix, particularly when program cuts and consolidations impact constituents back home. The recent congressional foray into the transition of the TRACON at Palm Beach to Miami International is a perfect example of what should not happen . . . but does. FAA and Congress must make tough, unpopular decisions.

Let me turn now to one of the critical questions: How the collective "we" are going to pay for this transition? If the structural challenges I just described weren't hard enough, today FAA is forced to rely on an unstable revenue source for funding. Of course, the savings from FAA streamlining and smart-sizing will be used to fund the transition. In addition, Smart Skies supports bonding authorization for FAA to permit access to financial markets and ensure maximum leverage for available financial resources. Since the U.S. economy depends on an air traffic system that can accommodate the needs of all users, Smart Skies also advocates significant General Fund contributions. But experience teaches us not to expect too much from this source.

The real kicker—the grease in the fire you've all been waiting for—is Smart Skies' funding approach. It's the sensible approach long advocated by presidential commissions and leading economists, and now championed by the FAA and DOT and adopted by most of the major air traffic control providers in the world: user fees. This is an international solution to an international problem, and you're just the group to appreciate the significance of that statement.

For a moment, let's think about why user fees work and why major air traffic control providers, such as the United Kingdom, Canada, Germany, France and Australia have long used them to fund air traffic control. User fees provide a stable revenue source: Those using the system pay for the services they use and that money is used to develop, maintain, and enhance the system. Simple. Today Congress unquestionably controls FAA's funding and priorities through the federal budget process. Although ticket, fuel and waybill taxes pass to the Aviation Trust Fund and the general public "funds" the General Fund, the reality is that Congress has the final word.

Each year, Congress reduces the General Fund contribution and FAA receives less than the amount collected in aviation use taxes. For the past 15 years, the portion of FAA operating costs coming from the General Fund has declined, with only 20 percent coming from the fund in fiscal year 2005. To be blunt, those who say the

Trust Fund is healthy, wealthy and wise are ignoring the facts. They point to rising fare data and say, "Crisis averted"—but that ignores the fact that fares are highly cyclical and ebb and flow from one month to the next. In a study last month, GAO found that the uncommitted Trust Fund balance declined from about $7 billion at the end of 2001 to less than $2 billion at the end of 2005. GAO also found that if 2006 and 2007 revenues are below forecasted levels, the Trust Fund's uncommitted balance could reach zero by 2007. That doesn't sound healthy, wealthy or wise to me.

Opponents in business aviation talk as though user fees are some kind of a radical and untested concept—and one that was likely to victimize "the little guy"—or the weekend flier. Ladies and gentlemen, that's totally wrong on both counts. In fact, user fees are in place in most sophisticated ATC systems worldwide. They are a simpler as well as a fairer alternative to the current patchwork of ticket and flight taxes that are now used to fund ATC services.

In addition, as I hope everyone in this room knows, Smart Skies very clearly states that "Operators of piston-powered general aviation aircraft should continue to pay through their fuel tax mechanism." ATA has joined with NBAA, GAMA and AOPA in agreeing on this exemption from user fees. That's only fair. Operators of piston-powered aircraft interact with the ATC system in a minimal way. Therefore, they should pay less, while those using en route, oceanic and terminal services should pay considerably more. There is no need to change the system as it affects small piston-powered aircraft. This is not rocket science or voodoo—it's the system in place throughout the world.

Under the system that is in place today, airlines use two-thirds of ATC services, but they pay over 90 percent of the cost. That means they paid $9 billion last year. Let me say that again—they used 69 percent and paid 94 percent. Meanwhile, business aviation used 15 percent of ATC services, but paid just 4 percent.

And that's where we disagree with our aviation friends. ATA does not think that *all* general aviation—including million-dollar jets operated by private companies and others in the aviation business—should continue to pay far less than what it costs the FAA to deliver them safely through the airspace. It's a subsidy.

Now some people might think a smaller jet exacts a smaller cost, but the simple fact is: The size of the jet is immaterial in the ATC context. A business jet poses the same kind of challenge in the maintenance of air safety as a commercial jet, and represents an equal cost burden in ATC services. Tracked on radar, or seen from a satellite, and then transferred to a computer screen, a blip is a blip is a blip. Its volume that drives system costs today and will drive it tomorrow even more. The ATO can tell you, staffing and volume are inextricably linked. FAA—not ATA—estimates that general aviation, including business and corporate aviation, uses roughly 30 percent of system resources.

So where is any sense of fairness in the allocation of cost? Today a noncommercial Gulfstream IV flying from New York to Los Angeles contributes $545 to the Trust Fund through fuel taxes. An American 767 making the same flight pays more than $3,000, or almost $2,500 dollars more, even though they make use of the same ATC services. That's not fair. It's ridiculous.

Since operators of small piston-powered general aviation are exempt from our user-fee proposal, the user-fee controversy really shouldn't be their fight. The reality is that business aviation—not mom-and-pop operators and weekend warriors—is fighting user fees in the U.S. because they see their free ride threatened. Before coming here, I spent some time going through the Fact Book found at the NBAA's Web site. Here are some revealing statistics culled from the NBAA's 2003 Fact Book.

"Among the Fortune 500, 376 companies operate business aircraft."

NBAA represents the interests of 7,600 companies that "own, operate or support more than 9,500 general aviation aircraft used as an aid to the conduct of business."

According to NBAA, "the number of companies operating business aircraft in the United States has grown more than 60 percent, from 6,584 companies operating 9,504 aircraft in 1991 to 10,661 companies operating 15,879 aircraft in 2003," and I'm sure it's much more than that now. If I'm reading this correctly, according to NBAA in 2003 almost 16,000 business aircraft were operated in the U.S., or more than twice the number of aircraft in today's U.S. commercial fleet.

And finally, another fact from NBAA, more than 70 percent of all hours flown by general aviation are for business and commercial purposes.

So who is the much-advertised "little guy" who's at risk here? As I've already explained, it's not the owner of some little Piper Cub. Nobody's going after him or her. No, the supposed "little guy" in this tableau is none other than some of the biggest and profitable companies in the world—companies like Exxon Mobil, Anheuser-Bush and IBM, to name three with representatives on the NBAA board.

Now it may interest you to know that Exxon Mobil is—far and away—the biggest and most profitable company in the world. Helped by the good luck (for it) of rising fuel prices, Exxon Mobil earned $25 billion—that's billion, not million—in 2004 and $36 billion in 2005. Hurt by the bad luck (for them) of rising fuel prices, the two biggest U.S. airlines—American and United—lost $26 billion over the same two-year period. With just one year of Exxon's profits, we could wipe almost all the losses that U.S. airlines have sustained since 2001.

So pardon me if I feel a little bummed out at the thought of the airlines having to subsidize Lee Raymond and Exxon Mobil. When Raymond retired at the end of 2005 as Exxon's chairman and CEO, he also gained continued access to use of the company's corporate jets—to go on top of almost $350 million in compensation over the past few years. Is Lee Raymond a "little guy" who needs and deserves further subsidies?

Here are the numbers that help to put that into perspective. As I told you, business aviation now consumes 15 percent of ATC. That is nearly equal to the load on the system by American and United combined. If all users were truly paying for the cost of the services they consume, you would expect these two segments to pay about the same in fees and taxes. Not true. In fiscal year 2004, American and United paid $1.53 billion—that's billion—toward the cost of ATC services, while the pay-at-the-pump business aviation pumped in a measly $422 million. Hence the subsidy—amounting to more than a billion dollars—that goes from the airlines to business aviation—and the likes of Lee Raymond.

Sure, I understand why business aviation doesn't want to pay for ATC services. Who wants to pay "user fees" when you're getting a nearly free ride? But it's time—past time—for the U.S. to implement a system that fairly charges users for the services they use.

As it happens, that's exactly what the U.S. has long advocated in deliberations of the ICAO Air Navigation Services Economics Panel and other ICAO efforts.

In the long run, the transition to an efficient, sophisticated air traffic control and communications system will yield money-saving and productivity-boosting benefits for all of us, including business aviation. It is business aviation's best interests to join us in upgrading an ATC that serves no one well. It's time for all of us who are serious about the continued growth and prosperity of our air transport system as a whole to join together.

Comedienne Lily Tomlin once said: "We are all in this alone." Unfortunately, that comes fairly close to describing the attitude of different groups within the aviation community in recent years. But that is a destructive attitude and it is one of the reasons why the aviation industry as a whole has been terribly slow—even shamefully slow—on moving forward with modernization.

Let me close by reiterating the "bare bones" of my vision for FAA reauthorization and ATC modernization. I think you'll find that the aviation industry is in serious agreement as to what needs to be done: We need to adopt a sustainable, equitable funding mechanism; reduce the cost and increase the capacity and efficiency of the current system; and build a system that accommodates all system users and growth. We need to think, as Lindbergh did, in the broadest of terms—of what is good for the future of aviation as a whole.

We all know what it is that we must do. Now we must work together to turn what is eminently possible and desperately needed into a practical reality from which we will all benefit. It is our turn now to deploy the latest and best technology to the advancement of flight in all of its dimensions.

We share a common heritage. Surely, our destiny is not to squander our inheritance, but to build upon it, and, as Lindbergh said in his last book, *The Autobiography of Values*, to "acquaint more and more people with the adventure, ease and practical merits of flying."

Thank you.

❖

Address by James C. May, President and Chief Executive Officer, Air Transport Association of America.

Why You Hate to Fly

By Evan Sparks
The American, October 23, 2008

Thirty years ago this October, the era of affordable mass air travel was unleashed. Evan Sparks explains why this revolution stalled, and what can be done to finish it.

Airline complaint one-upmanship is an old standby of small talk—"You had to wait six hours at the gate? That's nothing! I was wedged between two linebackers and the in-flight movie was the latest from Larry the Cable Guy." But is air travel really this bad? Travelers seem to think so. One measure finds that customer satisfaction with airlines is at its lowest point in three years; and the 2008 Airline Quality Rating, an aggregation of consumer complaints to the Department of Transportation, reports that complaints were up 60 percent since 2007.

Airlines seem to give travelers fewer reasons to smile. By mid-2008, many airlines had begun aggressive campaigns to bring in more cash through fees. Several airlines devalued their frequent flier miles, hiked the fees to book a "free" ticket, and started charging for checked baggage. New fees were added so fast that Southwest Airlines began running ads touting the fact that they merely had not added any fees.

And if the fees weren't enough, fares are rising as airlines follow through on promised capacity cuts, trimming routes and frequencies. With fewer seats, passengers have fewer options and face higher fares to match record jet fuel prices.

But it's not just the airlines. The Federal Aviation Administration operates an air traffic control system that cannot keep up with demand for air travel, forcing delays in congested airspace and airports, especially in the northeast United States. Many airlines now add several minutes to a flight's travel time, thus lowering the odds of having the flight reported as delayed and lowering passengers' expectations.

The FAA is not the only agency aggravating travelers. The Transportation Security Administration, the hastily constructed bureaucratic response to the 9/11 terrorist attacks, has become what some experts call "security theater," a show of rigorous inspection whose primary function is to make us feel safer.

So if we increasingly hate air travel, who's to blame? The unlikely bogeyman du jour is airline deregulation, which culminated with the signing of the Airline Deregulation Act by President Carter 30 years ago on October 24, 1978. Long praised by economists as pro-competition and consumer-friendly, airline deregulation is now

Long praised by economists as pro-competition and consumer-friendly, airline deregulation is now under attack for allegedly hurting airlines and travelers.

under attack for allegedly hurting airlines and travelers.

For example, James Oberstar (D-Minnesota), the powerful chairman of the House Transportation Committee, warned the airline industry in April that "public patience is running out" and that Congress might feel the need to "reregulate" the industry. And in a speech at the Wings Club in New York in June, former American Airlines CEO Robert L. Crandall called for just that: "Three decades of deregulation have demonstrated that airlines have special characteristics incompatible with a completely unregulated environment." He proposed a slew of policy changes to ensure that airlines "earn the profits needed to sustain the huge investments essential to the industry's future"—including "modest price regulation . . . and a more accommodating stance toward industry collaboration."

But these assertions fly in the face of experience. Airline deregulation has had remarkable benefits. Alfred Kahn, known as the "father of airline deregulation" for his service as chairman of the Civil Aeronautics Board (CAB) as well as his forceful case for widespread deregulation in the 1970s, estimates the consumer benefits at $5 billion to $10 billion per year. Fares over the past 30 years have fallen dramatically in real terms—by as much as 40 percent since 1980—while passenger traffic has spiked.

To be sure, efficiencies gained through new aircraft, advanced computer reservation systems, and increased passenger totals also helped. But many of the productivity improvements in the post-regulation era stemmed from competitive pressures unleashed by deregulation. Indeed, Clifford Winston, an economist at the Brookings Institution, says recent shocks to the aviation system might have been even worse under regulation.

If airline deregulation is not responsible for the litany of woes expressed by passengers today, what might explain it? One hint can be found in a 30-year-old warning. In 1978, Kahn was under pressure to restrict airline operations to correspond with air traffic control and airport capacity. In a speech at the time he said, "There is no guarantee that freer competition on the airline side of the equation—that is the part that creates the demand for airports [and air traffic control]—alone will solve these problems. On the contrary, it will stimulate more air travel. . . . My moral is simply this to the FAA: If you are going to follow economically irrational policies, don't ask the CAB to bail you out by doing the same thing."

According to this view, airline deregulation is an unfinished reform: while unleashing airline competition, it did not provide for a competitive aviation infrastructure. Air traffic control, airports, and congestion management remain organized not much differently than 30 years ago. And despite deregulation's benefits, this is where our current problems reside.

The good news for our aviation system is that many of its problems have so-lutions at the ready. These solutions—from airport management and congestion pricing to air traffic control reform—have been tested, often with great success, overseas. They may hold the key to bringing our aviation infrastructure into step with the promise of airline deregulation.

Airports for Sale

The United States lags behind the world in seeking out efficient airport manage-ment and investment solutions. Here, airports tend to be owned and operated by cities, port authorities, or other government agencies. The exceptions are so rare that they stand out: Indianapolis International Airport, managed until 2007 by Brit-ish airport company BAA, and Chicago's Midway Airport, now for sale.

Many other countries, from Latin America and Europe to East Asia and Aus-tralia, have experimented extensively with airport privatization, often with salutary effects on competition and infrastructure investment. The experiments comprise an innovative array of corporate arrangements, from independent government corpo-rations to nonprofits and private companies with significant government stakes to entirely privately owned ventures.

Australia and New Zealand are home to some of the most advanced experiments in privatization. They have seen widespread private ownership and light-handed regulation of airports that "work quite well," according to a recent volume on airline infrastructure released by the Brookings Institution. In Canada, nonprofit corpora-tions have achieved government goals to expand airport capacity, especially in To-ronto and Vancouver. A list of the world's busiest airports includes several that are privately owned and operated to some degree, including London's Heathrow Airport (BAA), Bangkok's Suvarnabhumi Airport (Airports of Thailand), Frankfurt Interna-tional Airport (Fraport), and Amsterdam's Schiphol Airport (Schiphol Group).

One of the most common arguments against airport privatization is the experi-ence of BAA, which owns London's three main airports—Heathrow, Gatwick, and Stansted, comprising 91 percent of the capital's commercial aviation traffic. The UK Competition Commission has argued that its common ownership has stifled airport competition, neglected the needs of its airports' users, and impeded ade-quate investment. The BAA case proves the importance of competition among air-ports. If privatized to promote competition, London's airports would have had more incentives to invest in expanded capacity.

For a helpful stateside comparison, consider New York City and San Francisco. In the Big Apple, the three major airports—John F. Kennedy International, LaGuar-dia, and Newark Liberty International—are owned and operated by the Port Au-thority of New York and New Jersey. In the San Francisco Bay area, a similarly ex-pensive and densely populated area, the three main airports are owned and operated by different authorities. The published average landing fee at New York's airports is 73 percent higher than at San Francisco International Airport, which finds itself competing with the even cheaper Oakland and San Jose airports.

Crowd Control

The skies are crowded—and I'm not just talking about legroom. In 2006 and 2007, snarled skies and tangled taxiways dominated headlines. A storm had thousands stuck in Dallas; snow stranded hundreds of passengers on JetBlue planes at JFK. A "passenger's bill of rights" that would guarantee minimum levels of food, drink, air, and customer service picked up steam in Congress, and congressional committees dragged airline executives in front of C-SPAN cameras to berate them. And the costs of congestion are enormous. The New York City comptroller's office estimated that delays at New York area airports ate up almost $200 million in lost productivity in 2007.

But while Congress pins the blame on aviation's private sector, the real cause of congestion delays is structural and political: an unwillingness to charge the true value of in-demand space. In this case, the space is runway capacity. Airports currently charge airlines landing fees on the basis of weight. This has prompted airlines to favor smaller aircraft, like so-called regional jets, over larger aircraft. The current structure, says Kahn, "gives enormous advantage to planes with fewer passengers at peak hours at congested airports." Hence the plethora of regional jets carrying fewer passengers at one of America's most crowded airports, LaGuardia.

Congestion pricing is a sensible solution long advocated by aviation economists. As Kahn says, "We used congestion pricing in regulating electric utilities in New York in the '70s!" In aviation, it has been studied since the 1960s. In practice, it would mean that crowded airports would charge higher runway use fees at the busiest times of day.

There have been signs of progress on the congestion pricing front, but significant obstacles remain. In July 2008, the FAA adopted a rule to allow crowded airports to introduce a revenue-neutral "peak-pricing model" into current weight-based charges. But airlines and consumer groups remain dead set against full-scale congestion pricing, the latter fearing that airlines will only pass on to travelers the increased costs. "All this will do is end up taking more money from passengers to line the airport's pockets, and that doesn't help," says Brett Snyder, an airline industry veteran and travel blogger. Yet congestion pricing will impose on airlines, and by extension travelers, the true cost of their trips.

The 2006–2007 congestion brouhaha resembles that of 1999–2000, when there were nightmare stories of travelers spending hours on grounded planes and when a passengers' bill of rights was also floated. That era of congestion ended with the September 11 attacks, which, in the months following, induced roughly a 20 percent decline in demand for air travel. This bought the aviation sector several years to deal with the underlying congestion problem: lack of capacity at airports and in air traffic control. These were not addressed, but the rise of $140-per-barrel oil may have a 9/11-style effect on the airline industry. According to Winston, "The 'crisis' of gas prices is going to end the 'crisis' of traffic delays."

If the industry capacity cuts of 2008 lead to breathing room on the congestion front, will we move forward in increasing infrastructure capacity to match future demand? Don't get your hopes up. Without an ongoing crisis, there is likely to be little public pressure for systemic aviation reforms. Congestion pricing should be thought of as a stopgap measure until we make deeper reforms, one of the most pressing of which should address the failure of the nation's air traffic control system to keep up with the demand unleashed by deregulation.

Traffic Jam

Air traffic control in the United States is administered by the Air Traffic Organization, a division of the FAA that employs a cadre of 14,000 air traffic controllers and 5,000 air traffic managers. Controllers are trained professionals who are, even under taxing circumstances, capable of manually separating and shepherding dozens of planes in the sky. Happily, the FAA has seen accident rates fall markedly.

But ATO is a troubled entity: it lacks a source of funding that corresponds to the services it provides; its labor relations are toxic; and safety concerns are beginning to rise. More important in the long run is ATO's persistent delay in making long-planned upgrades to the nation's air traffic control system—a collection of technologies known as "NextGen."

One explanation for ATO's problems is its ill-conceived financial structure. ATO is funded by taxes on jet fuel and airline tickets. Thus, revenue might fall if airlines introduce jets that are more fuel efficient. Aviation is a cyclical industry, so it sells fewer tickets during slowdowns, cutting ticket tax revenue. Moreover, ATO's revenue has nothing to do with actual use of the air traffic system. Many non-commercial aircraft use controlled airspace but pay no ticket tax; their contribution is from the jet fuel tax.

The agency has not come close to keeping up with demand for air travel. In fact, the FAA is on the verge of its largest personnel crisis since Ronald Reagan fired striking controllers en masse in 1981. The FAA hired a huge wave of controllers in the early 1980s to replace the strikers, and this generation is near retirement—without sufficient reinforcements.

The result, according to controllers' union president Patrick Forrey, is a "staffing crisis" leading to "an unacceptable compromise in safety." The FAA is also moving more controllers from the line to management, further diluting the pool of qualified staff. According to Melvin Davis, a controller in Southern California, "The FAA will tell you that staffing does not affect safety, and that is simply untrue."

At a hearing on June 11, air traffic controllers told Congress that their facilities are understaffed. They added that the chronic understaffing requires them to work six-day weeks, with new hires put in sensitive positions relatively early without intensive guidance. Fatigue, they said, is a growing concern. Concordant with the stretched situation, the rate of runway incursions—that is, an aircraft being on an active runway when it shouldn't—is rising. But Steven A. Wallace, a controller in Miami, reports that the FAA is "cutting" rates by waving the magic wand of terminology and relabeling some runway incursions as "proximity incidents."

'With User Pay Comes User Say'

The solution is not simply to raise controllers' salaries and hire more of them; it is to follow-through fully on the promise of NextGen. The FAA has bungled the crucial technological transformations that will modernize our aviation system. Is there an alternative?

Just as in the airport sector, many countries have privatized or partially privatized their air traffic control sectors. The United States is one of the few developed countries that still has a publicly owned and operated air traffic control system, unlike the autonomous government corporations of Australia, Germany, and New Zealand; the public-private partnership in Great Britain; and the fully privatized, nonprofit Nav Canada.

What has been the result of commercializing air traffic control? In a speech in Washington in February, Eugene Hoeven of the Commercial Air Navigation Services Organization said: "The ability to set fees in line with the service provided has introduced a new dynamic to what has traditionally been a bureaucratic approach to service delivery. Airline operators have rightfully demanded greater accountability— 'with user pay comes user say'—and a greater sensitivity to customer needs has developed. There is no longer any doubt as to who the customer is." As long as the charges airlines face don't correspond to the costs they impose on the system, U.S. air traffic control will be under little pressure to serve the system's users.

Is private-sector involvement in air traffic control a panacea? No one says so. For example, labor issues have not disappeared. Airservices Australia's union recently claimed that some of their facilities are so understaffed that only a few sick controllers means that facilities must temporarily close down. But even if Airservices Australia has not properly projected staffing needs, it is a poster child for how commercialization can provide a solid foundation for technological investment. The company is currently implementing cutting-edge technology to allow automated air traffic control.

And while the United States may not be ready for a privatization of the kind in place in Canada, it needs at a minimum to implement user fees for ATO. Such a change would make the organization more responsive to its customers' needs and concerns, provide a stable revenue source that corresponds to services used, and protect ATO from political influence. As Kahn concludes, "I don't think this problem's ever going to be solved until we take control away from members of Congress. . . .Government is simply incapable of doing it."

The Good News

The news about aviation isn't all bad. Airline pilot Patrick Smith, a columnist for Salon.com, talks up the good news about the cost of flying: "We have lost an appreciation for just how cheap and accessible flying has become. The fact that for a few pennies per mile we have the ability to zip ourselves halfway across the country, or halfway around the world, in a matter of hours, in nearly absolute safety, is almost entirely taken for granted."

And we've been zipping halfway across the country with a lighter carbon footprint, too, according to recent figures from the Environmental Protection Agency.

Benefits that aren't even anticipated today might come from enabling innovation in aviation infrastructure. According to Winston, "What we learn from airline deregulation is just how much was suppressed from innovation under government control." Neither he nor anyone else can fully estimate the benefits of, say, air traffic control privatization and the organizational and technological innovation that such a reform in the world's largest aviation market might stimulate.

After 30 years, airline deregulation has been remarkably successful. The U.S. aviation sector's very real problems are due not to the lack of regulation but to excessive or ineffective government involvement in other segments of the industry. By making its aviation infrastructure more competitive and efficient, the United States can spend the next 30 years building on deregulation's unmet potential.

❖

Evan Sparks, an associate editor at the American Enterprise Institute, blogs on aviation at EvanSparks.com.

Hell on a Tarmac

By Robert Verbruggen
National Review, August 4, 2008

Every frequent flier has his airline horror stories. Delays, missed connections, family members stranded on holidays, lost vacation time. Virtually all observers—from these frustrated passengers to policy wonks—agree that the industry needs to deal with airport congestion, over both the short and the long term.

But unfortunately, when it comes to what to do and how to do it, there are a lot of conflicting and powerful interests in play—the air-traffic controllers' union, the airlines, leisure- and corporate-aviation advocates, the Federal Aviation Administration. As a result, the federal government keeps kicking the can. Recently, Congress failed to reauthorize and update the FAA, instead extending its old budget for a few more months. It has done this several times in the last year.

Looking past special interests, however, it's clear what needs to be done. In the short term, the FAA and airports need to charge users in a way that discourages congestion. In the long term, the FAA needs to update its technology through a project known as NextGen; to do this quickly, safely, and fairly, a total overhaul of the agency is in order.

As it stands, the FAA does a decent job of supporting itself. In 2006, for example, only 18 percent of its budget came from general taxpayers; the rest comprised excise taxes collected from aviation users in various ways. This makes sense, as the FAA's service is for specific individuals and businesses, not the general public. But the FAA collects these taxes in a nonsensical fashion, and changes could ease congestion while funding NextGen—which is expected to cost airlines and the FAA, in total, something like $47 billion.

On a given route, pretty much every plane needs the same things, including direction from controllers and a runway to land on. But currently, flights are taxed at very different levels—for example, airline passengers pick up a huge part of the tab through ticket taxes, so a corporate jet can fly the same route as a commercial airline yet pay far less. According to a cost-allocation study by the FAA, corporate and leisure aviation drives 16 percent of air-traffic-control costs, but contributes only 3 percent of the taxes.

Airline lobbyists, perfectly reasonably, support closing this gap. One way to achieve this would be to replace the current system with user fees, where each plane pays for the services it uses. User-fee advocates include the FAA itself, which included them in its proposed modernization plan.

User fees provide more than fairness: They reduce congestion, and not just by making corporate jetting more expensive. Under the current system, airlines pay mainly by the passenger (the aforementioned ticket taxes and a per passenger "segment tax"), not the plane. Therefore, when an airline de-

> ***When flying imposes delay and congestion costs on others, those costs should be reflected in higher prices.***

cides to fly more small planes instead of fewer big ones, the fees don't reflect this. And as a result, there has been a remarkable increase in the use of small-capacity "regional jets" in recent years. Since regional jets cause the same congestion and use the same air-traffic-control services as bigger planes, this strains the system. User fees would discourage the use of regional jets.

"The average member of Congress doesn't appreciate that user fees can reduce congestion," says Dorothy Robyn, a principal of the Brattle Group, an economics- and financial-consulting firm. Robyn advised the Clinton administration on aviation issues, and recently wrote a paper on them for the Council of Economic Advisers. "The FAA never explained it, and the airlines haven't explained it. In all of [former FAA administrator Marion C. Blakey's] appearances arguing for user fees, she never drew the link."

User-fee advocates are typically willing to carve out an exception for recreational aircraft. "They don't fly in the same airspace as commercial and business jets," Robyn says. Robert Poole of the Reason Foundation, a libertarian think tank, supports a similar exception.

Despite their many advantages, user fees have received little political support. Even with an exception for recreational aircraft, the Aircraft Owners and Pilots Association opposes them, according to a statement, because "the imposition of user fees on any segment of aviation would inevitably lead to user fees for all." (Poole offers a more skeptical interpretation: The corporate-jet faction of the association, in an effort to avoid paying its fair share, is ginning up the recreational flying faction, which has "wealthy members in just about every congressional district.") When the House passed an FAA reauthorization bill—it was the lack of a Senate bill that held it up through September—there were no user fees.

The airports can do more to ease congestion as well. Aviators currently pay landing fees, but like ticket taxes they fail to address the problem: The fees are based on planes' weights. This isn't even a good way to assess wear and tear on the runway, because heavier planes can sometimes do less damage than lighter ones, depending on how the weight is distributed when they land. But more important, there is no extra charge for scheduling a flight to a busy airport at a peak time. An aviator can hold up traffic without bearing the cost of doing so.

There are a variety of pricing schemes that would ease congestion—auctioning takeoff and landing slots, charging more during peak times—but not a single airport in America uses them. The Air Transport Association, a lobby representing the major airlines, says it will sue if any airport does. Though the Department of Transportation claims airports may charge for congestion, the ATA disputes the DOT's authority to make such a determination.

The ATA worries that congestion pricing would make flying more expensive. It has even claimed that congestion pricing amounts to "artificially constraining demand." But when flying imposes delay and congestion costs on others, those costs *should* be reflected in higher prices. Also, there is a limited supply of runways available during busy times, so there's nothing "artificial" about letting the price mechanism sort out the mess.

As for the long-term project, NextGen, the FAA predicts about two decades of transition. NextGen's main accomplishment will be to overhaul air-traffic control—currently, controllers use an antiquated radar system to guide planes through the sky, but NextGen will install far-more-precise satellite GPS. Each pilot will know exactly where he is, and where other planes are, so aircraft can fly closer together with less help from controllers. Flights are expected to double over the next 20 years, and NextGen is expected to double to triple capacity over the same period.

But even though the end goal is clear, and there are good ideas for funding the initiative, implementation is a mess. For example, the FAA released a proposal last year that would have required most aircraft, by 2020, to be able to transmit (but not receive) their GPS coordinates. Air-traffic controllers are already on course to receive and use these coordinates by 2013, making life easier and cheaper for the FAA, but airspace users will see few benefits. It's not until pilots can receive other planes' coordinates in the air that they can access information about the situation around them, and the 2020 proposal had little to say about that. It did what almost nothing else could, and unified the various segments of the air-travel industry—in opposition.

"Let's say to buy a car, you have to pay $340 for GPS, but it won't work for a year. You'd say, 'Why would I buy the GPS now?'" says David A. Castelveter, vice president of communications for the ATA. "We're strong believers in the transition. The question is how we go about doing it."

Most observers suggest a gradual implementation that has immediate benefits to users, focusing on areas where GPS is most advantageous. "There are places where it can be used right now, where we don't have radar," says Patrick Forrey, president of the air-traffic controllers' union. "The mountains, the Gulf of Mexico, even the oceans of the world."

It's debatable whether the FAA, in its current form, is even capable of handling such a transition. The FAA both provides and regulates air-traffic-control services (an arguable conflict of interest), and relies on Congress for money. "What we need is an arm's-length regulator that's distinct from the air-traffic-control services. Almost every country in Europe, and Canada, Australia, and New Zealand, has done this," the Reason Foundation's Poole says. Poole also emphasizes freedom from the federal budget—the ability to charge users, and to issue bonds to fund modernization. A spun-off air-traffic-control provider need not be private, just a distinct government entity.

"We also need, as happens in Canada, these decisions to be thrashed out by a board that can control the investment plan and schedule. The board would include everyone—private pilots, business aviation, airlines—under some kind of adult supervision," Poole says. "If the small guys [i.e., recreational pilots] won't go along, you find a way to pay them off, and everyone's best interest is served if you have this all in place by 2012. You provide some kind of subsidy to help them get the equipment by a much quicker deadline. Those kinds of deals don't seem to be possible in the current system."

To make this a reality, though, lawmakers would have to overcome stiff opposition from the air-traffic controllers' union—which opposes privatization and sees a spin-off, says Forrey, as "one and the same thing." Forrey cites concerns about safety; he says the FAA will do a better job regulating itself than overseeing a spun-off agency. But there are other reasons the union would oppose an air traffic-control spin-off, and modernization more broadly, Poole says: "They have a history of dragging their feet on anything that would increase productivity. They want a bigger workforce in preference to a smaller one." There's no reason for existing controllers to lose their jobs, Poole adds, but the new system will make it possible to hire fewer new ones.

For airline customers, congestion is becoming more than a nuisance—it's a severe and rapidly growing roadblock to travel. To relieve the traffic jams at the airports, the government will need to set aside interest-group concerns in favor of market-based solutions.

5

Railways

A train moves through the Auburndale station in Newton, Massachusetts, one of 175 cities and towns serviced the by Massachusetts Bay Transportation Authority's Commuter Rail. In 2009 the Commuter Rail serviced approximately 143,700 passengers on weekdays.

Yesterday's Rails

By Paul McCaffrey

The United States possesses the largest railroad network of any country in the world. In total, the system measures around 225,000 kilometers of track and represents one of the greatest engineering feats in history. Among the most important achievements in the construction of this network was the completion, on May 10, 1869, of the First Transcontinental Railroad at Promontory Summit, Utah.

As railroad technology migrated to the United States following the invention of the steam-powered railroad in Great Britain in 1825, a vision of a railroad connecting the country from coast to coast began to develop. Writing in the *Western Emigrant* newspaper in 1832, Samuel Dexter declared, "It is in our power to open an immense interior country to market, to unite our eastern and western shores firmly together." Within this vision was a pronounced element of manifest destiny: the United States had yet to expand to the Pacific coast, but proponents of the railroad were certain that one day it would.

The need for a railway was obvious. The overland route across the continent by wagon was an arduous and costly one. The ocean voyage was equally problematic, necessitating a trip around Cape Horn or a complicated stopover in Panama. A railroad would shorten what was a months-long journey to one of several days.

An early champion of the railway, Asa Whitney was a merchant who had acquired a fortune doing business in China. Returning to the United States from Asia in 1844, he dedicated himself to the construction of the transcontinental railroad, seeing in the endeavor a way to bind the nation closer together and open it up to trade with Asia. Whitney suggested that the railroad follow a central route from Chicago, Illinois, to Northern California and that funds be raised through the sale of land along the route that would be granted to the enterprise by the federal government. Whitney's proposals were introduced in Congress in 1845, and he spent the next six years lobbying for the adoption of his plan. Even with the United States acquisition of vast sections of the west following the signing of the Oregon Treaty with Great Britain in 1846 and the conclusion of the Mexican-American War in 1848, it would be fourteen years before the project moved forward. Not even the discovery of gold in California in 1848 and the ensuing gold rush could persuade the government to act. Whitney's plans were rejected by Congress for the final time in 1851, and thereafter Whitney faded into the background, his life's mission seemingly unfulfilled.

In the 1840s and 1850s, the chief impediment to the transcontinental railroad was the question of its route. The country was deeply divided along sectional lines, between the North and South, free states and slave states. Each side wanted the railroad to run through its territory and Congress was deadlocked over the issue.

To facilitate a potential Southern route, the United States government signed the Gadsden Purchase in 1854, acquiring land from Mexico, but still construction on the railroad did not commence.

By the late-1850s, a successor to Whitney stepped forward to move the project closer to realization. Theodore Judah, a railroad engineer, and his team had designed and built the first railroad line west of the Missouri River, the Sacramento Valley Line, in 1856. Setting his sights on a transcontinental railway, Judah soon grasped that more than congressional support, the project needed investors.

Having surveyed a route through the Sierra Nevada Mountains, one of the major logistical challenges of the project, Judah gained the backing of "The Big Four," a wealthy circle of influential California businessmen, among them Leland Stanford, Collis P. Huntington, Charles Crocker, and Mark Hopkins. Charles Crocker's brother Edwin would eventually come aboard as well. These men not only had financial clout, they were also major figures in California's nascent Republican Party. Stanford himself would be elected governor in 1861. Together they would organize the Central Pacific Railroad, which would be tasked with building the First Transcontinental Railroad east through the Sierra Nevadas from its western terminus.

On July 1, 1862, President Abraham Lincoln signed the Pacific Railroad Bill. The legislation created the Union Pacific Railroad, which would be responsible for constructing the eastern portion of the First Transcontinental Railroad, building west from Omaha, Nebraska, the line's as-yet-undetermined eastern terminus. It also endorsed and funded the Central Pacific's efforts to build east from California. The government would subsidize the railroad companies with public land and cash bonds for each mile of track they laid.

On January 8, 1863, the Central Pacific commenced construction in Sacramento, the railroad's western terminus. Though finally underway, the project suffered from slow progress. Labor was in short supply due to the ongoing American Civil War. Meanwhile, financial maneuvering within both the Union Pacific and the Central Pacific created an atmosphere of mistrust. Alienated from the other members of the Central Pacific's board, Judah went searching for new investors. Stricken with illness, he passed away in New York City on November 2, 1863, his project still unfinished.

The Union Pacific officially broke ground on December 2, 1963, but for the next few years had very little to show for its efforts. Rail lines only began to be laid in earnest in 1865. Through a series of stock schemes, Thomas Clarke Durant had gained control over the Union Pacific and manipulated the company for his own financial gain, devising intricate schemes—including the 1872 Credit Mobilier scandal—to fleece investors and enrich his own wealth. Thanks in large measure to Durant's expensive and ethically problematic lobbying campaign, Congress passed a second Pacific Railway Act, which, among other measures, vastly expanded the lands granted to the railroads.

The labor shortage started to ease with the conclusion of the Civil War in 1865, and the Union Pacific pressed westward with work crews composed mainly of Irish Americans, many of them Civil War veterans The Central Pacific meanwhile turned to Chinese American laborers—6,000 in total—who had the difficult task of tunneling and blasting through the mountainous terrain of the Rocky Mountains.

The era was not a happy one for the Native American tribes of the Great Plains. Displaced from their lands, harassed and massacred by the army, some tribes sought to stop the railroads in their tracks, sabotaging equipment and staging raids.

To ramp up the pace of construction, Durant hired General Jack Casement to supervise the company's work crews and brought in Grenville Dodge to serve as chief engineer in 1866. For the next three years, amid labor strife, financial maneuverings, and Native American unrest, among other challenges, the Union Pacific and Central Pacific laid hundreds of miles of rail. Upon its completion, the First Transcontinental Railroad measured nearly 1,800 miles in length.

Following painstaking negotiations, the Union Pacific and Central Pacific agreed to join their tracks at Promontory Summit. On May 10, 1869, before a crowd of dignitaries, Leland Stanford hammered in the ceremonial Golden Spike connecting the Central Pacific and Union Pacific lines. As his hammer struck, telegraph wires transmitted the news to San Francisco and New York, where on signal, cannons saluted the achievement. The long-awaited First Transcontinental Railroad was complete.

Some 143 years later, the American railroad network serves two main purposes: moving freight and moving passengers. As a mode of transport, trains enjoy certain advantages over automobiles and airplanes. A freight train is three times more energy efficient than a truck, while passenger rail travel is approximately 30 percent more fuel efficient per passenger mile than auto travel. Compared to airplane travel, trains use about 20 percent less energy.

Freight-carrying railroad companies are divided into three classes based on their annual revenues. The seven or eight biggest operations fall into the Class I category and account for over 90 percent of all railroad freight revenues. All told, Class I lines own and operate over 140,000 miles of track. The largest Class I carrier in the country is the storied Union Pacific Railroad. The rest of the railroad freight industry consists of around thirty Class II companies, which are regional or shortline operations, and about 320 Class III local-line haulers. Together these carriers transport over 40 percent of the country's freight.

Passenger train service in the United States is largely the province of the National Railroad Passenger Corporation, commonly known as Amtrak. A product of the 1970 Rail Passenger Service Act, Amtrak was formally established by the federal government the following year. It has since consolidated all United States intercity passenger train service under its auspices. Currently, it connects over 500 destinations in forty-six states. Operating along a network of roughly 22,000 miles of track, Amtrak owns and operates about 650 miles of rail, much of which it shares with local commuter lines. The vast majority of the Amtrak network is composed of rail owned and maintained by freight companies. Amtrak receives funding from the federal government in excess of $1 billion each year. Though a perennial target of budget cutters in Congress and threatened from time to time with complete defunding, Amtrak set a record in 2011, carrying over 30 million passengers.

The principle hub of Amtrak service is the Northeast Corridor, which connects the major cities of the region from Washington, DC to Boston, Massachusetts. Inspired by the high-speed rail (HSR) networks of Western Europe and East Asia, Amtrak has been experimenting with similar service in the Northeast Corridor with its Acela train. Though the Acela does qualify as HSR according to American standards, it only reaches its peak speed of 150 miles per hour on a short stretch of track and averages a mere seventy-seven miles per hour between Washington and New York and sixty-seven between New York and Boston. Certain HSR trains in Spain, meanwhile, average 146 miles per hour. The slow speeds in the Northeast Corridor are due to aging and obsolete infrastructure as well as terrain and traffic considerations.

Outside of the Northeast Corridor, Amtrak service depends on tracks owned and maintained by freight companies. Such rail lines are designed principally to move cargo—not passenger trains or HSR. For HSR to work elsewhere, entirely new tracks would have to be laid.

To spur the development of American HSR, as part of the American Reinvestment and Recovery Act of 2009, the administration of President Barack Obama awarded $8 billion directly to state and regional agencies to support the construction of HSR networks. The administration directed the money towards ten potential high-speed corridors it had identified throughout the country. Despite the outlay of funds, the president's vision is far from being realized. Cost estimates for the proposed HSR network run in the $200 billion range. The most ambitious project, an HSR line between Sacramento, the old western terminus of the First Transcontinental Railroad, and San Diego, has run into funding problems with the state government which, like many across the nation, faces difficult budgetary constraints. Politics has intruded on the effort, with Republican governors in Ohio, Wisconsin, and Florida rejecting their states' portions of the federal outlay, seeing HSR as a costly and wrongheaded investment. Their skepticism is shared among large segments of the public. As a consequence, the future of HSR in the United States is far from assured.

Though its fate remains in doubt, HSR will be the central topic in American railroad infrastructure for the foreseeable future. Just as the First Transcontinental Railroad dominated rail construction in the nineteenth century, HSR is poised to do the same in the early twenty-first. The Golden Spike was the culmination of decades of efforts by a diverse cast of idealists, industrialists, government operatives, and laborers. Their work was not always profitable—or ethical—but they accomplished their goal and transformed the country. Whether HSR proponents can perform a similar feat will be determined in the decades ahead.

The Case for
Not-Quite-So-High-Speed Rail

By Phillip Longman
The Washington Monthly, July 2011

The bad news: Republicans have torpedoed plans for American bullet trains. The good news: The Obama Administration is quietly building a slower, but potentially much better, rail system.

After concluding some business in Frankfurt, Germany, recently, I found myself with a day to kill and decided to use it to tour the historic Cologne Cathedral, about 120 miles away. I could have rented a car and driven through traffic on the autobahn for about two hours, but instead I decided to walk a few blocks from my hotel and board Intercity-Express #616. The sleek bullet train left Frankfurt's magnificent nineteenth-century main terminal on time and sped along a super-engineered, bee-line right-of-way completed in 2002 at a cost of $5.6 billion. The scenery wasn't much, as we were often in tunnels built to keep the line straight and fast. But the ride was smooth, quiet, and comfortable, even at 180 miles per hour, and in a mere fifty-six minutes the train arrived on time to the second within steps of the Cologne Cathedral. The fare was $109.

You might expect me at this point to proclaim, like so many Americans who have sojourned in Europe, Japan, or China on gleaming bullet trains, that what the United States needs now is a crash program to catch up with our peers in building high-speed rail for the twenty-first century. And, for the record, I will proclaim that. It's a vision almost all progressives have come to share, even as conservatives increasingly denounce it as creeping socialism, social engineering, or worse. But I'll make an important qualification that should inform the increasingly partisan debate about high-speed rail in this country—one that is illustrated by my trip back to Frankfurt later that afternoon.

Having arrived in Cologne faster than I needed to, I decided to take the longer, more scenic route back to Frankfurt, which costs just $72, riding the old West Rhine Railway. Begun in 1844, it's a conventional railway that twists and turns mostly along the banks of the Rhine, passing beneath many high-perched castles and vineyards. It also provides access to such midsize cities as Koblenz and Mainz, and to such bucolic spots as the famous Rock of Lorelei, all of which the new high-speed rail line misses in order to save time.

Because of its more circuitous route and local stops, and because passenger trains on the Rhine Valley line also have to share tracks with many freight trains, these trains are slower than those on the new high-speed line. Yet they still max out at about 100 mph, which means that they only take a bit more than an hour longer to go from Cologne to Frankfurt even as they serve more population centers in between. The line is vibrant, with local and express passenger trains passing through any given station every fifteen to twenty minutes. By European or Asian standards, this service doesn't qualify as high-speed rail, but it is faster on average than most American railways, and frequent enough to provide vital connectivity throughout the Rhine Valley.

My point? Yes, bullet trains speeding at 180 mph or more from major city to major city are great for business execs in a hurry and on an expense account. But the more conventional, cheaper, "fast enough" high-speed rail lines like the West Rhine line are the real backbone of the German passenger rail system and that of most other industrialized nations. And it is from these examples that America has the most to learn, especially since it now looks as if the U.S. isn't going to build any real high-speed rail lines, except possibly in California, anytime soon. In an ironic twist, between the mounting concern over the state and federal deficits and growing Republican and NIMBY opposition to high-speed rail, the Obama administration is being forced to settle for incremental projects that will only bring passenger rail service up to the kind of standards found on the West Rhine line. And that's a good thing, provided Republicans don't succeed in killing passenger trains in the United States altogether, as they are increasingly wont to try.

The debate over high-speed rail in the United States has become akin to that over organic food. Most people can't define exactly what it is, but they tend to have strong, almost theological opinions about whether it's morally good, elitist, impractical, and/or politically correct. Progressives are likely to tell you that high-speed rail is necessary to reduce global warming, prepare for "peak oil," and overcome "auto dependency." The Obama administration plays to this growing progressive consensus by proudly proclaiming that it has set in motion projects that will bring high-speed rail to 80 percent of the U.S. population within twenty-five years.

Meanwhile, especially since the elections of 2010, conservatives have been rallying their troops in full-throated opposition to any and all government spending to improve passenger rail service, often portraying it as another step on the road to serfdom. Though many Republicans, such as Kay Bailey Hutchinson of Texas, have strongly supported Amtrak over the years (especially for service in their own backyards), we now see a new breed of Republican governors in Florida, Ohio, and Wisconsin all making a big show of waving away billions in federal stimulus dollar for rail improvements in their states.

So how about we all calm down, chuck the theology, and look practically at what should be the future of passenger trains in the U.S.?

To do that, we need to start by defining what we mean by high-speed rail. An extreme example is the French National Railways' *train à grande vitesse* ("high-speed train"), or TGV, which in 2007 set a world record of 357.2 mph. In regular service, its average start-to-stop speed is typically a bit north of 170 mph, with top speeds of around 200 mph. I once had the opportunity to ride in the cab of a TGV between Paris and Lille, and even to hold the throttle. It was an unexpectedly harrowing experience, as the windshield repeatedly filled with the remains of unfortunate birds who failed to get out of the way in time. But back in the revenue seats, the experience is sublime. Even as the French countryside shoots by in a blur, you won't see so much as a ripple in your wine glass, and even the coach seats are bigger than what you would find in first class on an airplane.

The service has proven to be a great commercial success. As with other high-speed rail lines in Europe, it generates an operating profit. The capital cost of constructing the first TGV line between Paris and Lyon was recovered within twelve years, and newer lines are well on their way to paying for themselves as well. The social returns, in the form of reduced airport and road congestion, pollution, and energy use, have also been high, as have been the returns in the form of economic development. Lille was once one of the most economically depressed cities in France. Now served by high-speed trains that put Paris and Brussels just an hour away and London an hour and a half, as well as by other high-speed lines providing easy connectivity to other major Continental cities, Lille is no longer a dying "flyover city" but a quickly expanding commercial hub.

> *The debate over high-speed rail in the United States has become akin to that over organic food. Most people can't define exactly what it is, but they tend to have strong, almost theological opinions about whether it's morally good, elitist, impractical, and/or politically correct.*

But as great as it would be to have passenger service as fast and elegant as the TGV in the United States, there are many reasons not to put our first dollars into such an ambitious project. First off, building a truly high-speed rail system in today's America would be so expensive, disruptive, contentious, and politically risky that it just might not be possible. It would require, for example, securing brand-new rights-of-way, because trains traveling at more than around 125 mph can't share tracks with slower freight or passenger trains. This in turn would require using eminent domain to secure millions of acres of real estate, and these days, in the U.S., that would involve endless litigation, environmental review, and the innumerable other processes that always stand to derail any large-scale infrastructure project.

Plans to build a high-speed rail in California between San Diego and the Bay Area are now foundering for precisely this reason. Big showcase high-speed projects in Texas and Florida flopped in the 1990s for the same reason, plus another: the shifting currents of polarized American politics. Under the governorship of the late Democratic Governor Lawton Chiles, Florida committed to building a true high-speed line connecting Tampa, Orlando, and Miami. Both the government and private companies spent millions to conduct feasibility and environmental studies, survey the route, secure financing, and develop elaborate project management and business plans. But then, just as the project became "shovel ready," Florida elected Republican Jeb Bush governor, and he promptly pulled the plug despite widespread public support for the project. Last February the same thing happened again, when newly elected Florida Republican Governor Rick Scott decided to reject $2 billion in federal funds that the Obama administration wanted to use to revive the project that Chiles had set in motion more than seventeen years ago.

Quite apart from these bureaucratic and political barriers to an American TGV, there's also an economic question that needs to be asked for any given rail corridor: just how fast does high-speed rail need to go in order to gain a meaningful market share? The typical answer is "fast enough to beat air and auto travel times," but achieving that optimum speed is rarely just a matter of buying souped-up trains. Often boosting top speeds up to 180 mph or more, while requiring enormous increases in capital spending and geometric increases in energy use, does little to increase average speed, which is what really counts. Total trip times, especially on runs of less than 200 hundred miles or so, are typically far more affected by a train's slowest moments than its fastest. On Amtrak's forty-mile run between Washington, D.C., and Baltimore, for example, trains run as fast as 125 mph on some segments. But because all trains on the line must spend a long time creeping through the yard at Washington's Union Station and through antiquated tunnels under Baltimore Harbor, the average speed of even the fastest scheduled train, the vaunted Acela, is only 83.4 mph. Increasing speeds on the slowest segments of the line would do as much or more to shorten travel times as making the fastest speeds faster, and wouldn't require an expensive new right-of-way or new equipment.

As it is, Amtrak's service between Washington and Boston is already highly successful, even if it does not qualify as high-speed rail by world standards. The top speed obtained by any train is 150 mph, and that happens only in a brief segment of Rhode Island. The average speed is much lower, even to the point that the schedule today between New York and Boston is only nineteen minutes faster than that achieved by the New Haven Railroad's "Merchants Limited" in 1954. But today's service is fast enough for Amtrak to dominate the travel market among the intermediate points along the corridor. Tellingly, almost no one rides all the way from Boston to Washington, which takes seven hours on the Acela and costs more than flying. But the trains are nonetheless full despite steep fares, and ridership continues to mount.

That's because most passengers are traveling between intermediate points where existing train service is more than competitive with alternative modes, such as battling the traffic on I-95 or catching a flight. Compared to airlines, for example, Amtrak has virtually a 100 percent market share of passenger trips between Philadelphia and New York, a 60 percent share between Washington and New York, and a 50 percent share between New York and Boston. On each trip between Washington and Boston, more than half the passengers will get off at either Philadelphia or New York and are replaced by other passengers. From the travelers' point of view, it doesn't matter much whether the train goes 150 mph or even 300 mph, since they will only be on it for a short time anyway. What matters to them far more is that the trains are frequent, pleasant, reasonably priced, and reliable. Recently, after Florida rejected federal money for its high-speed project, U.S. Transportation Secretary Ray LaHood redirected $795 million to upgrade some of the most heavily used sections of the Northeast Corridor. This money will increase speeds from 135 to 160 miles per hour on critical segments, but much more importantly it will improve on-time performance and add more seats to accommodate the continuing surge in ridership.

This principle is also illustrated by Amtrak's highly successful "Cascades" service on the 187-mile line between Portland and Seattle. The Spanish-designed Talgo "tilt" train sets look futuristic, and with their on-board bistros and comfy chairs they are a joy to ride. But because they run on conventional track through mountainous country shared by freight trains, their current top speed is only 79 mph, and their average speed is just 53. Still, that's enough to make taking the train faster than driving, and ridership has swelled to more than 700,000 passengers a year. Using federal stimulus dollars plus state spending, work is currently under way to boost top train speeds to 110–125 mph, simply by adding better signaling and more sidings to let freight trains get out of the way. This incremental investment will also boost reliability and allow for increased frequency, which will further bump up ridership. But numerous studies show there is no point in making trains go faster than 125 mph on a segment this short because of the great cost involved and the limited gains to total trip times. Moreover, if a new bullet train line were built between Portland and Seattle, the tremendous cost of its construction would require fares too high for all but well-heeled business travelers to afford.

The same considerations apply even on much longer segments. In many instances conventional train service is, or could be, competitive with flying or driving, if only it were more frequent and reliable. For example, when I need to travel from my home in Washington, D.C., to Chicago, I am always tempted to take a sleeper car on Amtrak's "Capitol Limited," and frequently do. Though it never goes faster than 79 mph, the train is scheduled to leave Washington at 4:00 p.m. and to arrive in Chicago at 8:45 a.m. To make a morning meeting in Chicago by plane, I would either have to fly out the night before and rent a hotel room, or get up at some ungodly hour on the same day and arrive frazzled. Either way, taking the plane requires schlepping my way to and from airports on both ends, while also enduring the hassle and uncertain duration of airport security. In the wintertime, I'm also far more likely to be stranded by snowstorms if I take the plane, and, of course, dinner in the diner sure beats airplane food.

But while the Capitol Limited is fast enough to be more convenient than flying when it's on time, it frequently runs hours late, even in fair weather, due to competition with freight trains. So I can't count on it for business travel to Chicago unless my meeting is in the afternoon. Even with that poor track record, sleeper cars on the Capitol Limited are often sold out weeks in advance, such is the surging popularity of this way of travel among professionals who have had it with air travel. All Amtrak needs to build a much larger market share would be better on-time performance, and this, in turn, would require only incremental investment in new sidings and track capacity to make sure freight trains don't get in the way.

Frequency of service is also often more important than top speed. Only two passenger trains serve Cleveland, for example, and both come through, in both directions, between 12:59 and 5:35 a.m. It's surprising how many people use these trains nonetheless. Recently, after business in Cleveland that kept me there late, I decided to take a sleeper car home rather than spending an extra night in a hotel room and flying out in the morning. I counted some seventy-five people in the waiting room even at two a.m. Many more would be taking the train in and out of Cleveland if only there were reliable daytime service to nearby points such as Pittsburgh, Toledo, South Bend, Akron, Indianapolis, or Chicago, all of which could be reached by conventional trains in far less time, and at far less cost, than flying. (Sadly, Ohio Republican Governor John Kasich has rejected $400 million in federal stimulus funds that would have had such service up and running in short order. Republican Governor Scott Walker has waved away more than $800 million in federal money that would have brought similarly practical and thrifty passenger rail service to the Chicago, Milwaukee, Madison, and St. Paul corridor.) Providing connectivity to small towns and midsize cities that currently lack affordable air service, or any air service at all, is one of the most important potential benefits of passenger rail, and you don't need 300-mph bullet trains to pull it off.

Conventional trains running between Washington and such nearby cities to the south as Richmond, Charlottesville, Durham, and Charlotte already attract a growing ridership, and would attract a larger one if they were more frequent and reliable, as well as better integrated with trains running north of D.C. along the Northeast Corridor. The minimal investment needed in new track capacity would also improve freight service, thereby getting more trucks off the road and improving the driving experience for those who don't want to take the train. It also would likely spur a good amount of economic development. Midsize cities such as Lynchburg or Petersburg, Virginia, which once thrived because of their strategic position on the nation's rail map, might experience a real estate boom if it were possible to live there and still have easy access to the business opportunities and cultural amenities of Washington, Philadelphia, or New York. Projects currently under way will do the same for cities like Kalamazoo, Michigan, and Springfield, Illinois, by providing improved connections with Chicago. Making such incremental improvements might not stir the hearts of Americans the way eclipsing the French or the Chinese in high-speed rail might, but it's still a sensible course that will gradually start rebuilding a rail culture in the U.S. As more and more Americans outside the Northeast Corridor experience practical, reliable, conventional train service that beats flying or driving, the constituency for super-expensive, super-fast trains will build as it has abroad. Until then "fast enough" high-speed rail is good enough.

The Trouble with High-Speed Rail

By Liam Julian
Policy Review, April 2010

On the morning of April 16, 2009, President Obama, flanked by the vice president and the secretary of transportation, announced a plan to devote $8 billion of his economic recovery package (the stimulus), plus another $1 billion a year for five years, to fund high-speed rail corridors across the nation. "Imagine whisking through towns at speeds over 100 miles an hour, walking only a few steps to public transportation, and ending up just blocks from your destination," the president said. "Imagine what a great project that would be to rebuild America."

Nine months later, in January of this year, the administration specified where and how those billions of high-speed rail dollars would be allotted. The biggest winners were two long-planned bullet-train routes: One in Florida, designed to span the 80 miles between Tampa and Orlando, which took in $1.25 billion of federal money; and the other in California, a proposed system that would eventually connect Sacramento, San Francisco, Los Angeles, and San Diego, which collected $2.3 billion. The highly traveled Northeast Corridor route that currently stretches from Washington, D.C, to Boston received only $112 million.

Some commentators have praised the administration's funding plans, but the divvying has struck many other observers as odd. The biggest puzzlement is why a procedural impediment involving an environmental review resulted in the Northeast Corridor receiving so few federal dollars. "If we really wanted to have high-speed rail in this country, and have it be a great success" said Joseph Vranich, author of the books *Supertrains and Derailed*, "then what we would do is concentrate the funds on the New York-Washington corridor, which is the top corridor in the country." Amtrak's Northeast Corridor routes transport some 15 million passengers per year, and the nation's only purported high-speed train, the Acela, travels between Washington and Boston, but currently does so at an average speed of less than 80 miles per hour.

Obama has also been criticized by those who see trouble in the breadth of his high-speed rail ambitions. Robert Puentes, a senior fellow at the Brookings Institution, told *U.S. News and World Report*, "The advice was, pick one or two corridors and invest wisely." But instead, the administration is "spreading the peanut butter thinly all over the place." Other commentators have pointed out that the speedy trains that work in parts of Europe and Asia won't work in a vast United States, with its dispersed inhabitants. Robert Samuelson noted in a *Washington Post* column on the subject that the population density of Japan, for instance, is 880 people per square mile, while in America, there are just 86 people per square mile.

Can the Obama administration counter the naysayers with numbers and data? No, it cannot. For high-speed rail is simply an imprudent and inefficient answer to an unreal American transportation need. One has only to look at the history and development of the nation's most-advanced, Obama-touted high-speed rail projects—in Florida and California—to see that the administration's plan is merely a high-speed way to waste untold billions.

Florida

Welcome to the I-4 Corridor—a blazing, flat, 84-mile stretch along Interstate 4 that slices through the middle of the Florida peninsula between Tampa, on the west coast, and Orlando, inland, but only 25 miles from the Atlantic. In many ways the corridor divides Florida politically as well as physically, with big, brash, liberal counties like Broward (Fort Lauderdale) and Miami-Dade lounging below the asphalt strip, and more-rural, more-conservative counties, especially those clustered within the panhandle, situated above it. The corridor gained notoriety in the 2008 presidential campaign when it was widely reported that whichever candidate won the most votes between Tampa and Orlando would win the Sunshine State and, likely, the presidency. That turned out to be true. Though the race wasn't a close one, Obama did indeed pocket the most votes in Florida's contested band, and he went on to take the state and the White House.

Obama was back in the I-4 Corridor in January of this year, on the morning after his State of the Union address. In front of a raucous crowd inside a University of Tampa gymnasium, the president pledged to make central Florida the nation's high-speed rail pioneer. "We are going to start building a new high-speed rail line right here in Tampa," he said. "I'm excited. I'm going to come back down here and ride it."

Maybe he will, and maybe he won't, for the Sunshine State has a long and fraught history with high-speed rail. It goes back more than three decades, beginning in 1976, when the state legislature mandated a transit study that eventually concluded that constructing a high-speed line along I-4 Corridor would be feasible. In 1982, Governor Bob Graham visited Japan and was impressed by its Shinkansen bullet trains. Upon his return he authorized creation of the Florida High Speed Rail Committee, which subsequently released a report that found the state's infrastructure inadequate to handle future growth and recommended construction of a high-speed rail line.

Over the following decade, Florida flirted temperamentally with high-speed rail, occasionally conducting feasibility studies of a potential, expanded Tampa-Orlando-Miami route. But high-speed rail was expensive, and there was significant opposition to using tight state dollars to bankroll it. "That dog won't hunt," said Governor-elect Lawton Chiles in 1990, reacting to a plan to use state taxes to fund high-speed rail construction. But in following years, Florida's lawmakers came to realize that if superfast trains were ever going to crisscross their peninsula, the state would simply have to play a major role in financing them. With Florida's highways ever more clogged and deteriorating, with population growth confounding road expansion and repair plans, the legislature decided to commit $70 million per year for several years for the planning of a high-speed rail line.

Proposals were submitted, and in February 1996 the state selected Florida Overland eXpress (FOX), a consortium of four American and international companies, to construct a $6.3 billion French TGV (*Train à Grande Vitesse*, or "high-speed train") system between Tampa, Orlando, and Miami. The formal deal was signed in August, but it was a risky, rickety one that hinged on the federal government's willingness to give the state $300 million in cash and guarantee $5 billion in bonds. Washington worked as Washington tends to work—slowly—and after months of lobbying Congress with nothing to show for it, the high-speed rail deal was teetering. Florida politicians grew restive. One state senator, for instance, called the project a "boondoggle" and said that "the whole thing" made him "nervous."

During the next two years, Florida taxpayers devoted several million dollars to more studies of the feasibility of the proposed Tampa-Orlando-Miami line. But the studies were largely inconclusive; a *Tampa Tribune* reporter wrote in 1998 that despite all the examination "not much has been learned about whether trains traveling lickety-split between the trio of Florida cities can turn a profit." With federal support of the project still dubious, and with so many of its details still left undefined, newly elected Governor Jeb Bush killed the plan in January 1999, less than two weeks after taking office, saying that it would cost taxpayers too much for a gain too uncertain.

But though the FOX scheme was dead, bullet trains in Florida were not. An elderly southwest-Florida businessman named C. C. Dockery quickly resurrected the issue by spending $2.7 million of his own money to put a specific question on Floridians' November 2000 election ballots: Should the state Constitution be amended to mandate construction of high-speed rail? That year, when Floridians had such trouble voting for president, they had no trouble voting "yes" on Dockery's amendment.

Thus did the Florida Constitution come to command that construction of a high-speed rail line connecting the state's five largest cities must begin on or before November 1, 2003. Yet the amendment did not specify how the construction was to be paid for. And so, mere months before November 2003, the revitalized high-speed rail project again seemed hopeless: The state legislature was not going to put up hundreds of millions of dollars for it, and neither were private investors. And so Floridians again found themselves with an imminent opportunity to vote on a train-related constitutional amendment—this time, on one that would repeal the high-speed rail language that they had approved in 2000. Repeal that language they emphatically did, voting almost 2-to-1 for the new amendment.

Again, the dream seemed dead. But then President Obama swept into the Sunshine State, and Floridians began to dream once more.

There are many political reasons why Florida was the right place for Obama to launch his high-speed rail push. Florida is a swing state, for one. And when arguments about the effects of stimulus dollars matter, as they do, the original Tampa-Orlando route no doubt appealed to Obama because of its "shovel-readiness"; estimates are that construction can begin in late 2010. But many reasons for making Florida the country's high-speed rail showpiece are not political—they are practical. Florida is flat, which obviously simplifies construction and makes it less expensive. The state Depart-

> *A major concern is that potential passengers will be dissuaded from hopping aboard simply because the train won't take them anywhere near their final destinations.*

ment of Transportation also already owns over 90 percent of the Tampa-Orlando route's right-of-way—most of the phase's proposed high-speed rail track would run in the median of I-4 (some of it would also run along the medians of Interstate 275 and State Road 528). And unlike other tracks, the planned Tampa-Orlando line would accommodate only high-speed locomotives (not other, slower trains), and it would contain no grade crossings, which is unusual in American rail systems.

Yet the showpiece has its flaws, and not a few of them. The first problem is construction funding, which remains iffy. Florida estimates that building the I-4 Corridor route will cost $3.2 billion (many believe this number is too low). The state requested $2.6 billion in high-speed rail stimulus funds and was given $1.25 billion. So, though Florida has agreed to make available each year $60 million of its own money (despite a $3 billion state deficit), significant construction costs remain. "We asked for $2.6 billion and clearly that's what we need to implement this project," Nazih Haddad, Chief Operating Officer of Florida High Speed Rail, told the *Sarasota Herald-Tribune* in late January after the state learned how much federal money it would receive. Haddad told me he is confident that more federal money is forthcoming, and Obama has said that all his high-speed rail grants are merely "down payments." Indeed, the 2010 federal appropriations bill does contain another $2.5 billion for high-speed rail. Nonetheless, the Sunshine State is beginning to build a multi-billion-dollar rail system without knowing where much of the money is coming from. That fact is at least a tad disconcerting.

More importantly, assuming the train is ready by 2015, when it is scheduled to begin service, who will ride it? A major concern is that potential passengers will be dissuaded from hopping aboard simply because the train won't take them anywhere near their final destinations. Good public transportation in Tampa and Orlando is nonexistent, and so it would seem that any rail system connecting the two cities must deposit its riders in several urban locations, including the downtown districts. But the I-4 Corridor route does not do this. In fact, to call it a Tampa-Orlando route is rather disingenuous because the trains will avoid Orlando entirely—the last stop heading east is the Orlando International Airport, some ten miles outside of town.

There is also the plain fact that, while it is estimated that the train ride will last 55 minutes with stops, it takes only 90 minutes to drive the same distance. If a potential high-speed rail passenger in Tampa factors into his trip the time required to get to the city's train station (which could easily take an hour), park his car, purchase tickets, and wait for the train, he would probably decide to drive to Orlando. If he then considers that were he to take the train he would arrive not in Orlando but at Orlando International Airport, which could leave him tens of miles from his final destination (14 miles from Amway Arena, where the Orlando Magic play, for example), and that he would arrive there without a car and with no good way of getting around the city, he would definitely decide to drive to Orlando. In a late-October 2004 editorial titled "Going Nowhere Fast," the editors of the *St. Petersburg Times* wrote that Florida had "spent nearly three decades studying high-speed transit to no particular avail." After years of research there was still "almost no evidence" that a high-speed rail route "would serve large numbers of riders," especially because Florida's major cities were not "adequately prepared to transport bullet train riders to their final destinations." Six years on, and nothing about this situation has changed.

Tampa and Orlando are not dense cities like New York or Washington, D.C.; rather, they are sprawling urban areas encompassing many cities. The Tampa Bay area covers some 2,000 square miles, and Greater Orlando spans over 4,000. Their 5 million residents are far-flung. Not only do these people like their cars; they need their cars. And so do tourists, who might use the proposed high-speed train to travel from Orlando's airport to Disney World, where a station is planned, but who will still need to rent a car to get just about anywhere else, including anywhere remotely near the beach. What's more, the need for high-speed rail from Orlando airport to Disney World is hardly obvious. It's about 25 miles, or less than the distance from Washington's Dulles Airport to the White House. The Florida Department of Transportation estimates 2,715,500 annual passenger-trips in the high-speed rail route's first year of operation and 3,120,000 in its fifth year. Those numbers are wildly hopeful.

And who will pay to keep the I-4 Corridor trains running, even if they're mostly empty? Haddad said that ticket sales will cover operating costs, but Randal O'Toole, of the Cato Institute, disagrees. "Fares won't come close to covering the operating costs," he told me. "They never do. I'd be surprised if in Florida they even cover half." A 2009 *Florida Times-Union* article gives backing to O'Toole's assessment, noting that "Ticket sales at affordable prices don't cover all the operating costs of any railroad."[1] When pressed, Haddad seemed to at least allow the possibility that ticket sales wouldn't be sufficient. But even if they aren't, he said, there's always that annual $60 million in state funds to make up the difference. At least for a while.

Carl Hiaasen, the *Miami Herald* columnist and longtime witness to Sunshine State wackiness, nailed it. Florida's high-speed rail's "prospects for profitability are the same today as they always were: Nil," he wrote recently. The "money delivered by President Barack Obama . . . should have come with a note: 'Here's a gift from Uncle Sam. Now go build yourselves something you can't possibly afford to operate.'"

California

To go from San Francisco to Los Angeles is no picnic. You could drive, but traffic will be nasty, and the fastest route, Interstate 5 through the Central Valley, will still take six hours on a good day. A scenic ride on California State Route I, which hugs the Pacific coast, will take you nine or ten hours. Flying is quicker, of course (about one and a half hours from takeoff to touchdown), but then you have to deal with all the airport hassles, and a one-way ticket costs $70. How about the train? Well, the Amtrak Coast Starlight chugs between Los Angeles and Oakland (you can then switch trains or take a bus into San Francisco)—a journey that lasts about eleven hours and costs 60 bucks.

No surprise, then, that Californians have an attraction to high-speed rail. The state first broached the subject in the early 1980s, when a private company proposed building a 130-mile bullet-train line between Los Angeles and San Diego. That project eventually sputtered out, though, after encountering a combination of logistical snafus and political opposition. In 1996, talk of bullet trains was revived when the California Intercity High Speed Rail Commission, a panel formed by Governor Pete Wilson, released a proposal for a statewide high-speed rail system— a route that would eventually run between Sacramento and Los Angeles, with the first segment connecting Los Angeles and San Francisco. The panel estimated that total construction costs would be either $18 billion (for a VHS system, which would travel at 220 mph) or $26 billion, for Maglev, which could reach speeds of 310 mph and shuttle passengers from L.A. to San Francisco in two hours. The California High Speed Rail Authority was established to begin the actual planning process, and in 2000, it put forth its plan for a 700-mile network that would serve more than 42 million annual riders by 2020, with trains reaching speeds of 220 mph, and with an updated construction cost of $25 billion.

But prospects for high-speed rail in the Golden State quickly lessened. Although the California legislature had voted to place on the November 2004 ballot a $10 billion bond measure for high-speed rail construction, a new governor, Arnold Schwarzenegger, supported subsequent legislation successfully postponing that measure (he also slashed the High Speed Rail Authority's budget). Moreover, the estimated cost to build the system had ballooned in just four years from $25 billion to $37 billion. The High Speed Rail Authority's previous work also came under fire for being, as an *Oakland Tribune* reporter put it in late 2004, "not just sloppy, but misleading." A ballot measure that would've asked voters in 2006 to approve fundraising for the rail system was again postponed, while disputes over the proposed route (Pacheco Pass? Altamont Pass? Both?) had become ubiquitous and heated.

High-speed rail's end seemed near. But then, revitalization. In November 2008, in the midst of a massive state budget shortfall, a worldwide economic crisis, and home foreclosures galore, California voters approved Proposition 1A, a $10 billion bond measure—a down payment on the Los Angeles to San Francisco portion of a new high-speed rail system. With that vote, and with the Obama administration's recent promise of $2.3 billion, thoughts of high-speed rail in the Golden State have come roaring back.

California does not have the same advantages that Florida's I-4 Corridor does— for instance, California will need to make major land purchases and build some 24 passenger stations—but it does have many of the same drawbacks. In fact, in California, the drawbacks are perhaps even larger. The biggest is cost.

Florida believes that it will need $3.2 billion to construct the I-4 Corridor route. Estimates of what it will cost to build California's system started at $25 billion and have since exploded. In 2008, the state guessed that it would require $45.4 billion to build the entire system and $30.7 billion for the first phase, Anaheim to San Francisco. But the newest, inflation-adjusted estimates now put *just* the price of the Anaheim to San Francisco route at $42.6 billion. California expects to receive about $18 billion from the federal government; so far, Washington has donated a mere $2.3 billion. The state also expects to receive $12 billion from private investors, but the High Speed Rail Authority has provided scant evidence that it can raise anywhere near that amount. Californians are beginning to wonder: With our state's budget gap currently at $20 billion, how much more may we be asked to pay to get these trains rolling?

There are other problems, too. In a February 28, 2010, article in the *Los Angeles Times*, reporters Rich Connell and Dan Weikel wrote that one-way ticket prices between Los Angeles and San Francisco have risen "from $55 to $105." The increase "shows healthier surplus revenue, which may appeal to private investors. But estimated ridership falls by about one-third, to about 40 million annual boarders in 2030." The High Speed Rail Authority's projected annual ridership number, now 40 million, has fluctuated over the years from a low of below 40 million to a high of nearly 100 million. Now, for the first time, its estimates are being widely questioned. "This just smells funny," state Senator Alan Lowenthal, a high-speed rail supporter, said in February. "We've never understood their models."

Lowenthal chairs the Senate's transportation committee, which is beginning to examine the projected ridership figures. It should. A September 2008 report from the Reason Foundation concluded that California's ridership projections at the time were "absurdly high—so much so that they could well rank among the most unrealistic projections produced for a major transport project anywhere in the world." The report continued: "Under a passenger-mile per route-mile standard, the CHSRA [High Speed Rail Authority] is projecting higher passenger use of the California system than is found on the Japanese and French HSR [high-speed rail] networks despite the fact that these countries have conditions that are far more favorable to the use of HSR." Such untamed overestimates make it probable that the rail line will "fall far short of its revenue projections, leading to a need for substantial additional infusions of taxpayer subsidies." That is a major predicament, especially because such subsidies are illegal. The $10 billion bond measure that passed in 2008 expressly prohibits any public operating subsidy for California's high-speed rail.

Adding to the ridership doubts is the fact that California's cities, like Florida's, are sprawling. Without a car, it's not easy to get from one place to the next. The Reason Foundation report notes that "the San Francisco urban (urbanized) area's transit market share is 3.8%, Los Angeles is 1.6%, San Diego 1.2%, San Jose 0.8% and Sacramento 0.7%," which means that "the overwhelming majority of HSR trips are likely to require a car at one or both ends to complete the trip in a reasonable time and with reasonable comfort."

Other setbacks came in January, when the California Legislative Analyst's Office, the legislature's nonpartisan watchdog, issued an evaluation of the High Speed Rail Authority's most recent business plan. It found the following:

- The rail plan offered an "uninformative timeline" and presented an "inconsistent order of events."

- The rail plan contained "no risk management strategy." For instance, it addressed "the risk of incorrectly forecasted ridership with one sentence," murkily noting that "the risk 'would be mitigated by policies that continue to draw people to reside in California and encourage high-speed rail as an alternative mode of transportation.'"

- The rail plan did not "provide any numerical ranges nor confidence intervals for projections contained in the plan (such as cost, revenues, or ridership)." Thus, "the risk of not realizing the forecasted ridership, revenues, or costs is unknown."

These conclusions are simply devastating. Perhaps the most-damaging among them, even though it's not particularly new, is that the High Speed Rail Authority's latest business plan contains no realistic outline of how California will pay to build a high-speed rail system. And so the ridership problems, political problems, route problems, timeline problems all become secondary—none of them matters if billions of construction dollars never materialize.

At this point, it seems likely that Florida will build an 80-mile route that nobody will use. In California, it seems likely that several billion dollars will go toward constructing a high-speed rail system that will never be finished and never be operational, because the requisite money can't be found.

A Billion Here, a Billion There

Nonetheless, the Obama administration pushes onward, encouraging states such as Florida and California to concoct bogus high-speed rail plans and then dispersing billions of dollars to them. All the while, nobody has an accurate idea of what these scattered high-speed systems will actually cost the country, all total, in the end. History shows that official construction estimates are usually lowballed big-time. A 1990 evaluation by the U.S. Department of Transportation of 10 major American rail transit projects found that their average cost overrun was about 50 percent; the real costs of seven of the ten projects were between 30 and 100 percent higher than their original estimates. A 2003 study carried out at Aalborg University in Denmark evaluated 258 transport infrastructure projects completed in 20 nations on five continents between 1927 and 1998. It found that the costs of nine out of ten projects were underestimated, and that for rail, actual expenses were some 45 percent higher than predicted. Ridership projections are typically way overshot, too, though not as whoppingly so as in Florida and California.

The designers of Florida's and California's proposed high-speed rail routes say that ticket sales will pay for their respective system's operating costs. No doubt those who are planning lines in other American corridors will say the same. The claims are surpassingly dubious. Only two dedicated high-speed railways in the world—one connecting Tokyo and Osaka, and the other between Paris and Lyon—have ever broken even on their initial and ongoing expenditures. And many European high-speed rail systems that are deemed cost-effective actually receive lots of extra help. A 2008 study, commissioned by Amtrak's Office of the Inspector General, notes that European passenger railways often count the government funding they receive as revenue, and that some systems receive "off-balance sheet" public funding, "typically provided for staff and pension obligations, debt service, restructuring, and past capital investments." The report concludes that, when all is said and done, "European Passenger Train Operations operate at a financial loss and consequently require significant Public Subsidies." They require far more in subsidies than Amtrak, in many cases, and Amtrak is subsidized at $32 per passenger. In 2008, Amtrak lost $1.1 billion.

The economics of high-speed rail do not work, especially in America. Could this be why the Obama administration habitually makes its case for domestic bullet trains by ignoring numbers and appealing to history? Transportation Secretary Ray LaHood has said that "President Obama's vision for high-speed rail mirrors that of President Eisenhower, the father of the Interstate highway system," and others, including the vice president and the president himself, repeatedly make the same comparison. But the analogy is inapt for several reasons, one of which is that U.S. highways serve all 50 states (not ten dispersed corridors) and the average American travels those roads for thousands of miles each year. According to Randal O'Toole's calculations, if the proposed high-speed rail routes were to be built, the average American would ride them for fewer than 60 miles annually.

Americans have recently digested federal expenditures of hundreds of billions of dollars. Is it possible that the country's taxpayers, many of whom will never in their lifetimes ride a bullet train, will remain unbothered as tens and probably hundreds of billions of dollars more are allocated to high-speed rail experiments in districts far from their own? Is it possible that these taxpayers will countenance the squander in order to achieve the president's "vision for high-speed rail in America"? It is possible, but it is unlikely—and it is unwise for the administration to bet on the long-term willingness of Arkansans, Minnesotans, Alabamans, etc. to continue funding its high-speed rail reverie.

❖

1. In 2008, Acela did make a profit. It's debatable whether $170 for a round-trip Acela ticket is "affordable," but it is certainly far, far more than Floridians will pay to travel between Tampa and Orlando.

Fast, Faster, Fastest

By Jaime Rall
State Legislatures, March 2010

Americans love trains.

They evoke nostalgia for a golden age of industry when our cities grew up around rail lines and passenger trains were the fastest, most dependable and most luxurious way to travel.

The rise of commercial aviation and the interstates in the mid-20th century sent passenger rail into a steep decline. The nation now has only two-thirds the rail miles it had in 1916, and some passenger routes take hours longer today than they did during the Great Depression.

Fast-forward to 2009 when President Barack Obama announced his vision for high-speed, intercity passenger rail: Sleek, fast trains similar to the advanced systems in Europe and Asia that will whisk Americans hundreds of miles without the hassles of airports or highway traffic.

"The president's vision has captured the public's imagination, and recent boosts in federal funding for high-speed rail initiatives have raised hopes that the vision will become a reality," says New York Senate President Pro Tem Malcolm Smith. "Suddenly, high-speed rail is a high-profile transportation issue."

But many questions remain unanswered and the rhetoric is flying. Those who advocate passenger rail see it as an environmentally friendly and much-needed option that will transform how Americans travel. Others warn it will be an expensive boondoggle that cannot deliver on its promises. The question facing the states is whether investing in high-speed rail is smart public policy.

What Is High-Speed Rail?

The term "high-speed rail" is often associated with Japanese "bullet trains" and the Train à Grande Vitesse or TGV in France, both of which travel at average speeds of more than 260 mph on some routes. In 2008, Congress defined high-speed rail more modestly as "intercity passenger rail service that is reasonably expected to reach speeds of at least 110 mph."

Today, only three routes are high-speed by this definition: the Keystone Service in Pennsylvania, the Empire Line in New York and the Acela from New York to Washington, D.C. Even these trains attain high speed only on small portions of track.

Unlike more advanced systems around the world, which run on grade-separated, dedicated tracks, American passenger trains almost always share track with slower freight trains and also contend with curving tracks, old signaling systems and other obstacles.

Federal Policy

Since World War II, federal transportation investment has focused on highways and aviation. Unlike those modes, passenger rail has no dedicated revenue source or trust fund. And the discrepancy between rail and highway investment is striking. From 1990 to 2007, Congress provided $4.17 billion for high-speed rail development. In contrast, federal-aid highways received more than nine times that amount—more than $39 billion—in 2007 alone.

Since 1992, 10 "high-speed rail corridors" have been federally designated, based on their potential for development. They are in California, Florida, Pennsylvania, Texas-Oklahoma and New York, as well as the Midwest, Pacific Northwest, Southeast, Gulf Coast and New England. Along with the Northeast Corridor from Boston to Washington, D.C., these routes reach 34 states and total more than 9,500 route miles.

Those who advocate passenger rail see it as an environmentally friendly and much-needed option that will transform how Americans travel. Others warn it will be an expensive boondoggle that cannot deliver on its promises.

States have long advocated for federal funds for state-supported, intercity passenger rail. In 2008, the passage of the Passenger Rail Investment and Improvement Act signaled a major federal policy shift. The act reauthorized Amtrak, required national and state rail plans, and approved nearly $5 billion over five years for three new grant programs for intercity and high-speed rail.

Administration Backing

Last April, Obama called for robust, efficient high-speed rail service in 100- to 600-mile intercity corridors. He also confirmed that the designated corridors were potential recipients of federal funding.

There was nothing new in talking about high-speed rail. The real innovation from the current administration was not naming the corridors or identifying the grant programs, but providing far more money than what was previously authorized.

An $8 billion "down payment" from the American Recovery and Reinvestment Act was provided through existing grant programs to jump-start the nationwide improvement of passenger rail. In December, Congress approved $2.5 billion more for high-speed rail in FY 2010 appropriations—$1.5 billion more than the president had requested. More funding is expected from federal budgets over the next four years and from legislation authorizing federal surface transportation programs.

States in Motion

States quickly pursued the new money. For the initial $8 billion in federal stimulus money, states submitted 259 applications for a total of $57 billion.

In January, the U.S. Department of Transportation awarded the $8 billion in grants to 31 states to develop 13 routes across the country. These included funds for smaller projects and planning, to lay the groundwork for future development.

Most of the money was awarded to develop new, large-scale high-speed rail programs. California received $2.25 billion and Florida $1.25 billion to build new, dedicated, European-style systems between the states' major cities. Seven Midwest states received a total of $2.62 billion to upgrade existing lines to make them faster and better serve existing markets.

The state role in passenger rail can include infrastructure planning, development and funding. Left without a federal funding partner for decades, however, many states have had limited or no passenger rail programs. In 2005, only about half the states had dedicated rail offices in their transportation departments, and some of those were handling solely freight—not passenger—systems.

Still, that means about half the states are actively supporting passenger rail, despite 50 years of federal financial neglect. As of 2005, at least 22 states were subsidizing Amtrak, passenger rail or commuter rail with state money. Many states—including California, Florida, Illinois, New York, North Carolina, Pennsylvania, Virginia and Washington—have established rail governance structures. In 2009, Texas joined them by legislatively creating a rail division, partly to catch up with development efforts in other corridors.

Even in states with plans for high-speed rail, development efforts have stalled in the absence of federal funding. California and the Midwest coalition have been planning their systems for more than 12 years, the Pacific Northwest since 1992, and the Gulf Coast states since 1982. For some of these states, the Obama initiative is finally getting their projects moving.

Any federal funds will come with clear expectations for state involvement, according to Joseph Szabo, administrator of the Federal Railroad Administration. "While FRA writes the checks, it is really state DOTs that will have responsibility for implementing these programs," he says.

State legislators also have a key role, says Minnesota Senator D. Scott Dibble. They need to "oversee and provide the policy framework and the political leadership. Legislators need to pay attention and engage at the state, regional and federal levels. The alternative is to have this issue completely pass you by."

On the Right Track?

Amid all the enthusiasm for high-speed rail, questions remain about whether it is a smart policy choice. Advocates of high-speed rail have claimed it can relieve highway and airport congestion, lessen greenhouse gas emissions, limit dependence on foreign oil, and support economic growth. But some—including the Reason Foundation, the Cato Institute and Harvard economist Edward Glaeser—have suggested high-speed rail cannot deliver on these promises.

Part of the problem is that predictions about high-speed rail are based on uncertain estimates of its costs and ridership. Models often use data from Asia and Europe, which have only limited applicability to the United States. They also sometimes project other variables decades into the future, such as population growth, fuel prices, economic growth and airfare costs.

Here's what we do know: First, high-speed rail is an expensive proposition. Incremental improvements in the Midwest will cost $3.1 million per mile; California's new, faster system will be about $65 million per mile. Most systems will require substantial up-front public investments and perhaps long-term operating subsidies.

Second, the public benefits of those investments will vary by project, and those benefits are hard to predict.

High-speed rail may work best in corridors with large, dense populations and congestion on existing modes of transportation, and where frequent, reliable service can be provided, according to a study by the U.S. Government Accountability Office.

Even in those areas, however, economic viability is not guaranteed.

"As these initial dollars are put on the table," says Dibble, "we need to be very rigorous in making sure that we are building the right facilities and that the business cases are very sound.

"High-speed rail can be a fantastic investment for the economy, for individual lives, and for the environment," he says. "But investing in a project that is a failure will affect the whole movement toward building a robust nationwide passenger rail network."

Success will depend on the basics, says Florida Senator Paula Dockery. "The key is that the trains have to run on time, be clean, be safe, and take the people where they want to go. If you make it easy to use, it becomes a viable alternative."

In a time of fiscal crisis, high-speed rail likely will be weighed carefully against other spending priorities, including existing, underfunded transportation infrastructure. With scarce state funds, few in-country rail experts and no existing high-speed rail industry, states that want these systems may find it challenging to develop the capacity and expertise to do their part.

This leaves state policymakers in a familiar situation: Making difficult decisions based on competing priorities, careful deliberation and often conflicting information.

"The long-term success of rail in this country and in your individual states and regions," says Karen Rae, the railroad administration's deputy administrator, "depends upon state legislatures understanding the goals of the program, the potential benefits, and then just doing the tough thing you do all the time: figuring out how that fits into your larger transportation goals."

The Future of High-Speed Rail

Although high-speed rail may be gaining momentum, its future is uncertain.

Building a national high-speed rail network would take decades of sustained federal commitment. Though the $10.5 billion given so far is a start, the National

Surface Transportation Policy and Revenue Study Commission estimated the capital cost of reestablishing the national passenger rail network by 2050 at over $357 billion. Without a dedicated funding source, high-speed rail projects must compete with other demands on federal funds and may give way to other policy priorities in the future.

"Whether or not the enthusiasm of this administration will grow into a sustainable, long-term program, only time will tell," says New York's Smith.

Minnesota's Dibble thinks there is momentum building.

"The excitement, imagination, and possibilities that are out there for building a comprehensive network of high-speed, intercity passenger rail," he says, "really speaks to the need to create a much more reliable program with the kind of political and institutional commitment that will stand the test of time."

Speeding Around the Globe

Talk about high-speed rail in the United States often refers to the model systems in Asia and Europe.

Even President Barack Obama made the point last year. "All of you know this is not some fanciful, pie-in-the-sky vision of the future," he said. "It's been happening for decades. The problem is it's been happening elsewhere, not here."

Here is a quick picture of what's happening elsewhere.

- Japan unveiled the world's first high-speed rail line in 1964: the Shinkansen bullet train between Tokyo and Osaka, which averages 150 mph. Since then, seven other high-speed lines have been added, both before and after privatization in 1987. The system currently serves about 300 million passengers per year and continues to expand based on a national master plan. Right now, a new Tokyo-Osaka line is being built to carry passengers at more than 300 mph.

- France opened its first Train à Grande Vitesse or TGV line from Paris to Lyon in 1981. In 2007, a TGV train broke the world speed record at 357 mph. Every year, more than 100 million passengers ride the 1,180 miles of TGV, which connect major cities in France and link to Germany, Belgium and England. France is currently pursuing a plan to build 1,200 additional miles of high-speed rail before 2020.

- Spain's first high-speed rail line, from Madrid to Seville, opened in 1992; more people now travel between those cities by rail than by car and air combined. In 2007 and 2008, additional lines were built from Madrid to Barcelona and Valladolid, and from Córdoba to Malaga. Today, the 981-mile system serves 9 million passengers per year. Spain's most recent national transportation plan calls for $103.9 billion to develop 5,592 miles of high-speed rail.

- China has embarked on the fastest expansion of high-speed rail in the world. The country started its service only three years ago and plans to invest more than $1 trillion to develop more than 8,000 miles of high-speed rail by 2020. Last year, China unveiled the world's now fastest high-speed train, which averages 217 mph. By 2012, China will have spent $300 billion and may have more miles of high speed rail service than any other nation.

True high-speed rail that travels at more than 150 mph requires exclusively dedicated track with no grade crossings, no freight traffic and no sharp curves. These systems are costly. France invested $10.6 billion and Spain $1.3 billion in passenger rail in 2003 alone; Japan spends about $2 billion a year on the Shinkansen. So far, only California and Florida plan to build similar systems in the United States.

❖

Jaime Rall covers high-speed rail and a range of other transportation issues for NCSL, and co-staffs the new NCSL High-Speed Rail Working Group.

Amtrak Needs Stronger Spending Controls

By John Hayward
Human Events, December 20, 2010

Amtrak is one of the big money sinks for taxpayer cash. The subsidized rail system loses about $1 billion a year, which means taxpayers cough up roughly $40 for each passenger it carries. You would expect a shaky operation with huge subsidies to work under strict oversight, but Amtrak executives have long had other ideas.

ICG Fired

In June 2009, the inspector general of Amtrak, Fred Weiderhold, completed a report that concluded the "independence and effectiveness" of the inspector general's office was being "substantially impaired" by Amtrak management, as reported in the *Wall Street Journal.* Coincidentally, Amtrak management chose that moment to conclude Weiderhold's career. He was paid over $300,000 to sign what amounted to a non-disclosure agreement on his way out. The Amtrak brass tapped Lorraine Green, formerly vice president for human resources, to be his replacement.

Amtrak has a long history of doing things the organization would happily pay $300,000 of your money to keep quiet. Executives have filed false accounting reports to paint fanciful pictures of operational health, intermittently punctuated by sudden announcements that doomsday is imminent unless more subsidies are supplied. *Politico* says Weiderhold found over $100 million in mismanaged legal fees from 2002 to 2005, yet was sacked because he was "no longer the effective inspector general that our company needs," as an internal memorandum put it.

Grassley and Issa Probe

Sen. Chuck Grassley (R.-Iowa) and Rep. Darrell Issa (R.-Calif.) had a feeling Welderhold might have been cashed out because he was a bit too effective. They also noticed the Amtrak board removed Weiderhold without notifying Congress at least 30 days before his dismissal, as they are legally obligated to do. Weiderhold was given 24 hours to clean out his desk, then skedaddle with his severance check stuffed in his breast pocket. Last week, Grassley and Issa released a report of their findings, and it's not pretty.

"Amtrak failed to comply with the Inspector General Act for way too long," Grassley said. "Forcing its inspector general out of office without notice or Consultation with Congress is only the latest example. Naming an interim inspector general from Amtrak management with no relevant experience only added insult to injury. All of this undermined the independence of the Office of Inspector General. Like any entity that receives billions of tax dollars, Amtrak needs independent oversight and I hope this controversy has helped Amtrak learn that valuable lesson."

I find myself less hopeful than the senator. He's obviously right about the crucial importance of independent oversight when billions of tax dollars are on the line. When taxpayers get tired of subsidizing Amtrak, where do we go to vote it out of existence?

Accounting Shenanigans

Liberals always trumpet "infrastructure" as one of the vital reasons for perpetual tax and spending increases. Well, Amtrak is infrastructure, and look at how it's managed. Oversight is difficult in massive government agencies. How is a guy like Weiderhold—very good at his job, according to everyone except Amtrak brass—supposed to stand up to a board of entrenched bureaucrats waving a pile of freshly printed bills in one hand, and a non-disclosure agreement in the other? He's not the only inspector general to get rough treatment after asking too many questions in this administration. Remember Gerald Walpin, the AmeriCorps inspector general sacked by President Obama and smeared as an Alzheimer's patient when he objected? Grassley and Issa remember him, naming him in their report on Weiderhold.

> *Amtrak has a long history of doing things the organization would happily pay $300,000 of your money to keep quiet.*

The ultimate "oversight" of a corporation is the market, and a disinterested government apparatus that enforces clear regulations. Private companies have been dissolved for the kind of accounting shenanigans Weiderhold uncovered at Amtrak. Corporations with Amtrak's inept business model rapidly implode from their losses. Try hanging around at an Amtrak depot and asking the passengers how much they paid for their tickets. Every one of them will give you the wrong answer, because none of them will include the $40 average taxpayer subsidy. In the chaotic fusion of government and industry, no one knows what anything actually costs. The least government can do is keep an unblinking eye on the people who are spending our money to provide things we would not purchase voluntarily.

6

Seaports and Waterways

(Robert Nickelsberg/Getty Images)

A cargo container vessel is tied up at a pier in the Port of Los Angeles-Long Beach June 3, 2004, in San Pedro, California.

A New Era of Growth for America's Seaports

By Paul McCaffrey

In a national referendum held on October 22, 2006, the people of Panama overwhelmingly approved a $5.25 billion project to expand the Panama Canal. The expansion plan includes the construction of a third set of locks along the waterway and the widening of the canal's channels so that larger ships can pass through. When completed in 2014, the revamped Panama Canal is expected to have twice its current shipping capacity. The expansion, which is poised to transform the American shipping industry, has set off a scramble among the major ports of the eastern United States to build the necessary infrastructure to berth, load, and unload the larger vessels that the new canal will accommodate. West Coast ports will be affected as well. This race to prepare for what a renovated Panama Canal will bring has illuminated many of the strengths and weaknesses of port facilities in the United States.

In 2011, the US imported approximately $2.2 trillion worth of goods from overseas—much of it from Asia—and exported about another $1.4 trillion. Whether entering or leaving the country, most of this cargo was processed in an American port facility and transferred from oceangoing ships to ground transport, or vice versa. The top ten US harbors accommodate about 85 percent of all exports. The three largest American harbors by volume are the ports of Los Angeles, Long Beach, and New York-New Jersey. Los Angeles and Long Beach, situated right next to one another, are the busiest ports in the nation, but could stand to lose container ship traffic once the Panama Canal project is finished.

The sheer volume of cargo coming from and going to American ports highlights how essential port facilities are to the US and global economy. Yet, according to a January 2012 report by the World Economic Forum, US harbors rank 22nd in the world, well behind the leading ports of Asia. Indeed, of the top ten global ports, six are in China, none are in the US. In one year, the port of Shanghai processes more cargo than the top seven American ports combined. According to former Pennsylvania governor Ed Rendell, the fifty-nine busiest US ports can only operate 35 percent of the time. "Other countries understand that port innovation and capacity is key to competitiveness in an export-driven economy," he stated. "Policy-makers in Washington need to make smart infrastructure investments a priority, because if we don't, we will only fall further behind the rest of the world."

More than any other development, the Panama Canal expansion has demonstrated how American ports have to evolve if they are to survive. Currently, Panamax-class ships measuring 965 feet long and 106 feet wide and requiring a draft of around 40 feet are the largest vessels capable of navigating the canal. Major US ports on both coasts have the channels, depth, cranes, and transit networks to handle ships of this size.

But the New Panamax or post-Panamax ships are 1200 feet long, 160 feet wide, and require drafts of up to 50 feet when fully loaded. New Panamax vessels can transport two to three times the cargo of traditional Panamax ships. While Long Beach and Los Angeles, among other West Coast ports, have the necessary infrastructure, only one facility on the East Coast—the Port of Virginia, in Norfolk—is currently equipped to process fully loaded New Panamax vessels, while the Port of Baltimore is expected to be ready by 2014. In all the other shipping centers, the harbors may not be deep enough or the channels wide enough by then.

The Port of New York–New Jersey has the necessary depth, but the Bayonne Bridge, which connects the New York City borough of Staten Island to New Jersey, will need to be raised if the new ships are to safely pass beneath it. A project to raise the bridge 64 feet is expected to take five years and cost in excess of $1 billion. Meanwhile, proposed dredging projects in Miami and Savannah to make their harbors ready for New Panamax ships have met with resistance from environmental groups and face funding issues. If these harbors are not equipped for the larger vessels by the time the Panama Canal renovations are complete, they may end up being bypassed altogether and could, some worry, lose much of their business as supply chains are rerouted. In response, Norfolk and Baltimore could take up an ever-larger share of East Coast shipping traffic. Of course, even if a particular port can handle New Panamaxes, it's not clear if the connecting road and rail networks can handle the increased cargo load that the ships will carry.

Along with many East Coast ports, West Coast harbors could be in for some major changes come 2014. The Port of Los Angeles processed 7.94 million shipping containers in 2011. Setting an all-time record for a US harbor, Los Angeles readied 2.11 million containers for shipment overseas. With the nearby Port of Long Beach, the two facilities handled around 14 million containers in 2011, and about 40 percent of all US imports.

The dilemma posed by the Panama Canal expansion to the West Coast ports is a complicated one. Currently, much of the cargo from Asia headed to the eastern US is unloaded in western harbors, transferred to truck or train, and sent on to its destination. While quicker than going through Panama and on to an eastern port, cross-country rail and truck transport is expensive. Once the canal can accommodate New Panamax ships, with their increased load sizes, these costs will look even more onerous to shipping companies. Many expect that more ships from Asia will bypass western ports like Los Angeles and Long Beach altogether once the revamped canal is complete.

Along with the challenge of increasing capacity and preparing for the expanded canal, there are ongoing security and environmental concerns at the port facilities. Prior to the September 11, 2001, terrorist attacks, port security focused on collecting customs duties and inspecting for drugs, counterfeit goods, and other banned products. Terrorism was not on the radar. "Every major commercial seaport before

9/11 was porous. They were vital engines of the US economy and few people were looking at security at all," Jay Grant, chief executive of the International Association of Airport and Seaport Police, commented. "Today, we're not perfect, but someone is always watching. Someone is always paying attention."

After 9/11, there was widespread fear that terrorists might smuggle a nuclear weapon into the US through its ports. At the time, the ports had no structures in place to counteract such threats. Over ten years later, things are much different. In 2002, Congress passed the Maritime Transport Security Act, which mandated that port facilities and transport vessels institute screening procedures, conduct risk assessments, and implement various other security measures. One component of the new law was the Port Security Grant Program (PSCP), which allotted funds to the port facilities to upgrade their security systems. Since the PSCP came into effect, the federal government has paid out nearly $1.7 billion to protect vital maritime infrastructure, and the port facilities have built up robust security operations. To deal with the nuclear threat, the federal government has mandated that by July 2012, all shipping containers bound for the US must be scanned for radiological material at their port of origin.

As concerns about proposed dredging projects in Miami and elsewhere demonstrate, port facilities projects face environmental challenges as well. The ports of Los Angeles and Long Beach, for example, were notorious for their contributions to air pollution in Southern California. Emissions from idling ships, trucks, and trains accessing the harbor had a drastic effect on human health. According to a *New York Times* report, residents of the neighborhoods in the immediate vicinity of the ports suffered from increased health risks. In response, the port authorities, in coordination with the local government, instituted a number of measures that have apparently helped to cut down on emissions. They have phased out diesel trucks and brought more environmentally friendly locomotives into service. They have also adopted incentives to encourage the container ships visiting the port to reduce their emissions.

Meanwhile, US inland port facilities and waterways face challenges both distinct from and similar to those on the coast. All told, the US inland waterways network serves forty-one states, including sixteen state capitals. It includes about twelve thousand miles of waterways that are navigable by commercial barges and managed by the Army Corps of Engineers. This network is divided into four systems: the Mississippi River, the Ohio River Basin, the Gulf Intercoastal Waterway, and the Pacific Coast (or Columbia River). The Mississippi River system is by far the largest of the four, composing about 75 percent of the total 12,000 miles. The Ohio River is next largest at roughly 2,800 miles, while the Gulf Intercoastal contains about 1,109 miles and the Pacific Coast 596 miles. Within the system are around 257 locks, which help make stretches of water more navigable by raising and lowering their depth.

At interior ports, security is somewhat less of a concern since they are not the first points of contact with foreign cargo. Interior ports do not handle massive ocean-going vessels, and process much smaller loads, so their infrastructural requirements are less onerous. The system of interior ports in the US does not have to undergo major adjustments ahead of the Panama Canal expansion.

Nonetheless, though barge transport is considerably cheaper and less environmentally damaging than rail or truck transport, the inland and intercoastal waterways network suffers from perennial neglect. About half of the revenue for the system's upkeep is raised through a tax of 20 cents per gallon of gasoline that is levied on commercial transport operators that run barges on about 11,000 miles of the system. This money is then deposited into the Inland Waterways Trust Fund (IWTF), which the Army Corps of Engineers accesses for lock repair projects and other initiatives. Annually, around $90 million is raised through these fuel taxes. Another $90 million or so is allotted to the Corps via congressional appropriation.

This revenue has not been enough to maintain the locks. In 2006, 47 percent of the locks overseen by the Corps were deemed obsolete. That percentage is expected to increase over the next decade. A lock is designed to have an effective lifespan of about fifty years. Yet, of the 257 operating on US inland waterways in 2009, ninety-two were sixty years or older, while thirty dated back to the nineteenth century. Since each lock repair project costs in the neighborhood of $50 million, the Corps can't fix them fast enough. Unless more funding is brought to bear, by 2020, more than 80 percent of the locks are expected to be outmoded. Based on these conditions, in its 2009 Report Card on American Infrastructure, the American Society of Civil Engineers (ASCE) gave a grade of "D–" to US inland waterways, and called for $50 billion in funding over the next five years to bring the system up to standard.

The common theme among both coastal harbors and inland port facilities and waterways is the need for renewed and well-planned investment. In capacity and technology, US ports fell behind their global counterparts decades ago. Despite such deficits, they have still managed to do the job. The Panama Canal expansion could change that. Certain harbors, if they don't adapt in time, may become obsolete altogether. Faced with that prospect, the various port authorities and their government partners are finally taking steps to update their operations. Whether these measures will suffice to save some ports from irrelevance is unclear. However, the Panama Canal expansion has unquestionably opened up a challenging new era for port facilities in the United States.

The Shipping News

By Phillip Longman
The Washington Monthly, July 2010

Start moving freight by water again, and we'll use less oil, emit less carbon, cut highway traffic—and perhaps even save St. Louis.

Every four days, a 4,200-horsepower tugboat, having crossed the Gulf of Mexico from Brownsville, Texas, slips into the ship channel off Egmont Key at the mouth of Tampa Bay. The vessel pulls a single barge. On board are stacks of metal containers ranging in length from twenty to fifty-three feet. Few of the bathers along the beaches of nearby Fort De Soto Park are likely to take much notice of such a routine sight, much less associate it with a green-energy future. But there is a connection, and it will help protect places like the Gulf floor from the sort of drilling that now threatens the region with environmental catastrophe.

The tug and barge are operated by a privately held company called SeaBridge Freight. If you hire SeaBridge to move a container between northern Mexico and the southeastern United States, a truck will pick the container up, and a truck will deliver it to its final destination. But rather than use a truck to make the entire journey, the company will load your container onto a barge and ship it across the Gulf of Mexico. This water route saves 690 miles of driving, takes no longer than trucking door to door, and consumes much less oil.

According to SeaBridge's president and CEO, Henry P. "Hank" Hoffman, a SeaBridge barge on a recent sailing carried containers loaded with 420,000 metric tons of cargo of all descriptions, from chilled orange juice to automobiles and mechanical assemblies. Making the run from Brownsville to Tampa Bay consumed 9,000 gallons of diesel fuel. If trucks had made the move, Hoffman notes, they would have consumed more than 53,000 gallons of diesel fuel. Needless to say, such conservation does wonders for a reduction in oil use.

Waterways used to be the most important avenues of transport in the United States. Today, however, only 4.7 percent of our current freight (as measured in ton-miles) moves by water, most of it low-value, bulky materials such as grain and coal. Compare this to the European Union, in which 40 percent of all domestic freight (also measured in ton-miles) moves by coastal shipping and inland waterways.

Boosting that abysmal market share, as a handful of companies like SeaBridge are trying to do, would require no sacrifice from the average American, and it would provide dramatic economic and environmental benefits. Barges use just over a quarter as much diesel fuel as a semitruck in moving a ton of freight. If only 30 percent of the freight that currently goes by truck went by barge instead, it would result in a reduction in diesel fuel consumption of roughly 4.7 billion gallons. This is equivalent to conserving more than 6 percent of the total end-use energy consumed by U.S. households, including heating, cooling, and lighting. To put it another way, the energy savings would be equivalent to turning off every household appliance in the state of Texas. Yet no one would have to do so much as turn down the air conditioner, ride a bike, or even install a fluorescent bulb.

It gets better. A rebirth of domestic water transportation would roll back the nation's reliance on trucks, the fastest growing source of U.S. greenhouse gas emissions. That's in addition to many incidental benefits, from boosting the Navy's sealift capacity to improving rescue efforts for disasters like Hurricane Katrina and the earthquake in Haiti. Moreover, by getting containers off trucks and onto a marine highway, it promises to make driving safer and faster for the rest of us, while also significantly reducing the need for highway repairs and new road construction.

The case for using our waterways begins with plain geography. Writing in 1783, George Washington observed that he was increasingly taking "a more contemplative and extensive view of the vast inland navigation of these United States," and that he "could not but be struck with the immense diffusion and importance of it." The United States is unique among nations in being blessed not only with three extensive coastlines and abundant natural harbors but also with 25,000 miles of navigable lakes and inland waterways, thanks both to what Washington and his generation called "Providence" and to the investments made by subsequent generations of Americans in locks, levies, and other improvements.

Today, it is impossible to account for why most U.S. cities sprang up where they did without considering the role played by access to navigable waters. By 1825, completion of the Erie Canal connected New York harbor to the Great Lakes, and soon a great trade of cordwood, flour, and wheat flowing east, and manufactured goods and imported foods flowing west, enabled New York City to surpass Philadelphia as the nation's largest and richest city. By 1840, more than 500 steamboats plied the Ohio-Mississippi-Missouri river system, opening up the bustling new frontier of river towns described by Mark Twain. The most strategically located of these grew into great cities like St. Louis and Minneapolis-St. Paul. Of the country's top twenty-five metropolitan areas today, twenty-one are either on coastal harbors (such as New York, Boston, Los Angeles, and Seattle) or on broad inland waterways (such as Chicago, Pittsburgh, and Little Rock).

Well into the twentieth century, the U.S. still made extensive use of coastal and inland water shipping. As late as 1958, the Coastwise Steamship Company picked up rolls of newsprint from mills at Port Angeles and Camus, Washington, delivering them up and down the Pacific coast. Into the 1960s, trucks, trains, and automobiles moving between Michigan and Wisconsin still used an extensive fleet of ferries to cross Lake Michigan rather than take the long way through congested Chicago.

For the past fifty years or so, however, the U.S. has barely made use of its natural competitive advantage in domestic water transportation. This might seem like the inevitable by-product of progress. In reality, though, the decline of domestic water transportation was neither inevitable nor progressive. By the late nineteenth century, railroad barons captured control of many canals and coastal shipping companies and did their best to put them out of business. While this contributed to the decline of the maritime industry, the most important factor was the long post–World War II era of cheap energy and a rapidly expanding, deeply subsidized interstate highway system. As the price of trucking became artificially low, new factories and warehouses came to be built without regard to water access, thereby accelerating the move away from fuel-efficient ships and barges. But now that extended period of secure, abundant oil and open, well-maintained interstates has ended. So, too, has our innocence of the environmental damage and threats to human health. This makes it high time to tackle the waste and inefficiency that pervades the 10 percent of U.S. gross domestic product involved in freight logistics.

Today, most high-value freight moves by truck. For trips of under 500 miles, this makes sense. Trucks are fast and convenient. But most of our trucks are traveling distances of thousands of miles. To take just one example, 58 percent of the large trucks moving through the junction of I-90 and I-290 near Buffalo, New York, are on trips of more than 500 miles. Together, these long-haul trucks are responsible, according to the Federal Highway Administration, for creating 367,000 hours of delay each year at this single choke point alone.

As soon as trucks are deployed for long hauls, the disadvantages pile up. For one thing, trucks are wasteful. If you're hauling a ton of freight by truck, a gallon of fuel will only move it 255 miles. Haul it by railroad, and a gallon will take it 413 miles. Haul it by towed barge, and a gallon will carry it a full 576 miles.

Trucks are also by far the dirtiest form of ground transportation. A tugboat plying inland waters can typically move a ton of freight more than 51,000 miles before emitting one ton of greenhouse gas. A truck, by contrast, releases nearly three times as much greenhouse gas over the same distance. (In fact, trucks are the economy's fastest growing source of greenhouse gas emissions. While greenhouse gas emissions from cars rose only 3.3 percent between 1990 and 2006, the amount spewing from medium and heavy trucks, which have increased in number and sit longer in traffic, increased 77 percent.) That's not even factoring in other emissions, such as cancer-causing nitrous oxides found in diesel exhaust, most of which comes from trucks. According to the Environmental Protection Agency, this pollution contributes to the premature death of 21,000 Americans a year.

When truck-related deaths don't come from pollution, they come from crashes. For every ton of freight they haul one mile, trucks have a fatality rate that is six times that of railroads and 155 times that of inland barges. Some 5,000 Americans die each year in collisions involving trucks.

Finally, trucks cause serious damage to the nation's highways, for which the rest of us pay. According to the latest available estimate from the Federal Highway Administration, the pavement damage caused by a forty-ton semitruck barreling down an urban interstate came to forty-one cents per mile in 2000, while the tolls and taxes its owner paid came to only nine cents per mile.

It's not just our interstates that suffer. State roads like New Jersey's Route 31 and Interstate 81 through the once tranquil Shenandoah Valley are inundated with truckers desperate to avoid I-95. Despite what may be many years of moribund economic growth in the wake of the Great Recession, freight tonnage on I-95 is projected to double over the next thirty years. Even the biggest fan of trucking knows this isn't sustainable.

So what do we do about our freight logjams? Adding more and more new lanes is, of course, one way to alleviate the problem. But routes such as I-95 are built on top of some of the country's most densely developed real estate. Just to widen I-95 to six lanes between New Haven and the Rhode Island border would cost $1 billion, while also causing additional construction-related delays for years.

> *The single most effective option that remains, then, is our vast network of waterways—if we just care to use them. Not only would they save money and fuel; they would even, in some cases, save time.*

Railroads are also an important option. (See "Back on Tracks," *Washington Monthly*, January/February 2009.) But, after years of downsizing, the nation's rail system today lacks the capacity to handle much more traffic than it already does, particularly if that traffic is going to move fast enough to be time competitive with trucks. Moreover, along many corridors, moving freight by rail competes with another important objective: restoring and improving America's high-speed passenger network. (The main reason why Amtrak is so frequently late is delay caused by freight trains.)

The single most effective option that remains, then, is our vast network of waterways—if we just care to use them. Not only would they save money and fuel; they would even, in some cases, save time. For example, a single truck driver moving a container from Boston to Orlando can make the trip legally in no less than fifty-four hours, given speed limits and mandatory thirteen-hour rest periods each day. By contrast, in just thirty-three hours, a container can be taken by truck from Boston to the port of New London, then placed onto a high-speed coastal freighter and shipped to the port of Charleston, and finally trucked from Charleston to Orlando, according to Stephen P. Flott, founder of SeaBridge, who has testified before Congress in support of the idea and may yet bring it to fruition.

To make this sort of thing happen is easier than it might sound. At its peak, truck traffic on I-95 was 32,000 trailers a day. With only thirty-three ships put into service, each capable of carrying 300 fifty-three-foot containers, the number of trailers on I-95 could be reduced by a third. The price tag wouldn't be prohibitive, either. At $50 million a ship, it would cost just $3.3 billion.

Better yet, because crafts plying coastal and inland waters are shallow draft, they could operate out of minor, neglected harbors like New London or New Bedford,

Massachusetts. With today's so-called "Roll-on/Roll-off" ships (RoRos), cranes aren't even necessary. Drivers just roll their trucks on board, and, if they want to, travel along with their rig, thereby satisfying their mandatory rest requirements as they float past such major choke points as the Boston-to-Washington megalopolis before taking to the road again to reach their final destination.

Nevertheless, despite all the inherent advantages of a marine highway system, market forces still aren't causing it to spring into existence. There are a few reasons for this.

One is that, in the midst of global recession, the current cost of energy is slightly too low to create the necessary critical mass for an upsurge in shipping. According to a study prepared for the U.S. Maritime Administration, even a minimal rise in energy prices would dramatically increase the cost of trucking while only marginally affecting the cost of water transport. For example, when crude oil costs $55 per barrel, the cost of moving a forty-foot container one mile by truck is about $1.75. But if crude oil goes up to $91 a barrel, the trucking cost jumps to $2.28 per mile. And if oil reaches $157 a barrel, the trucking cost jumps up to $3.24. By comparison, even if oil is at $157 a barrel, the cost of moving that same container one mile by barge is only twenty-eight cents, less than a tenth of the trucking cost.

One entrepreneur who is very aware of such calculations is Stephen J. Pepper, founder of Humboldt Maritime Logistics. Pepper is trying to start a service that would allow shippers to move containers by barge from the port of Oakland up and down the Pacific coast. At current fuel prices, he says, such a service is cost competitive with trucks, but only barely so. With even a modest uptick in fuel prices, though, the numbers would shift dramatically in favor of barge over truck.

Another reason that the maritime highway isn't farther along is that ill-considered public policies are working against it. Some of the wrongheaded ideas are obvious, such as tax rates on trucks that are too low to cover the cost of the damage they do to roads. Others are more obscure, but equally significant.

One important case in point is the so-called "harbor maintenance tax." Originally pushed by the Reagan administration, it requires that shippers pay a tax on their cargo value each time their freight passes through a U.S. harbor. The thought was that the money raised by this tax would go toward the cost of dredging and otherwise maintaining deep channel harbors. Instead, most of it has gone to finance the government's overall budget deficits. Worse still is the mechanism for how the tax is collected. Suppose that Federal Express wanted to save on fuel costs by using a truck ferry to move its container traffic between Windsor, Ontario, and Detroit, Michigan. Because of the harbor tax, the company would have to determine the value of each parcel in each container and collect from its owner a harbor tax of $1.25 per $1,000 of cargo value. This would not only be an administrative nightmare; it would also add up to serious money. If the total value of the cargo in a container came to $500,000, the total harbor tax due would be $625. By contrast, if the container traveled by truck over the more than eighty-one-year-old, highly congested Ambassador Bridge between Windsor and Detroit, no tax would be due, and the toll would be only $3.25 per axle.

Marine highway advocates also complain bitterly about a piece of legislation called the Jones Act. Originally passed in the 1920s, the Jones Act requires all ships used in domestic service to be built by domestic shipyards. The rationale for retaining this policy has been that the U.S. needs a shipbuilding industry to support the needs of the U.S. Navy—a consideration that has merit. But building a commercial ship in the U.S. today typically costs twice as much as building it in South Korea. This isn't because of the difference in labor costs; it's because South Korea builds so many ships for world markets that it can use highly standardized, assembly line processes that achieve vast economies of scale, much as the U.S. did in building the famous "Liberty Ships" of World War II.

But here a win-win solution exists—one that doesn't disturb the Jones Act but still allows water transportation a fair shot at the competition. The Navy, it turns out, is very interested in seeing a surge in shipbuilding, and it may even be willing to help pay for it. During the 1980s and '90s, when America's merchant marine was fading, the Navy spent $6 billion acquiring ships it could use for transporting troops and supplies around the world. Today, many of these ships are nearing the end of their service life, and the Navy would like to have new RoRo ships suitable for off-loading tanks, trucks, and other vehicles in shallow, often undeveloped harbors.

The Navy could, of course, just put out bids to have its fleet of aging RoRos and other freighters replaced. But that would compete with the cost of modernizing its submarine fleet and other aging warships. How much better it would be, says Jonathan D. Kaskin, who directs the Navy's Strategic Mobility and Combat Logistics Division, if the United States once again had a robust merchant marine fleet plying domestic waters—a fleet whose ships could quickly be leased by the Navy if they were needed for emergency service?

"A commercial ship is fully capable of meeting our military [sealift] requirements except for minor enhancements," says Kaskin. Better yet, he notes, if the U.S. developed a marine highway system, the cost of shipbuilding overall would go down. "I see the marine highway as an option," Kaskin says, "and there may be resources that the Department of Defense could devote to it." Just as Eisenhower could not sell the country on the value of interstate highways without pointing to their military purpose, national security needs may be just what is needed to get the marine highway system moving.

In April 2010, Secretary of Transportation Ray LaHood announced his support for a "Marine Highway Initiative," stating that, "For too long, we've overlooked the economic and environmental benefits that our waterways and domestic seaports offer as a means of moving freight in this country." The funding available for this initiative, however, is a mere gesture—just $7 million in grants, plus $58 million in one-time stimulus money. Meanwhile, the president's budget for 2011 calls for $41 billion in highway spending. The Obama administration does not seem to get the full range of opportunity that domestic water transport offers for advancing the national interest across the board. So let's try to envision the virtuous cycles that would be set in motion by reviving our waterways.

One virtuous cycle would begin in 2015. That is when a project to widen the Panama Canal is scheduled to be completed. It will allow today's super-large ocean-going vessels to fit through the canal and travel directly between Asia and both the Gulf and Atlantic coasts of the United States. Today, containers traveling from Asia typically move through West Coast ports and are then trucked or carried by rail to inland destinations. But containers moving on mega-ships through the Panama Canal could be off-loaded in ports such as Houston or New Orleans, where, thanks to the Mississippi River system, they could be hauled to cities like St. Louis, Minneapolis, and Pittsburgh by low-cost, energy-efficient barge. Or they could travel to deepwater ports such as Newark and be trans-loaded onto smaller coastal ships serving destinations up and down the eastern seaboard.

In another virtuous cycle, barges would beget barges. That is to say, as the volume of coastal and inland water transport increased, so too would its time competitiveness with trucks. Today, once a week, a new service known as 64 Express moves containers up and down the James River between the port of Hampton Roads and Richmond, Virginia. Only those who can afford to wait currently use it. But many more companies would use the service if it ran more frequently. With containers from Asia flowing directly into Hampton Roads, that's exactly what would happen.

Meanwhile, today's diesel-powered tugboats and coastal ships could become even cleaner by converting to natural gas, as has already been done on a limited scale. Unlike trucks, ships don't require a vast fueling network, since they have the space to carry large tanks of natural gas on board. If trucks at the same time became relegated to mostly short-haul service, this would make it more practical for them to convert to natural gas as well.

And we can imagine a final virtuous cycle coming into play. As the economic and environmental case for domestic water transport increased, land-use patterns would change. More factories and warehouses would spring up in places that offer easy access to navigable waters, whether it was in East St. Louis's once thriving but long troubled real estate along the Mississippi River, or Cleveland's squandered waterfront property along Lake Erie, where today just about the only remaining economic activity occurs in a deeply subsidized sports stadium on the weekends. As banal as talk of barges and freighters might at first seem, the rebirth of domestic water transport promises a much stronger and sustainable America—one that uses, and lives in harmony with, the bounty of waterways that first made it great.

❖

Phillip Longman is a senior research fellow at the New America Foundation and the author (with Ray Boshara) of The Next Progressive Era: A Blueprint for Broad Prosperity.

Shipping Out of the Economic Crisis

By Jan Hoffmann

The Brown Journal of World Affairs, Spring/Summer 2010

During the last 60 years, international trade has been outgrowing the world's gross domestic product. Indeed, this elasticity has become stronger over time. Since the 1990s, the volume of trade has grown three times faster than the world economy—as long as times were good. By the same token, during the financial crisis the downturn in trade was even stronger than the slump in production. In 2009, the world's GDP decreased by 2.2 percent, while trade dropped by 14.4 percent as traders and factories used up their inventories. Forecasts for 2010 and 2011 are again positive, and trade is expected to grow at about twice the rate of output. Nevertheless, the volume of trade will for many years remain far below the level consistent with its pre-crisis trend. This is particularly bad news for those who make a living out of transporting this trade by sea—in terms of volume, 90 percent of global trade is moved in this way.

Transport is one of the cornerstones of globalization. Together with telecommunications, trade liberalization, and international standardization, the increased efficiency of port and shipping services has made it easier to buy and sell merchandise goods, raw materials, and components almost anywhere in the world. According to the *Journal of Commerce,* "despite all the headlines and political bluster surrounding the World Trade Organization, [North America Free Trade Agreement], and other trade pacts, the real driving force behind globalization is something far less visible: the declining costs of international transport."

The maritime business itself is arguably the most globalized of all industries. The service providers are rarely citizens of the nations whose cargo they move. A simple commercial transaction may easily involve people, services, and property from more than a dozen different countries: a Greek-owned vessel that is built in Korea may be chartered to a Danish operator who employs Filipino seafarers via a Cypriot crewing agent. The ship is registered in Panama, insured in the United Kingdom, and transports German-made cargo in the name of a Swiss freight forwarder from a Dutch port to Argentina, through terminals that are concessioned to operators from Hong Kong and Dubai. On its journey, the vessel may have repairs done in a Portuguese yard, bunker fuel in Spain, and transship containers—to be reloaded on a different ship on a different destination—in Brazil. International standardization, an important component of globalization in general, is crucial to the shipping industry. Without standardized containers, globalized intermodal networks would not be possible.

Furthermore, standardization enables the application of United Nations regulations on safety and training to apply on all international waters.

Shipping in Circles

Shipping has been hit particularly hard by the economic crisis. The downturn in trade has directly led to a rapid decline in demand for transport and related services. For example, port traffic in the world's largest container ports, Singapore and Shanghai, decreased by 13.5 and 11 percent, respectively, in 2009. Yet, in spite of this downturn in demand, the shipping fleets' capacity has been expanding throughout 2009, as vessels ordered in earlier years continued being delivered by the world's shipyards. Between January 2009 and January 2010, the world fleet's total container carrying capacity increased by 5.7 percent. The dry bulk tonnage for the transport of coal, iron ore, and grains increased by 9 percent.

The supply side's response to changes in demand is never immediate (Figure 1). Between 2002 and 2004, demand for containerized trade grew faster than the supply of container carrying capacity, so the industry ordered new tonnage. This tonnage is usually delivered two to three years later, and since 2006, the supply of container ships has been growing faster than demand. In 2009, the difference in growth rates amounts to a staggering 15 percentage points.

Figure 1—Growth of demand and supply in container shipping, 2000–2009 (annual growth rates)

	2000	2001	2002	2003	2004	2005	2006	2007	2008	2009
Demand	10.7	2.4	10.5	11.6	13.4	10.6	11.2	10.9	4.4	−9.7
Supply	7.8	8.5	8.0	8.0	8.0	10.5	13.6	11.7	10.9	5.7

Source: UNCTAD Review of Maritime Transport 2009, updated with data from Clarkson Container Intelligence Monthly (January 2010). Clarkson's forecast for 2010 is +5.2 percent for both demand and supply.

The resulting oversupply of tonnage has led to a significant drop in container freight rates, which decreased by one third between the end of 2008 and the end of 2009. A similar picture emerges in dry bulk shipping, where the cost of chartering vessels went down by more than half.

The low freight and charter rates, combined with the downturn in trade volumes, have led to historical financial losses for the operators. The world's largest container shipping company, Maersk Line, reported a loss of $2.1 billion in 2009. Hanjin Line lost $1.1 billion during the same year, Neptune Orient Line lost $741 million, and similar losses were recorded all across the industry. The shares of container carriers today are worth two-thirds less than at their peak in 2007.

The maritime business has long been known for being cyclical. In times of growth and high profits, ship owners have positive cash flows and order new capacity. This capacity, however, takes time to deliver. There are waiting times because the shipyards' order books tend to be full in times of prosperity; any new construction will only be commenced two to three years after being ordered, and then the construction itself can take up to a year. When the industry was booming earlier in the present decade, each year the world saw historical records of new vessel orders. These vessels are still being delivered today—and thus, in spite of the economic crisis, the world fleet is still expanding. The resulting surplus capacity and the shipping companies' negative cash flows led to a standstill of new orders during most of 2009.

While the dimension of the current boom and bust cycle of the shipping business is extreme, the cyclical nature of the shipping business as such is not new. It has been compared to the "pig-cycle" that was discovered in 1930s in Britain. It basically implies that this boom-and-bust is mostly self-inflicted by the shipping industry. The production of new output responds to changes in price—but only after a time lag, and this time lag is itself the cause of future price changes. Ideally, new vessel additions would arrive in a steady flow, but in practice, investment in a new vessel capacity follows the pig-cycle. Intensive new activity occurs at the peak of

> *While the dimension of the current boom and bust cycle of the shipping business is extreme, the cyclical nature of the shipping business as such is not new.*

the highly profitable boom period, only to see new ships become available at the height of the bust, which is effectively made worse by the delivery of the new ships.

In a nutshell, even without the current economic crisis, the huge order book of new ships would, by today, have led to an oversupply of tonnage and a corresponding decline in vessel prices; and this has been made worse by the economic downturn. In the case of container ships, for example, the fleet is forecasted to continue to grow over the next four to five years, and most of this growth is on account of ships that can carry more than 8,000 20-foot containers. Vessels of this size did not even exist before 2004. Specifically, there are 156 container ships of more than 10,000 20-foot containers due to be delivered by 2013, compared to only 34 ships of that size in service in February 2010. With regards to dry bulk vessels, the current order book stands at two thirds of the existing fleet.

How the Industry Adjusts to the Crisis

Freight rates and second hand vessel prices react immediately to a change in the supply and demand balance. The supply of new capacity, however, reacts much more slowly. The industry has five ways to adjust its supply to a decline in demand. Firstly, it will immediately stop ordering new tonnage. Secondly, it may demolish vessels. Thirdly, it may, to some extent, terminate or postpone existing orders at the shipyards. Fourthly, vessels may slow steam, thus reducing the effective capacity supplied by the existing fleet. And finally, the industry may temporarily withdraw existing tonnage from service.

Stopping of New Orders

Orders of new ships have practically come to a standstill. In 2007, 535 container-ship vessels were contracted, 208 units were ordered in 2008, yet in 2009 there were only two new orders. As regards dry bulk ships, there was a certain year-end surge in orders at Chinese shipyards, mostly from Chinese owners and Chinese financing.

Demolitions

Already at the outset of the crisis, some analysts highlighted that ship-scrapping is potentially one of the few shipping-related businesses that may benefit from the economic crisis: "The ship-recycling industry is now experiencing its largest growth period in history, after the financial crisis saw rates for many vessel types collapse. With a threefold increase in ship-scrapping expected globally this year, and more than 1,000 ships destined for the breakers' yards, there are now fears that existing yards cannot handle the workload." Although there were capacity constraints at the scrap yards, 2009 did in fact see a surge in ship recycling as ship owners sold their vessels as scrap metal. Notably, China saw a record in tonnage imported for scrapping. Nevertheless, the growth was lower than initially expected. As prices for scrap metal are very low, many vessel owners prefer to hold on and lay off their ships rather than scrap them, hoping for better times to come. The demolition of existing tonnage will not be enough to compensate for the downturn in demand and for the new tonnage that is still leaving the world's shipyards. While a record of 180 mostly smaller containerships with a combined capacity of 330,000 20-foot containers were sold for demolition in 2009, this still amounts to just 2.5 percent of the existing fleet in terms of capacity—compared to an order book of 36 percent of the fleet.

Termination and Rescheduling of Orders

Since the beginning of the crisis, numerous orders at the world's shipyards have been rescheduled. The specialized shipping press reported a "dearth of new orders with the renegotiation of existing contracts now taking up more of shipbuilders' time than new enquiries." Activity in the container ship market in 2009 focused "primarily on the restructuring of the existing order book, as possible cancellations and renegotiations of existing deals become an increasing issue."

Accordingly, the forecasts for delivered vessels were adjusted downwards each month. In January 2009, one leading analyst still projected that capacity would increase by 13.1 percent during the following year, while 12 months later the reported annual growth only amounted to 5.2 percent. In the end, shipyards were somewhat more flexible than most analysts had initially expected. Some shipyards were more flexible than others, notably those that only existed on paper and were only greenfield projects when the orders had been placed.

Even as numerous deliveries were postponed, most were not cancelled, as shipyards would not agree to losing the business completely. The shipbuilder Daewoo SME, for example, announced a 44 percent increase in 2009 net income as deliveries jumped by more than half. Some shipyards helped their clients finance the ships through leaseback schemes. In early 2010, the fleet capacity of the world's top 20 container lines is still on course to expand by more than a third over the next four years.

Slow Steaming

Slow steaming means that the voyage speed of ships is reduced, which then makes it necessary to employ a larger number of ships to maintain the same frequency. Employing nine or ten vessels on a service that usually only requires eight ships has two main potential advantages: first, it reduces the need to lay off ships, and second, it saves fuel. During the economic downturn, shippers were not too concerned about delays in the delivery of goods as they were mostly aiming to reduce their inventory anyhow. However, the impact on voyage times is significant: at 25 knots (nautical-miles per hour) a typical East-West voyage time is 16 days, whereas at 14 knots it extends to 29 days. This was not a major problem for shippers when they were using up their inventories, but as the economy is now picking up, traders and factories will no longer accept the longer delivery times.

The Idle Fleet

Many surplus vessels are not effectively deployed and are instead laid off or idle. As of early 2010, 12 percent of global container carrying capacity is idle and anchored at different harbors. Put differently, today there are more than 500 container ships idled at anchorages around the globe, and double that quantity still due to be delivered. Although the economy is picking up, the surplus tonnage will remain for years to come.

As ships are temporarily withdrawn from service, actual fleet deployment, i.e., the assignment of container ships to trade routes, has effectively decreased during 2009. The container capacity deployed on the main trade routes between East Asia and Europe and between East Asia and North America was 20 percent lower in January 2010 than one year earlier.

Interestingly, the reduction in fleet deployment was less drastic on major South-South routes as trade among developing countries has been affected less by the economic downturn than most of the developed world's trade. The deployment between southern Africa and East Asia went down by only 7 percent; between East Asia and South America it decreased by 13 percent, and the fleet deployment between southern Africa and South America actually increased by 3.4 percent during 2009. This reflects the positive role that developing countries and South-South trade in particular are playing in favor of the global economic recovery.

Consolidation: Adjustment in the Long Term

In previous periods of low profits, we saw significant consolidation in the container shipping industry. In the U.S. during the 1990s, Sea-Land was taken over by Maersk (Denmark), American President Lines by NOL (Singapore), and parts of Crowley by Hamburg Süd (Germany). Since the start of the current crisis, profits have not only been low, but actually mostly negative. Nevertheless, all of the top 25 companies have been able to maintain their independence—over the last couple of years there have been no mergers or acquisitions among them.

Still, the currently incurred losses cannot be sustained. Some government agencies and industry associations are already seeking ways to assist member companies, but find themselves confronted with competition (antitrust) authorities. In the European Union, for example, the Competition Directorate is contesting a government loan guarantee for the container carrier Hapag-Lloyd. A scheme by a group of European container ship owners to jointly manage capacity was similarly contested by the Competition Directorate. In the long run, there is probably no way around further industry consolidation.

Bouncing Back and the Countercyclical Side of Shipping

While ship owners and yards are thus still struggling to cope with the oversupply of tonnage, perspectives on the demand side are improving. The United States economy grew at its fastest pace in six years in the fourth quarter of 2009, expanding by 5.7 percent as companies scaled back their attempts to cut inventories. U.S. container ports reported higher imports in December 2009 than in December 2008, marking the first year-over-year monthly increase in containerized imports in two and a half years. China Shipping Group reported a better-than-expected 18.1 percent increase in carried cargo volumes in January 2009, with year-on-year growth reaching 32.2 percent. Once inventories are back to their pre-crisis stocks, these exceptional growth rates will return to normal levels.

Supply Meets Demand

Importers and factories that are now posting new orders overseas are in a lucky position, as there is ample spare capacity to transport their goods, and freight rates are far below the peaks of 2008. While the oversupply of tonnage has had a negative impact on the transport industry's profitability, it has had mostly positive implications for importers and exporters.

Waiting times in ports and freight rates have significantly fallen, bringing some relief to traders in the form of lower transport costs and smoother operations. Shipping one ton of dry bulk cargo over 1,000 nautical miles by sea in early 2010 cost between $4 and $7 as compared to $10 to $16 in 2008.

In a way, the pro-cyclical investment patterns of the shipping industry effectively act as a countercyclical corrective mechanism to international trade. While the economy was overheating and trade boomed, high freight costs and port congestion on occasion acted as a break that somewhat spoiled the party. As the business world and policy makers look to the next annual meeting of the World Economic Forum in Davos in 2011to discuss how to revive global trade, they will be happy to note that transaction costs today are relatively low and there is no shortage of capacity to carry the reviving trade in goods.

A notable exception has been port congestion in relation to the Chinese demand for iron ore, which continued to increase in 2009. This resulted in a large proportion of the fleet calling at the exporting ports of Australia, Brazil, and India, as well as the importing Chinese ports, pushing up vessel waiting times and freight rates. At its maximum on 26 June 2009, almost one-fifth of the specialized fleet was reported to have queued outside a port in one of those four countries.

Seizing the Opportunity: Countercyclical Private Investment

Exceptions prove the rule. In container shipping, Asia's largest carrier, Evergreen, is the only top 20 company with a currently empty order book for new vessels, though it is now planning to acquire 100 new container ships. Evergreen seems to have predicted the onset of the crisis back in 2006 and refrained from placing new orders, when many of its rivals were still expanding.

In general, countercyclical ordering makes a lot of sense. Ordering new ships at the low point of a cycle will be cheaper, delivery can take place earlier, and the company will have new and modern ships at the moment demand revives. The flip side to this approach is that it is risky; the cost of financing will be high, just as a higher cash deposit may be required to offset the high risk. Still, there appears to be a lot of truth in the old (and perhaps cynical) saying that a successful ship owner does not earn money on transport, but on buying and selling vessels at the right moment.

Countercyclical Public Investment

Many port capacity expansion projects have been put on hold, deferred, or cancelled over the past year. This is dangerous, as a lack of port infrastructure investment today may ultimately turn into a serious problem when trade resumes its positive growth.

Private sector investment in transport infrastructure and services is well known for being pro-cyclical: in times of booming trade, operators plan for expansions, investment increases, and the number of projects grows; in a downturn, investment projects are put on hold. Given the time lag between planning an investment and its actual conclusion, especially for large infrastructure projects that require extensive feasibility and environmental impact studies, it is important to keep in mind the long-term requirements for a country's foreign trade to expand. A decline in transport investment today will inevitably entail capacity restrictions on trade in the medium-term future.

While many economic stimulus packages aim at short-term measures to stimulate economic demand and employment, some measures in these packages also target long-term and innovative investments in public infrastructure or aim at closing investment gaps. Many of these investments are in transport infrastructure, such as the building or upgrading of roads, waterways, and railroad infrastructure, as well as the dredging of seaports.

Recognizing the need to support private investments, governments also provide guarantees for private investment, accelerate the approval processes of projects, and encourage public-private partnerships for infrastructure. In the long term, timely investments in transport and trade facilitation lead to increased throughput and frequency of transport services, resulting in lower freight costs and improved connectivity. Unfortunately, investment in public infrastructure has in the past often lagged behind requirements, leading to capacity shortages in ports and other transport infrastructures. The economic crisis and the national stimulus packages and support programs by international development banks provide an opportunity to advance investment in these areas. As much private investment is put on hold, public investment should fill a gap and build the capacities countries need for the economic recovery. Such investments will become a strategic component to overcome the crisis when made part of anti-cyclical expansionary fiscal policies to promote recovery through trade.

The Further Emergence of China in Maritime Businesses

To some extent, the shipping cycle may look like history repeating itself. Yet with every such cycle, some lasting change takes place, and in the context of the recent "financial crisis," the emergence of China on the market for ship finance could be such a lasting change.

If we remind ourselves that the current economic crisis started out as a "financial crisis" for the shipping business, it is particularly interesting to note that Chinese banks have lent billions of dollars to ship owners since the banking crisis started in September 2008. They thus replaced traditional sources of financing from Germany and the United Kingdom and helped owners to take delivery of previously ordered ships.

Developments in China are particularly noteworthy with regard to the supply of, and demand for, shipping services. On the supply side, Chinese shipping companies are among the fastest growing, and the country is host to the most important container and crane manufacturers. On the demand side, Chinese containerized exports make up a quarter of the world total, and Chinese ports are among the fastest growing in the world.

China is one of the few countries that participates in almost all maritime subsectors, such as ship building, port operations, nautical schools, ship scrapping, and vessel owning and registration. However, this does not mean that Chinese-owned ships will necessarily use the Chinese flag, or that only they will be deployed to transport national trade. Forty percent of the Chinese-controlled fleet is registered in China (i.e., uses the Chinese flag) versus the 60 percent that use a foreign flag. More than half of the Chinese-controlled fleet are dry bulk carriers, followed by oil tankers, general cargo vessels, and relatively few container ships.

China depends on the international shipping industry for its exports of goods. Through a combination of expanding its domestic shipyards (shipyards in Shanghai recorded a 50 percent increase in the value of exports in 2009) and becoming a key provider of international ship financing, the country is making sure that there will always be sufficient shipping capacity to transport its foreign trade at low freight costs.

Protecting Energy on the Water

The relationship between maritime energy supply and private security

By Stephen L. Caldwell

Journal of International Peace Operations, November 1, 2011

This article provides an update on threats to the maritime energy supply—such as tankers and offshore platforms—and discusses related developments regarding efforts to increase the use of privately contracted, armed, security personnel (hereafter "private security"). The increased use of private security is especially pronounced off the coasts of Somalia and Nigeria. These developments may be of particular interest to those working in peace and stability operations that are involved with private maritime security companies.

Importance of the Maritime Energy Supply

Industrialized nations' economies and security are heavily dependent on oil, natural gas, and other energy commodities, and the maritime environment plays a key role in both transportation and production of these natural resources. Ocean tankers transport about half of the U.S. crude oil supply, the source of gasoline, jet fuel, heating oil, and many other petroleum products. Because of their importance to industrialized nations' economies and national security, energy tankers, along with offshore infrastructure, have become the targets of terrorists and pirates.

Threats to Energy Tankers

The tankers that transport oil and gas face a number of threats and variety of attacks. The tankers travel on routes that are determined in advance and that lead them through chokepoints that limit the tankers' ability to maneuver away from possible attacks. Terrorist attacks, though rare, are one of the threats to energy tankers. In 2002, a suicide boat attacked the French supertanker M/V Limburg in the Red Sea near the Bab al Mandeb strait. In 2010, there was another incident involving the supertanker M/V M Star in the Arabian Sea near the Strait of Hormuz, which is also suspected to have been a terrorist attack.

In addition to the threat of terrorist attacks, tankers also face the more common obstacle of piracy. Pirates threaten tankers transiting one of the world's busiest shipping lanes, near key energy corridors, and the route through the Suez Canal. The

From *Journal of International Peace Operations* 7, no. 3 (2011): 12–16. Copyright © 2012 by International Peace Operations Association. Reprinted with permission. All rights reserved.

vast areas at risk for piracy off the Horn of Africa, combined with the small number of military ships available for patrolling them, make protecting energy tankers difficult. According to the International Maritime Bureau, 30 percent of vessels reporting pirate attacks worldwide from 2006 through 2010 were identified as tankers. As shown in the table below, pirate attacks against tankers have tripled in the last five years, and the instances of piracy against tankers continue to rise. From January through June 2011, 100 tankers were attacked, an increase of 37 percent compared to tankers attacked during the same time period in 2010.

Threats to Energy Infrastructure

Energy infrastructure, whether shore-side or offshore, also faces various threats. Port energy terminals face risks because they must provide access by land and sea, and because they are sprawling installations often close to busy population centers. In contrast, offshore energy infrastructure is vulnerable because it is often located in open waters, many miles away from security force assets and responders.

In 2004, terrorists attacked an offshore oil terminal in Iraq using speedboats packed with explosives, killing three U.S. military personnel. As documented in an earlier *Journal of International Peace Operations* article (see "Maritime Violence, Crime and Insecurity" by Peter Chalk, November-December 2008), Nigeria has become a case-study in attacks targeting maritime energy infrastructure. The article estimated that these attacks have shut down one fifth of Nigerian oil production. Since then, the U.S. Office of Naval Intelligence and media sources have continued to report attacks against maritime energy facilities in that region.

Number of Tankers Attacked by Pirates, 2006–2010

Type of Commodity	2006	2007	2008	2009	2010
Bitumen	0	1	0	2	2
Chemical/Product	35	52	55	69	96
Crude Oil	9	25	30	41	43
Liquefied Natural Gas	0	1	0	1	1
Liquefied Petroleum Gas	4	5	6	5	7
Totals	**48**	**84**	**91**	**118**	**149**

Source: International Maritime Bureau [Note: Chemical/Product tankers include oil products other than crude oil]

One of these more recent attacks occurred in August 2011, when gunmen exploded a bomb at the Dibi flow station operated by Chevron Nigeria Limited. The Deepwater Horizon explosion in April 2010, while not the result of an attack, showed the potential catastrophic consequences of an attack on offshore energy infrastructure. The explosion resulted in 11 deaths, serious injuries, and the largest oil spill in the history of the United States. By the time the well was sealed nearly three months later, over 4 million barrels of oil had spilled into the Gulf of Mexico.

Private Security

Some of the attacks discussed above, particularly the pirate attacks, have led the maritime industry to increase its employment of private security to protect vessels. Earlier, when piracy was first escalating off the coast of Somalia, the shipping industry and governments expressed concerns about the use of private security on commercial vessels. Of particular concern, especially with regards to energy tanks carrying flammable cargo, was the possibility that the level of violence could escalate. Now, there is much more support, or at least recognition, of the use of private security, particularly as piracy continues to escalate. To date, Somali pirates have failed to hijack any vessels with private security aboard. Realizing the inability of navies to guarantee protection across the broad area in which pirates operate, many in the maritime industry have changed their positions and now support the use of private security on a case-by-case basis. At a recent meeting of the U.N. sanctioned Contact Group On Piracy Off the Coast of Somalia it was estimated that the industry was already employing 65 private security firms with 350 persons on vessels. Similar estimates for private security working on offshore energy facilities, such as off the coast of Nigeria, are not available.

> *In addition to the threat of terrorist attacks, tankers also face the more common obstacle of piracy.*

National governments have been more reluctant to embrace private security, but are feeling pressure from the shipping industry. Reuters reported this summer that an oil and gas shipping company notified the Netherlands it could no longer sail under that nation's flag unless it changed its national regulations to allow the use of private security. The United States was one of the first nations whose sovereignty laws allowed for the use of private security. The U.S. Coast Guard has approved the use of such teams on U.S.-flagged vessels that operate in or travel through the high-risk waters of Somalia, as long as their vessel security plans have been updated to reflect self-defense systems that meet the mandated risk assessment. Other national governments are listening to the shipping industry and accepting their requests when risks may require the use of private security.

At a February 2011 meeting of the multinational Contact Group's Working Group 3 on Shipping Awareness, the United Kingdom agreed to lead an intercessional correspondence group to develop guidelines for the employment of private security. At a May 2011 meeting of the International Maritime Organization (IMO) Maritime Safety Committee, interim guidance was issued on the use of "privately contracted armed security personnel" on board vessels in high-risk areas. In September 2011, this guidance was revised and further disseminated. The interim guidance is in Signatory Companies. As with the issue of drafting the standards, the governance and oversight mechanism for the ICoC would never be able to replicate or even approach the level of maritime expertise in terms of both operations and law that is present within the IMO. Given the unique and international nature of maritime transport, intimate familiarity with the practical, operational and legal issues is vital for dealing effectively with maritime security. The ICoC requires that Signatory Companies be certified (and governed) by the governance and oversight mechanism. Given the absence of maritime expertise in the Temporary Steering Committee developing the governance and oversight mechanism, it is unclear how maritime security companies will fit into the eventual system. It will certainly be a challenge moving forward to keep the governance of Signatory Companies under one umbrella, though with a flexible approach and a willingness to allow for guidance from established international sources, such a feat should be within reason.

Fifth, there is no mechanism at the moment for amending the ICoC. The Code does not provide for amendments until the governance and oversight mechanism is up and running. This means there will be some time yet before the Code could be changed, by either direct amendment or the addition of a maritime-oriented annex. While the former approach would address the issues discussed above quickly and simply, the latter could do so as well while also providing some additional guidance. The present discussion has focused on issues pertaining to the existing Code, but such difficult matters as the relationship between private maritime security providers and the master of a vessel, obligations regarding responding to distress signals in high risk areas, and other uniquely maritime complications go beyond the obvious differences that will arise in implementing the Code in maritime operations.

Finally, it is important to note that the provision of private maritime security is not exclusive to anti-piracy operations. Much of the commentary surrounding and most of the efforts regarding the regulation of maritime security have focused on anti-piracy operations, particularly off the coast of Somalia. The services offered by private security providers in the marine environment transcend such a limited focus and must be considered comprehensively in this discourse so as not to create a patchwork system of regulation that only deals with one maritime security issue at a time.

The field of maritime security is growing and maturing rapidly. Though, as has been discussed, there are a number of substantive challenges interfering with the parsimonious inclusion of private maritime security services under the ICoC, none of those challenges is prohibitive. So long as the complexities and distinctions pertaining to maritime security are kept in mind, there is no reason why maritime security should not currently and in the future be considered to fall under the principles articulated in the Code. Indeed, the enthusiastic uptake of the ICoC with maritime security providers should be welcomed, applauded and, in due course, accommodated to ensure that such services are clearly covered by the Code and sensibly addressed in the follow-on processes.

❖

Stephen L. Caldwell is the Director for Maritime Security Issues at GAO, and provides related studies and testimony to congressional committees.

The Battle of the Ports

By Jeffrey Spivak
Planning, May 1, 2011

Currently, when a new Target, Office Depot, or similar big box outlet opens in metropolitan Dallas, Atlanta, or Columbus, Ohio, much of the stock—everything from clothes to clocks, most imported from China—arrives in the U.S. at one of the Los Angeles area's busy ocean ports.

In just a few years, though, those household and business products may journey from China to the stores in a different way, on a new generation of supersized ocean vessels that bypass the West Coast. These freighters will cut across a newly widened Panama Canal before docking at a port along the East Coast or Gulf Coast. This prospect is setting off a competition among eastern and southern ports, all eager to become the go-to destination for Asian imports.

Almost every ocean and gulf port in the eastern and southeastern U.S.—from New York to Miami to Houston—has projects under way or in the planning stage to prepare for expected growth in international trade. Even some smaller ports have gotten into the act, among them, Wilmington, North Carolina; Mobile, Alabama; and Gulfport, Mississippi.

The improvements run the gamut: digging deeper channels, building new container terminals, adding cranes to handle larger ships, and enhancing highway and rail connections. The Port Authority of New York and New Jersey has approved a $1.3 billion project to elevate a landmark bridge. Savannah is pursuing funding for a $62.5 million plan to dredge its long channel. Miami has found public and private partners for a new $1.1 million tunnel. Even Wilmington has a $2 billion wish list.

A Birthday Present

All these plans revolve around the current expansion of the Panama Canal, the 48-mile waterway that connects the Atlantic and Pacific oceans. The $5.25 billion project is scheduled to be completed by August 15, 2014, the centennial of its original opening. For years now, the canal locks have been unable to accommodate the ever-larger ocean carriers, some of them longer than three football fields (and the Navy's longest aircraft carrier).

These huge vessels carry almost three times as many shipping containers as the freighters currently passing through the canal are capable of carrying. Containers unloaded from just one giant ocean vessel fill up the equivalent of more than 20 trains or 3,000 semi-trailer trucks. Seaports "touch everything in our lives, everything we eat, everything we sit on, everything we do," says Richard Barone, director of transportation programs at the tri-state Regional Plan Association in New York City.

The U.S. Maritime Administration predicts that the canal expansion "will lead to a significant increase in container traffic calling at the Gulf Coast and eastern ports."

That outlook is shared by many others in the shipping industry. Drewry Supply Chain Advisors, a London-based maritime consulting firm, has estimated that with the expansion up to 25 percent of the present cargo base of the western ports could shift to eastern and southern ports in the decade to come. Even West Coast port officials acknowledge that some shift is likely to occur.

All told, East Coast and Gulf Coast port expansion plans compiled by the Maritime Administration, the Southern Legislative Conference, and other sources total almost $20 billion, with nearly half of the projects scheduled for completion within the next five years. To put those dollars in perspective, the federal government has estimated that capital spending at all U.S. ports in the 60 years from 1946 to 2006 amounted to $31 billion.

"I'm seeing more port activity on the East Coast right now than in the 25 years I've been involved in this industry," says Charles Clowdis, managing director of North American markets for IHS Global Insight's Global Commerce and Transport Group. "You talk to all the port directors, starting with Houston and going along the Gulf and up the East Coast, and they all say there's going to be a dramatic impact from the Panama Canal expansion, and there's a rush to take advantage of the changes."

Game-Changer

The Panama Canal, which was designed to cut shipping distances in half between the East and West coasts, was a treacherous undertaking. The construction project, started by the French in 1880 and finished by the U.S. in 1914, resulted in the removal of at least two hundred million cubic yards of earth and rock—the equivalent of more than 40 Hoover Dam projects. In the process, more than 26,000 workers died from tropical diseases such as malaria and yellow fever.

The canal consists of a series of artificial lakes and channels, and three sets of thick-walled locks (almost 60 feet at their base) whose gates can be closed to regulate water level. Ships are raised or lowered more than 80 feet during a day-long passage through the locks. For more than half a century, virtually every commercial ship could fit through the locks. But in the past few decades, shipping companies have been building progressively larger tankers and cargo freighters, spawning the term "Post-Panamax" to describe vessels too large to go through the canal.

"If the canal didn't do something, it would have been at capacity and verging on obsolete," says Theodore Prince, a port consultant and board member of the International Transportation Institute at the University of Denver.

The expansion project, funded by private financing and higher canal tolls, involves building two new sets of locks adjacent to existing ones on the Pacific and Atlantic edges, plus deepening and widening miles of channel between the locks.

The construction project, started by the French in 1880 and finished by the U.S. in 1914, resulted in the removal of at least two hundred million cubic yards of earth and rock—the equivalent of more than 40 Hoover Dam projects. In the process, more than 26,000 workers died from tropical diseases. . . .

The new locks are 40 percent longer, 60 percent wider, and 43 percent deeper than the existing (original) locks. They will be able to accommodate ships with 12,000 TEU (20-foot-equivalent unit) containers, almost triple the 4,500 TEU containers that ships are now limited to in the canal.

Kurt Nagle, president of the American Association of Port Authorities, has called the Panama expansion a "game-changer" for seaports in the U.S. So has David Matsuda, maritime administrator for the U.S. Department of Transportation. And Rodolfo Sabonge, vice president of research and analysis for the Panama Canal Authority, last year told a conference of the Council of Supply Chain Management Professionals that the authority anticipates container volume through the canal to double by 2015.

Ports on the East and Gulf coasts expect to receive a major share of that growth. The Port of Virginia anticipates an immediate 20 percent boost in cargo once the canal expansion is completed. A study for the Port of Savannah predicted Asian import tonnage through the canal would jump 80 percent at the port between 2010 and 2020.

Not all experts foresee such a dramatic jump. They note that travel from Asia to the East Coast through the canal will always be slower than the direct route to West Coast ports. Asaf Ashar, codirector of the National Ports and Waterways Institute at the University of New Orleans, describes the canal expansion as "a change but not a game-changer."

Still, it's a shift that will play out across the interior of the country, in midwestern markets such as Columbus, Cincinnati, and Indianapolis; in southeastern markets such as Memphis and Atlanta; in Florida's booming metro areas; and in Dallas and Houston. In all these metropolitan areas, retail stores and industrial plants are mostly served by railroads and trucks that deliver freight from West Coast ports. The question now is whether the advantages of East Coast ports will win the day.

It's the Money!

The main advantage is cost. Water transportation is almost always less than rail and truck transportation, and ever-larger ships offer great economies of scale by spreading costs over more units of freight moved per ship. The cost of transporting a 20-foot-long container from Hong Kong to the eastern U.S. through a Los Angeles port and then by rail and truck is roughly $3,500, according to Drewry Supply Chain Advisors. The firm estimates that shipping a container would cost $250 to

$1,000 less if it were loaded on an 8,000-TEU ship, sent through the Panama Canal, unloaded at an East Coast port, and then hauled by rail and truck to a midwestern or southern destination.

Other estimates are less definitive, with some figuring savings of as little as $60 per container. And, of course, there's a trade-off in travel time. Shipping to the East Coast can take up to a week longer in ship and rail time than going through the West Coast, according to industry experts. Still, ProLogis, a developer of distribution facilities, wrote in a report last fall: "Given a choice, many shippers today are leaning toward a delivery service that costs less and is more reliable, even if the delivery time were slightly longer."

Another attraction of eastern ports is the emerging distribution network. Several eastern railroads and private developers have been building giant intermodal logistics centers in the east-central U.S., in locations ranging from Columbus, Ohio, to Dallas and Kansas City, to Memphis. These logistics centers act as centralized hubs, where containers arrive by rail from East Coast ports and are then sorted and transferred again to trucks, which take them to warehouses, stores, or manufacturing plants.

Two railroads, the Norfolk Southern and CSX, each recently upgraded their rail lines—the Heartland Corridor and the National Gateway, respectively—so they can move double-stacked containers on flatbed cars between the East Coast and the Midwest. Referring to Norfolk Southern's project, Russell Held, deputy executive director of development at the Virginia Port Authority, says, "One of our advantages is that we can reach the entire region east of the Mississippi. The Heartland Corridor gives us a direct shot at Columbus and Chicago."

One other factor working in favor of eastern ports is a history of instability and congestion at the Los Angeles and Long Beach facilities, which handle more than a third of the total U.S. container trade. Truck traffic in and around the ports is worsening, and the lack of available land has limited the construction of new warehouses. In addition, labor disputes have led to shutdowns and threats of strikes over the last decade, and there have been some complaints about rising shipping costs.

"The upward trajectory of port and rail costs from West Coast ports to the Midwest makes this transportation unsustainable at today's shipping rates," Craig Mygatt, senior director of trade and marketing in the U.S. for the Maersk Line shipping company, said at a meeting of the American Association of Port Authorities earlier this year. "If nothing changes, this international intermodal cargo will continue to shift to the East Coast," and other places. "Widening of the Panama Canal will accelerate the trend."

Recognizing the eastern advantages, some retailers are already diversifying their shipping supply chains, at least for products that aren't needed in stores immediately. "You don't want to rely entirely on Los Angeles-Long Beach. You don't want to have all your eggs in one basket," says Jonathan Gold, vice president of supply chain and customs policy for the National Retail Federation in Washington, D.C.

Catch-Up Needed

But are the East Coast ports ready for an influx of new business?

Consider the Port of New York and New Jersey. To reach New Jersey's marine terminals, container ships round Staten Island, then turn south into the Kill Van Kull channel and cruise under the landmark Bayonne Bridge, named for the New Jersey city it serves. The bridge is known for its long, gracefully arching steel truss, but its most distinguishing feature for shippers is its 155-foot clearance from the waterline. That's no longer high enough for some of the largest container ships, which tower 175 feet above the water. In 2009, the NYK shipping line's 4,886-TEU Nebula was riding too high to pass under the bridge and had to divert to Norfolk, Virginia. Another time, the 6,400-TEU Regina Maersk had to have its communications mast detached to fit under the bridge.

At the Port of Jacksonville, an Asian shipping company pushed back the opening of a $300 million container terminal by at least two years, waiting for the St. Johns River to handle larger ships. Across the U.S., inadequate channel depths constrain almost 30 percent of port vessel calls, a U.S. Army Corps of Engineers study determined in 2009. "The changeover in fleets [to larger freighters] is happening at a faster rate than people expected," says Richard Barone, the transportation director at the Regional Plan Association in New York.

This issue is becoming increasingly important as the Panama Canal expansion looms. Ports today need only 40 feet of channel depth to handle the largest ships coming through the canal. But a loaded 8,000-TEU ship sits 46 to 47 feet deep in saltwater and a foot deeper in freshwater. This draft requires a channel depth of close to 50 feet, and only one top East Coast container port is at that level now—the Port of Virginia in Norfolk. "Depth is absolutely critical," says John Martin, an international maritime market consultant who has done hundreds of port studies in the U.S. "A port's viability increasingly depends on the ability to attract a major carrier. You don't want a constraint."

Eighteen ports along the East and Gulf coasts are already deepening their channels or pursuing plans to do so, according to the U.S. Army Corps of Engineers. Numerous ports are also building or planning new terminals and wharfs, and some are adding highway connections to interstates and installing new overhead cranes that are longer than a football field.

In New Jersey, for instance, the New York-New Jersey port authority is dredging its channel to 50 feet, and it recently approved raising the Bayonne Bridge 65 feet rather than demolish and rebuild the structure. In Georgia, the Port of Savannah is midway through an eight-year, $500 million expansion that will nearly double its container capacity, and it is pushing ahead with a dredging project that will deepen its channel from 42 feet to 48 feet. In South Carolina, the Port of Charleston is building a $525 million container terminal on a former U.S. Navy base that, when completed in 2016, will increase the port's handling capacity by almost half. And as part of a $600 million upgrade plan, Alabama's Port of Mobile has opened a $300 million container terminal and completed a turning basin enlargement for Post-Panamax ships.

Then there's the $2 billion in new projects planned for the port of Wilmington, North Carolina, according to a Southern Legislative Conference survey of ports. "The expansion of the Panama Canal is the tool to help us build on our port," says Stephanie Ayers, director of planning and development for the North Carolina State Ports Authority.

These projects illustrate the ports' high hopes. It's unclear, however, whether they will be completed in time for the opening of the Panama Canal's new locks. The governmental reviews required for Savannah's dredging project stretched over more than a decade, involving interests ranging from the commercial fishing industry to environmental groups in neighboring South Carolina. "It's been a political logistics nightmare," says Tom Thomson, executive director of the Chatham County-Savannah Metropolitan Planning Commission, "but it was necessary to ensure that all the issues were addressed to the community's satisfaction."

Who Will Pay?

Major port projects typically require congressional approval and federal funding, and several port authorities were counting on the federal government's proposed fiscal year 2012 budget to kick-start their expansion plans. The ports of Savannah and Miami requested $105 trillion and $75 million, respectively. The two received a total of $600,000. The Port of Charleston couldn't even get $400,000 for a dredging feasibility study.

The fact is, with the federal deficit-cutting climate in Washington, D.C, getting funding for port projects could become more difficult. For one thing, the Harbor Maintenance Trust Fund is tapped every year to help offset the federal deficit. For another, Congress has sworn off the earmarks, or individual projects requested by lawmakers, that were a major source of port funding. "There is too much competition for scarce federal dollars," says Russell Held of the Virginia Port Authority.

In response, port authorities are turning to the private sector, with some success. New terminals are being developed as public-private partnerships, with public agencies contracting with shipping companies to build and then manage the operations. Some infrastructure improvements also involve private investors. The $1.1 billion Port of Miami tunnel, a road intended to bypass downtown congestion by linking the port to an interstate highway, is being financed through the state of Florida, Miami-Dade County, a federal government loan program, and a consortium of banks organized by Meridian Infrastructure, an international private infrastructure fund.

But as eastern ports vie for funding and a greater share of business, their West Coast competitors aren't exactly standing pat. Western ports and railroads will fight to keep or regain their Asian trade market share, a panel of port executives and consultants declared at an East Coast maritime conference last fall. The Port of Long Beach intends to spend $4 billion over the next decade to modernize and expand its container handling facilities. "Our best way to compete against the Panama Canal and the all-water route is to invest in our infrastructure projects," Alex Cherin, then the managing director of trade relations and port operations at the Port of Long Beach, told a U.S. Maritime Administration conference last year.

Ultimately, many observers foresee West Coast port business as continuing to grow, although not as fast as the East Coast's. "The West Coast will no longer be the gorilla," says John Vickerman, a port strategic planning consultant in Virginia. With an increasing volume of Asian imports and limited capacity for growth at the Los Angeles and Long Beach ports, "converging economic and trade forces now favor growth on the East Coast."

❖

Jeffrey Spivak is a senior research analyst at the HNTB Corporation, a transportation design and engineering firm based in Kansas City.

7

Future of Transportation

(AP Photo)

A maglev train runs Monday, September 25, 2006, in Shanghai, China, which has the world's only commercially operating maglev.

Navigating America's Transportation Infrastructure into the 21st Century

By Paul McCaffrey

Over the next few decades, the American population, like the national economy, is expected to grow at a rapid pace. This growth poses a host of challenges for the US transportation grid. Each component of the national transit network—rails, waterways, airports, mass transit systems, and roads—will have to increase capacity by a significant margin. In the process, each will confront a host of safety, environmental, congestion, and funding issues.

How this expansion will be accomplished, what it will look like, and whether or not it will entail a moderate or wholesale transformation, is not entirely clear. Among the central questions is the role of the automobile. As one of the principal drivers of the national economy and culture for the past seventy-five years, the automobile occupies a central place in American life. Yet dependence on the car has a number of costs associated with it. Tens of thousands of people are killed each year in automobile accidents. Fuel emissions exact a toll on both the environment and on human health. Traffic congestion saps the economy of billions of dollars each year. Reliance on foreign oil also creates a number of complicated foreign relations dilemmas. High gasoline prices, in turn, can act as a major drag on the economy, placing a heavy burden on people's wallets.

There are some who contend that the automobile may already be on the way out, given that per-capita car use is on a downward trajectory. According to one 2008 study, the annual total vehicle miles traveled (VMT) in the United States began to decline in 2007. That process was likely accelerated by the recent recession, though the ensuing recovery may have reversed it.

Whether VMT is increasing or declining, technological innovation is helping to ameliorate some of the excesses of the automobile. Not only are vehicles more fuel efficient, an increasing number of cars use hybrid engines, or run on alternative fuel. Through January 2012, over 2 million hybrid vehicles were sold in the United States. If gasoline prices stay high, that number can be expected to rise. The move from traditional to hybrid and alternative-fuel engines is reflected in municipal bus systems as well, where diesel- and gasoline-burning vehicles are being augmented by vehicles equipped with greener technology. Rather than being replaced by other forms of transportation, the automobile may instead be evolving with the times.

Indeed, judging by US Department of Transportation (DOT) spending, the automobile is not going anywhere. In 2010, of the $97.5 billion in funds dispersed by the DOT, 65 percent was spent on roads, highways, and bridges. Approximately 16.5 percent went to aviation and airport infrastructure; 13 percent to mass transit systems; 3 percent to railroads; 0.5 percent to ports and waterways. An estimated 2 percent went to miscellaneous expenses.

Though technological advances may lead to cleaner, more fuel-efficient, and safer vehicles, they do not cut down on the number of automobiles on the road. A growing, car-dependent population will increase traffic congestion in the years ahead, particularly in urban areas, and traffic jams are expensive. According to 2009 estimates, for example, congestion cost the US economy $115 billion, wasting 4.8 billion hours and 3.9 billion gallons of fuel.

Congestion is most severe in major cities. Even well-established mass transit systems are not a panacea against gridlock. According to 2010 estimates, for example, New York City and Washington, DC, two municipalities with robust public transportation networks, topped the list of the nation's most congested cities.

The problem of traffic has puzzled urban planners for decades. Building more roads and highways—increasing capacity—tends to be a short-term solution. Soon enough, the new roads are just as jammed as the old ones. In busy downtown areas, on the other hand, there is often no space to construct additional roads. On the highways, commuter lanes, reserved for cars with two or more people in them, have been used to encourage carpooling and decrease the number of vehicles. More recently, planners have installed reversible lanes where the flow of traffic can be turned backward depending on the volume of vehicles traveling in each direction.

Keeping drivers informed of conditions so that they can avoid traffic backups is also a common tactic used to reduce congestion. Electronic signs transmit road conditions to drivers, alerting them of possible delays. New technologies in the form of global positioning systems (GPS) and mobile phone applications that detail traffic conditions are now routinely deployed by the drivers themselves.

Over the past few decades, many cities around the world have embraced road space rationing to limit rush hour traffic or reduce air pollution. In road space rationing, certain vehicles, often depending on their license plate numbers, are restricted from use on particular days or during particular rush hours. While widely in practice throughout Latin America, road space rationing is not expected to catch on in the United States anytime soon. Thus far, it has only been considered on a theoretical level.

What has been seriously contemplated—at least in New York City and several other municipalities—is congestion pricing. The city of London adopted a form of congestion pricing known as "cordon pricing" in 2003. Drivers wishing to enter downtown London during business hours were required to pay a fee. Although not without its critics, the initiative led to reduced traffic and emissions, while generating considerable revenue for the city. As a consequence, the program was expanded in 2007. Stockholm, Sweden, and Singapore, among other cities, have since adopted similar systems.

In the US, however, London-style congestion pricing has yet to be put to use. In 2007, New York City mayor Michael Bloomberg proposed charging vehicles entering the borough of Manhattan below 86th Street during weekday business hours. Despite the promise of a large federal subsidy, his plan was rejected by the state legislature and its prospects remain cloudy. San Francisco and Chicago have weighed similar congestion pricing initiatives as well, but their plans have yet to advance beyond the preliminary stages.

Though congestion pricing has not been deployed in the United States, variable toll and parking prices have been embraced. Certain toll roads increase their fees during rush hours, for example, and some municipalities are varying what their parking meters charge depending on supply and demand. During busier hours on crowded thoroughfares, drivers can expect to pay more to park.

Beyond reductions in gridlock and emissions, one of the main selling points of congestion pricing is that it generates revenue that can then be reinvested in transportation infrastructure, whether in roads and bridges, subways, light rail, or other forms of mass transit. Cash-strapped city governments are eager for any transit money they can get. Indeed, of the many challenges confronting transportation infrastructure in the years ahead, the funding issue is likely to be the most difficult one.

Many fear that if infrastructure is not properly funded it will threaten US competitiveness in the global marketplace. In 2010, the World Economic Forum (WEF) ranked the United States 23rd in the world in infrastructure quality. Currently, the United States spends around 2.4 percent of its gross domestic product (GDP) on transport and water infrastructure, while Europe averages 5 percent, and China 9 percent. Established by Congress in 2005, the National Surface Transportation Policy and Revenue Study Commission analyzed anticipated American transport needs over the next fifty years. According to its 2008 estimates, $255 billion in annual investments would be required to both maintain the existing infrastructure and to build the necessary improvements. Despite these figures, less than half the money the commission believes is needed is currently being spent each year.

The federal government, states, and municipalities are all under severe budgetary constraints. The political environment, meanwhile, is prone to gridlock. In the federal sphere, over the past five years, for example, federal funds for high-speed rail (HSR) projects have been rejected by several states, while the Federal Aviation Administration (FAA), which oversees American air transit, was shut down for nearly two weeks in the summer of 2011 due to partisan wrangling between Congress and the White House.

In addition to political gridlock, revenues are diminishing. The federal government is responsible for about 25 percent of all transportation infrastructure funding. The rest is provided by state and local authorities. Much of the money from the federal government for roads, bridges, and mass transit is raised through a tax on various transport fuels. The federal tax rate on a gallon of gasoline has been 18.4 cents since 1993. The money generated from these taxes is then deposited into the Highway Trust Fund (HTF) and used to finance various transit projects throughout the country. But as fuel efficiency and gas prices have increased, fuel tax revenue has declined, meaning there's less and less money to invest in transport infrastructure.

Faced with the revenue shortfall, planners and politicians have been grappling with potential solutions. Due to the high price of gasoline, and a widespread aversion to raising taxes, an increase in the fuel tax does not seem likely. Like congestion pricing, revenue-generating measures that work in other nations may meet with resistance in the US. Some politicians have proposed a tax on oil producers, others a tax on miles driven. Regardless, these proposals have yet to be implemented and their future prospects are doubtful.

Public-private partnerships, as well as simple privatization initiatives, have been touted as solutions to the infrastructure-funding shortfall. In 2005, for example, Chicago entered into a partnership with a multinational consortium, leasing the Chicago Skyway toll road—and its maintenance—for the next 99 years in exchange for over $1.8 billion. Other states and municipalities have followed Chicago's lead, spinning off toll roads to private companies. These measures are somewhat controversial, with opponents wary of ceding public infrastructure to for-profit companies.

With government funds not forthcoming, many have suggested that an infrastructure bank might help raise the necessary financing for transport facilities. According to the latest proposal put forward by US President Barack Obama, the National Infrastructure Reinvestment Bank would borrow $60 billion in federal funds to finance infrastructure improvements throughout the nation. The bank would base its lending decisions on strict cost-benefit analyses carried out by experts, offering money only to the most-deserving initiatives—those likely to recoup the bank's investment—bringing a private-sector efficiency to public infrastructure. Supporters of the measure believe that the seed money provided by the government could catalyze up to a half a trillion dollars in private investment, revitalize the US transit grid, and create over a million jobs.

A European Investment Bank (EIB) is already in operation in the European Union (EU). A joint endeavor of all the EU states, the EIB holds hundreds of billions of dollars in capital with which it finances projects throughout the Eurozone. Before offering the loans to start a particular initiative, the EIB conducts a cost-benefit analysis, like the one envisioned in Obama's plan, to determine whether the endeavor is cost-effective and meets EU standards.

President Obama is not the first politician to champion a national infrastructure bank for the United States. Proposals have been bouncing around in Congress since 2007, and some states have created their own. The California Infrastructure and Economic Development Bank, or I-Bank, for example, has been in operation in varying capacities since 1994. Nevertheless, the current Congress has failed to act on the president's initiative.

The next several decades are important ones for American transport infrastructure. What sort of transportation grid will develop remains a matter of debate. Will the automobile retain its central role, or will mass transit and rail networks take up a larger share? Will we invest in first-class twenty-first-century transportation facilities, or will funding shortfalls and political gridlock leave us with a crumbling and obsolete twentieth-century system that is stretched beyond its limits? The answers to these questions will likely depend on how much the public and the politicians are willing to put up with, and what sort of solutions they are willing to fund.

Leap, Not Creep

Delivery and deployment of vanguard
technologies promise to lead the way to faster, safer,
better highway construction.

By Kathleen A. Bergeron
Public Roads, January/February 2008

In June 1956, President Dwight D. Eisenhower signed the law that brought about
the interstate system, one of the largest manmade structures in history. In 2006, the
highway community and Americans everywhere celebrated the golden anniversary
of this staggering engineering achievement. But many parts of this system of concrete, asphalt, and steel are now a half century old and beginning to show their age.

In August 2005, President George W. Bush signed into law the Safe, Accountable, Flexible, Efficient Transportation Equity Act: A Legacy for Users (SAFETEA-
LU). Among a number of other actions, the new law established a pilot program,
Highways for LIFE (HfL), to promote innovations and new technologies for building highways faster, safer, of better quality, and in a way that minimizes congestion—in short, to breathe new life into the interstate system and other parts of the
National Highway System.

Now, the Federal Highway Administration (FHWA) is advancing the HfL program, highlighting and deploying vanguard technologies to cut through the unfamil-
iarity, inertia, and other factors delaying adoption of leading-edge practices. FHWA
established dedicated teams with dedicated funding to market innovations to State
and local transportation stakeholders. The way the Nation's highways are built and
maintained could evolve significantly.

Need Is There, but Not the Money

From the day President Eisenhower signed the Federal-Aid Highway Act of 1956,
many of the pavements on the interstates were built for 20- to 25-year lifespans.
The designs of the day anticipated conditions that were much less demanding than
today's reality. Trucks are carrying heavier loads, and the sheer volume of traffic
using the system is several times greater than anticipated. As a result, the system
needs a makeover.

However, two cold facts stare that need in the face. First, funding for a nationwide construction effort is not there. Bringing the transportation system (including

highways) up to par would take some $50 billion in additional funding, according to a 2003 estimate by the American Public Works Association. Not only is that amount not available, but projections anticipate less, not more, funding in the future, based on current financing systems. The traditional approach of taxing gasoline on a per-gallon basis at the pump is less effective today than it used to be. In the past, when vehicles averaged 4.3 kilometers per liter (10 miles per gallon), a motorist could drive 161 kilometers (100 miles) on 38 liters (10 gallons) of gasoline. At a tax rate of 5 cents per gallon, that trip would generate 50 cents in taxes. Today, with vehicles getting 12.8 kilometers per liter (30 miles per gallon), that same 161-kilometer (100-mile) trip would generate only 17 cents. Vehicles powered by alternative fuels such as electricity are cutting that amount even more. Further, with gasoline prices near $3 per gallon, legislators are wary of proposing increases in fuel taxes, which have been the core of highway funding. That means just maintaining current spending levels will be a challenge.

Second, such a massive construction effort would have an enormous impact on the National Highway System, including countless work zones delaying commuters, freight haulers, and other travelers. Further, the potential for injuries to both workers and highway users would increase with the proliferation of new work zones. And the public already is showing signs of work zone fatigue. FHWA's most recent national driver survey revealed that the public's feelings about new highways have changed since the early days of the interstate program. Back in the 1950s and 1960s, when the interstate system was young, people clamored to have a section of the system built near their communities. The promise of being able to drive coast to coast without a stoplight was a strong draw.

Today, with highways experiencing problems with available capacity, the public equates new construction anywhere on the system with increased congestion, not less. According to *Moving Ahead: The American Public Speaks on Roadways and Transportation in Communities*, a 2001 report on findings from three national surveys performed by FHWA the year before, "A small but growing segment of the traveling public is dissatisfied with major highways. Both travel delays, which are due to traffic congestion and roadwork, and pavement conditions may contribute to this growing dissatisfaction . . . Work zones are especially critical as travelers view road repairs as a major reason for traffic delays."

The highway community is aware of motorists' perceptions. The logic follows that a way of building highways and bridges needs to be developed so that the impact on drivers is minimized, such as building them faster, in off hours, or away from the traveling public.

Another approach is to build highways to last longer and thus extend the interlude between one construction fix and the next. Safety is an ongoing concern for the public and the highway community; therefore, each construction project should incorporate the latest safety innovations as a matter of practice. Simply replicating a bridge or section of highway built decades ago might not be the best solution given current conditions. As in the past, cost is still a consideration. So the highway community needs a solution that incorporates all of these: roads built faster, safer, of better quality, and in a way that minimizes congestion—and at lower cost. All require one thing: innovation.

Lesson from the Past

Highway agencies have seen the benefits of innovations from their earliest days. In a 1999 article in *The New Yorker* magazine, Malcolm Gladwell, author of the book *The Tipping Point: How Little Things Can Make a Big Difference*, described the importance of the King Road Drag, a device that, at the turn of the last century, was used to smooth the ruts out of muddy rural roads. Smooth roadways provided access for the United States Postal Service®, which in turn brought the Sears, Roebuck and Co.™ catalog to people who had been isolated from much that the commercial world had to offer, from washing machines to the latest styles in clothing.

Thus, a small device for road grading created dramatic socioeconomic change in rural America. Wrote Gladwell: "Here was the dawn of the modern consumer economy . . . The [catalog], as economists have argued, represented a radical transformation in the marketing and distribution of consumer goods. But, of course, that transformation would not have been possible unless you had parcel post, and you couldn't have had parcel post unless you had rural free delivery, and you could not have had rural free delivery without good roads, and you would not have had good roads without D. Ward King [inventor of the drag]."

Barriers to Implementation

Today, highway research on technological advances is big business. The Federal Government itself spends a half billion dollars each year on highway research. These expenditures include work conducted at FHWA's Turner-Fairbank Highway Research Center (TFHRC), research by consultants and contractors, and scanning tours to other countries to identify innovations that might be used in the United States.

Hundreds of devices—from D. Ward King's King Road Drag, a device to smooth the ruts out of muddy rural roads, to the latest laser-guided paving machines—have been developed and put into use over the past century. But how long does it take for an innovation to move from the laboratory to state of the art to state of the practice? Experience shows the journey can take not months or years, but decades.

A good example is FHWA's experience implementing Superpave™ technology, which produces ideal asphalt pavements using "recipes" individualized for the particular climate requirements of an area. The effort to implement Superpave began in 1992; 12 years later, the 50th State adopted the approach, finally completing implementation.

The implementation process can take a long time for a number of reasons. One might be the familiar refrain: "That's the way it's always been done." Processes become locked into standard operating procedures until someone realizes there is a better way and breaks the mold. Reasons vary as to why the highway community historically has not been quick to adopt innovations. One is limited staffing and funding for technology transfer and for delivering information and training on innovations and technologies to potential users.

Several years ago, a contractor responsible for delivering hot-mix asphalt to a highway site wondered how he could reduce the delivery time. Then one night, while watching television, he saw a commercial for a pizza company that promised delivery in 30 minutes. The next morning, he called the company to find out how it made deliveries so fast. If the drivers could deliver pizzas within 30 minutes, he should be able to learn something from the restaurant chain about how to schedule drivers and plan routes. Specifically, the contractor learned where to get better maps and then hired college students to pencil in street numbers on the maps to speed delivery. The lesson here is that sometimes new and better approaches can come from someone with a totally different perspective.

The process of putting innovations into use costs money. Marketers know that persuading consumers to change their buying habits and try an innovative product is an extensive, costly process. So it is with the highway community. Suppose that a new design concept for a specific bridge is needed. At least two people need to be provided with knowledge: the State department of transportation (DOT) construction program manager, who will possibly need a cost-benefit analysis for selecting the new design; and a bridge engineer, who will want to see the concept in operation, on a real bridge built with the technique. Both will need training, the former in contracting for quality specifications for the new design and the latter on implementing the design onsite. There will be conferences, one-on-one discussions, and success stories in trade publications. Communications tools such as brochures, videos, and Web sites illustrating the benefits of the process could be helpful. All of that costs time and money.

Corporate Marketing Practices

One might well ask: Given the billions of dollars spent on highway research, how much money is dedicated specifically to getting innovations into everyday use by the various highway agencies, construction contractors, and consultants as they build and maintain America's highway infrastructure?

Major corporations likewise spend enormous sums on research and development (R&D) to come up with innovative products and services. But they also spend large sums persuading customers to buy those products and services, with a typical marketing budget being between 5 and 12 percent of gross revenues or corporate income. In many cases, those funds are expended through market research, product branding, and other targeted channels, including one-on-one sales, distribution and supply channels, or mass marketing techniques such as advertising or direct mail.

Just how high those costs can run is exemplified in the annual competition for attention via commercials on Super Bowl Sunday. The 2007 game set a new record at $2.6 million in advertising purchase costs for every time an advertisement aired for 30 seconds. The reason Super Bowl advertising costs are so high is that they promise one of the largest and most diverse audiences in the world.

Obviously, a large percentage of the budgets for making automobiles, breakfast cereals, laundry detergents, and other common goods is spent on marketing the product. But does that hold true in more research-intensive areas?

Perhaps the industry most noted for its R&D activities is computer technology and related hardware and software. Microsoft® might be the ultimate example in that industry. In its annual report for 2003, Microsoft noted that it spent $4.66 billion on R&D, but significantly more—$6.52 billion—on sales and marketing.

Clearly, corporate leaders understand that it makes little sense to spend billions of dollars developing a product if the buying public is not going to be made aware of it, adopt it, and use it. But the question remains: How much is spent on deploying highway innovations? The answer is: We don't know. Historically, deployment has not received the same recognition as R&D. That is where HfL comes into play.

Highways for LIFE

The HfL program came about after extensive market research by FHWA and passage of SAFETEA-LU. But what really got it started was publication of a special issue of *Public Roads* magazine in 2002.

Then-Deputy Secretary of Transportation Michael P. Jackson saw the July/August 2002 issue of *Public Roads*, which was dedicated to innovations in the use of concrete. The cover showed construction workers installing prefabricated concrete pavement slabs on the Tappan Zee Bridge toll plaza in Westchester County, NY, much as brick layers or tile workers might place flooring in a building or patio. Inside the issue were other innovations, from prefabricated bridges to self-consolidating concrete.

Jackson called the FHWA administrator and set up a meeting with engineering staff at TFHRC. The meeting was to be a simple 30-minute presentation, but it lasted 2 hours. At the end, Jackson told the group that he was impressed and that he saw the need to move innovations to implementation quickly as key to obtaining the highway system the Nation needed. He instructed the attendees to craft a plan for promoting such innovations. "Be bold and audacious in your thinking," he said.

The group looked at several approaches but wanted to solicit input from others in the highway community. In addition to numerous telephone calls, the group obtained input from representatives of State DOTs, trade associations, construction contractors, manufacturers, consulting engineers, and the driving public. Several sessions were attended by the U.S. Secretary of Transportation and the administrators of FHWA and the Federal Motor Carrier Safety Administration. Even in those early discussions, support was overwhelming for concepts that later would appear in HfL.

The Key to LIFE: Innovation

According to FHWA, the HfL program got its name from its purpose: "to advance Longer-lasting highway infrastructure using Innovations to accomplish the Fast construction of Efficient and safe highways and bridges." Innovation is a broad term that applies to all of the following: technologies, materials, tools, equipment, procedures and processes, specifications, methodologies, and practices used in the financing, design, or construction of highways.

A recent success story from Florida captures many of those elements. In 2006, the Florida Department of Transportation (FDOT) used prefabricated bridge elements and self-propelled modular transporters (SPMTs) to cut months off construction of the new Graves Avenue bridge in Volusia County. SPMTs are multiaxle, computer-controlled vehicles that can move in any horizontal direction while maintaining payload geometry and equal axle loads. In Florida, the SPMTs lifted the entire span of the old Graves Avenue bridge and moved it to the I-4 roadside—in just 22 minutes.

Two new concrete bridge spans then were built alongside I-4. After they were complete, they were installed over the highway using the SPMTs, reducing the need for road closures and disruptions to traffic. The first 43-meter (143-foot) span was installed over the westbound lanes of I-4 on June 4, with the second span installed over the eastbound lanes on June 10. The project marked the first time the SPMT technique was used in the United States to replace a bridge over an interstate highway.

"This accelerated construction technique allowed us to build the bridge's substructure and superstructure at the same time," says Amy Scales, resident engineer for FDOT's District 5. "We saved about 4 months over the course of this bridge project, greatly reducing the impact to drivers."

Instead of the weeks or months of lane closures and rolling roadblocks involved in traditional bridge building, FDOT detoured I-4 traffic for only 2 weekend nights and used roadblocks overnight on 2 nonconsecutive nights. The new bridge opened to traffic on August 7, 2006.

FDOT and FHWA hosted a delegation of about 100 transportation officials from across the United States and Canada at a June 9–11 conference in nearby DeLand, FL. Participants learned about the use of SPMTs for bridge construction and watched as the final span of the Graves Avenue bridge was installed.

Although initial costs of such projects can be higher, this can be offset by the reduced construction time and subsequent savings on personnel and traffic maintenance costs, as well as reductions in user costs. FDOT estimates that using the SPMTs cost an additional $560,000, but the shorter construction schedule resulted in $3 million in user savings.

"The project went well, and we would use SPMTs again," says Scales. "The technology is not for every project, but depending on the roadway, it can be worth it to speed up construction and get drivers back on the road sooner."

The HfL program, for example, includes provisions for studying how innovations currently are deployed and for finding ways of implementing them faster nationwide. Or, as FHWA Administrator J. Richard Capka calls it, moving to an approach that deploys innovations at the pace of a "leap, not creep." Faster implementation includes such steps as creating teams and plans for deploying specific technologies and then carrying those plans out; providing funding for State DOT projects that employ innovations; and working with private industry to develop nonhighway innovations for highway application.

Vanguard Technologies

When HfL leaders proposed faster deployment of highway innovations, they created three prototype teams to deploy vanguard technologies. The term "vanguard" was used because it represents the leading edge of a new approach. The specific technologies and practices the teams are promoting are prefabricated bridge elements and systems, road safety audits (RSAs), and techniques related to "making work zones work better."

HfL's purpose is not to develop new technologies; instead, it encourages adoption of high-payoff innovations that are available already but used infrequently.

Prefabricated bridge elements are manufactured away from or adjacent to the work zone and transferred to the construction site for installation. The prefabricated elements offer a variety of benefits, including faster implementation or construction cycles, decreased traffic disruption, improved work zone safety, greater durability, and, sometimes, lower construction costs. With RSAs, independent, multidisciplinary teams examine existing or future roadway sections to identify safety issues and opportunities for improvement. The concept of making work zones work better encompasses a suite of approaches that improve traffic flow and safety.

These innovations are dramatic changes in how highways are built, but the key for the HfL program is the process for deploying the technologies. HfL's purpose is not to develop new technologies; instead, it encourages adoption of high-payoff innovations that are available already but used infrequently.

What makes the vanguard approach different is that it is more aggressive than past deployment efforts. Rather than simply making a technology available, the teams develop marketing plans, create communications tools, and conduct activities such as one-on-one meetings, workshops, and product demonstrations for potential users. In addition, a guidebook on how to create a marketing plan for innovations was created and will be available through the "Highways for LIFE" Web site at www.fhwa.dot.gov/hfl.

Team members make deployment a job priority rather than a back-burner task they work on when time allows. They have funding for key elements such as training courses, manuals, and peer-to-peer programs.

Because of the high visibility of the teams in their respective disciplines, opportunities to partner with other groups have emerged. For example, the Technology Implementation Group within the American Association of State Highway and Transportation Officials is working with FHWA's RSA team, creating a synergy that promises even greater acceleration of deployment.

How successful has this approach been? The RSA effort, as an example, has generated results in dozens of States from Hawaii to New Hampshire in less than

3 years. The Arizona Department of Transportation, considered early on to be an "opportunity State," now has become the first State DOT to name a full-time RSA coordinator. The audit concept now is championed by local government agencies, law enforcement agencies, and a State attorney general's office. Other stakeholders, including the State Farm Insurance® company and American Automobile Association, are partnering with States and local communities to improve safety.

Likewise, prefabricated bridge elements and systems are being used across the country, with more States becoming involved all the time. Several product demonstrations have brought States' chief bridge engineers to construction sites to see how effective the technology can be, and many declare the approach to be something they definitely want to pursue. The work zone improvement effort is building a network of supporters as well, including a peer-to-peer program.

Now, another vanguard technology is being added. The new entry is prefabricated pavement slabs, the same technology featured on the cover of the issue of *Public Roads* magazine that started the HfL effort. This effort will be used as a training guide for others within FHWA, at State DOTs, and elsewhere in the highway community to learn the approach, with the first three technologies added as examples.

Ultimately, the goal of the HfL program is to dramatically improve the driving experience for Americans. Through rapid deployment of innovations, those improvements can be achieved sooner rather than later.

Repairs without Rivets

Carbon-fiber composites could
lead to quick fixes for old bridges

By David Appell
Scientific American, November 2007

Investigators still do not know exactly why the I-35 W bridge collapsed into the Mississippi River in Minneapolis on August 1, killing 13 people and injuring about 100. But a succession of less spectacular failures over the years has raised concern among the country's bridge engineers. New materials promise to make routine repairs less costly and intrusive, an important consideration in an era in which money for infrastructure is tight. "The days of letting a bridge deteriorate and then simply replacing it are going away," says Mark Hirota, a consultant with Parsons Brinckerhoff and a former bridge engineer for the state of Oregon.

According to a 2005 study by the American Society of Civil Engineers, 27.1 percent of the nation's bridges are either structurally deficient or functionally obsolete—a total of more than 160,000 bridges. The estimated cost to repair these bridges is almost $10 billion a year over the next 20 years. Built in 1967, the Minneapolis structure was a deck truss bridge with multiple steel girders and had been a concern among the state's transportation officials for years. After the collapse, U.S. Secretary of Transportation Mary Peters quickly called for an inspection of all the nation's steel truss bridges similar to the I-35 W span. A truss bridge, one of the oldest bridge types, is fairly simple in design and relatively cheap to build as compared with suspension and cable-stayed bridges, but engineers make no generalizations about types especially prone to sudden collapse.

Peters noted that initial inspections had raised concerns about stress on the I-35 W bridge's gusset plates, devices that attach steel girders together (with rivets, in the case of the Minneapolis bridge—other options are welds or bolts). She also cautioned states to carefully consider the added stress that repair and construction projects can place on a bridge. Some engineers have recently raised concerns about an incomplete understanding of how gusset plates tear out and fail, such as those expressed in a 2006 paper in the *Canadian Journal of Civil Engineering* by Robert G. Driver of the University of Alberta and his colleagues.

Cracks develop in steel girders and gusset plates because of fatigue and corrosion, and those as small as one eighth of an inch in width can lead to tearing and subsequent structural failure. Traditionally, engineers weld or bolt steel cover plates across these and larger cracks, but this approach has several disadvantages: it adds weight to the bridge, can require costly heavy machinery such as cranes, and often requires traffic diversions.

A possible quick-fix alternative is a new carbon-fiber-reinforced polymer. "It works almost like a Band-Aid," says Hamid Saadatmanesh, a professor of civil engineering at the University of Arizona. Saadatmanesh developed the material, called CarbonWrap, about six years ago and now sells it through CarbonWrap Solutions.

> *Traditionally, engineers weld or bolt steel cover plates across these and larger cracks, but this approach has several disadvantages: it adds weight to the bridge, can require costly heavy machinery such as cranes, and often requires traffic diversions.*

The polymer is made of woven filaments of glass, carbon and Kevlar, which are placed in a resin matrix. Its tensile strength—the force required to pull it apart—is about 200 tons per square inch, 10 times stronger than steel. The fiber costs $16 a pound and is attached to the bridge girders with a special epoxy. Patching a small girder crack would only cost about $200, including labor; doubling the layers increases the strength by about 30 percent.

"You don't need to drill holes," which can further weaken a structure, Saadatmanesh says. "Instead of taking eight hours" for a traditional patch, he adds, "you can do this in half an hour." In laboratory testing, Saadatmanesh says that CarbonWrap has held through the equivalent of about 10 million trips by a 35-ton truck. It resists corrosion, an important consideration given the galvanic currents that can be generated between metallic components on a bridge, and has withstood a pH 2.5 solution for two years. Steel would melt in just a few hours in such an acidic bath.

CarbonWrap has shored up water pipes and light poles, but it has yet to patch bridges—engineers are conservative by nature. "It takes a while to adopt a new thing," explains Taichiro Okazaki, a civil engineer at the University of Minnesota who is heading a team of researchers to examine the Minneapolis collapse. "New materials have to be very reliable, and it takes many years to develop trust." Bridge engineers have begun talking to Saadatmanesh's company, and Okazaki suggests that the first applications for CarbonWrap might be on small, lightly trafficked bridges, such as those found on golf courses. Such novel materials may play a crucial role in addressing the nation's aging infrastructure, although ultimately they cannot replace commitments to timely inspections, better designs and new bridges.

Maglev Ready for Prime Time

By Donald M. Rote and Larry R. Johnson
Issues in Science and Technology, June 2003

"Putting Maglev on Track" (*Issues,* Spring 1990) observed that growing airline traffic and associated delays were already significant and predicted that they would worsen. The article argued that a 300-mile-per-hour (mph) magnetic levitation (maglev) system integrated into airport and airline operations could be a part of the solution. Maglev was not ready for prime time in 1990, but it is now.

As frequent travelers know, air traffic delays have gotten worse, because the airport capacity problem has not been solved. As noted in the Federal Aviation Administration's (FAA's) 2001 Airport Capacity Enhancement Plan: "In recent years growth in air passenger traffic has outpaced growth in aviation system capacity. As a result, the effects of adverse weather or other disruptions to flight schedules are more substantial than in years past. From 1995 to 2000, operations increased by 11 percent, enplanements by 18 percent, and delays by 90 percent." With the heightened security that followed the September 11, 2001, terrorist attacks, ground delays have exacerbated the problem. The obvious way to reduce delays is to expand airport capacity, but expansion has encountered determined public opposition and daunting costs. The time is right to take a fresh look at maglev.

High-speed trains that travel faster than 150 mph have demonstrated their appeal in Europe and Asia. Although Amtrak has had some success with trains that go as fast as 125 mph on the Washington, D.C., to New York line, the United States has yet to build a true high-speed rail line. But interest is growing among transportation planners. Roughly half the states are currently developing plans for regional high-speed rail corridors. Pending congressional legislation would authorize $10 billion in bonds over 10 years to finance high-speed rail projects in partnerships with the states. However, due to the severe funding limitations, most of these projects are likely to pursue only incremental improvements in existing rail lines. Experience in Europe and Japan suggests that higher speeds are needed to lure passengers from planes and to attract new travelers.

Even though—or perhaps because—the Europeans and Japanese already have high-speed rail lines, they have been aggressively developing maglev systems. The Japanese built a new 12-mile maglev test track just west of Tokyo and achieved a maximum speed of 350 mph. They plan to extend the test track and make it part of a commercial line between Tokyo and Osaka. The German government approved the Transrapid System of maglev technology for development in the early 1990s and has been actively marketing the system for export. It recently announced funding of $2 billion to build a 50-mile route between Dusseldorf and Dortmund and a 20-mile connector linking Munich to its airport. Meanwhile, the Swiss have been developing a new approach for their Swiss Metro System, involving high-speed maglev vehicles moving in partially evacuated tunnels. China is building a maglev system to connect Shanghai with Pudong International Airport. This system should be in demonstration operation in 2003 and in revenue operation early in 2004.

The United States has also exhibited interest, but its progress has been slower. In 1990, the United States began a multiagency National Maglev Initiative that began with a feasibility analysis and was eventually to evolve into a development program. Although the initial analysis was promising, the effort was terminated in 1993 before any significant hardware development began. After a five-year hiatus, Congress passed the Transportation Equity Act for the 21st Century, which included a program to demonstrate a 40-mile maglev rail line, which could later be lengthened. Selection of a test site will be announced soon.

Maglev makes the most economic sense where there is already strong demand and where the cost of meeting this demand through expansion of existing infrastructure is expensive. Airports offer an appealing target. Current capital improvement projects at 20 major airports have a combined cost of $85 billion, enough to build 2,460 miles of maglev guideway at $35 million per double-track mile. This would be sufficient to connect maglev lines to airports in several parts of the country.

Maglev must also be compared with conventional high-speed rail. Maglev and high-speed rail costs are roughly equivalent for elevated guideways, the type of system most likely to be built. The added technology cost of maglev systems tends to be balanced by the fact that maglev vehicles weigh about one-half to one-third as much per seat as high-speed passenger trains, resulting in competitive construction costs. And because there is no physical contact between the train and the guideway in a maglev system, operation and maintenance costs are estimated to be between 20 and 50 percent less than what is required for high-speed rail systems. Maglev also has other advantages over rail systems: It takes up less space and has greater grade-climbing and turning capabilities, which permit greater flexibility in route selection; its superior speed and acceleration make it possible for fewer trains to serve the same number of people; and the greater speed will undoubtedly attract more passengers.

Lessons Learned

After looking at the progress of the technology, the history of U.S. government involvement in transportation infrastructure, and the experience of other countries that have begun maglev development, we arrived at the following key conclusions:

Performance: Speed counts. Ridership on ground transportation systems increases markedly with speeds that enable trips to be completed in times that are competitive with airline travel. Amtrak's incremental improvements don't cut it.

Economics: Maglev is cost-competitive with high-speed rail, yet provides greater speed, more flexibility, and the capability to integrate with airline/airport operations.

> *The added technology cost of maglev systems tends to be balanced by the fact that maglev vehicles weigh about one-half to one-third as much per seat as high-speed passenger trains, resulting in competitive construction costs.*

The physical connection to the airport is a necessary first step, but the benefits of maglev will not be realized until the next step is taken: integrating maglev with airline operations.

Government role: If maglev is to be a part of the solution to airport congestion, the advocate agency should be the FAA or the Federal Highway Administration, since maglev would primarily be accommodating air and highway travelers.

Public-private partnership: Private industry has long been a willing partner in development and deployment, but the federal government needs to demonstrate a long-term commitment if the private sector is expected to participate. In 1997, the Maglev Study Advisory Committee was congressionally mandated to evaluate near-term applications of maglev technology in the United States. The committee made the following recommendations for government action: a federal commitment to develop maglev networks for passenger and freight transportation, with the government as infrastructure provider and the private sector as operator; federal support for two or three demonstration projects; and federal or state funding for guideways and private financing for the vehicles, stations, and operating and maintenance costs.

Benefits of early deployment: The United States needs to have one or two operating systems to convince the nation that the technology is practical and to identify areas for improvement, such as new electronic components and magnetic materials, new aircraftlike lightweight vehicle body designs, new manufacturing and installation methods, and innovative civil construction techniques and materials.

Research: The nation needs long-term federal support for transportation system planning and R&D activities. In addition, since it is impractical to conduct R&D activities on a commercial line, it will be necessary to design a national test facility where innovations that affect system cost and performance can be fully evaluated under carefully controlled and safe conditions. This is no different from the research approach that other transportation modes have developed.

Fresh thinking: Maglev may best be thought of as an entirely new mode of transportation. It is neither a low-flying airplane nor a very fast locomotive-drawn train. It has many attributes that, if fully exploited, will provide speed, frequency, and reliability unlike any extant mode. It will add mobility even in adverse weather conditions and without the adverse effects of added noise and air pollution and increased dependence on foreign oil. If integrated with airline operations, it will augment rather than compete with the airlines for intercity travelers and will decrease the need for further highway expansion. It can be incorporated into local transit systems to improve intracity mobility and access to airports.

The future of high-speed ground transportation in the United States can be a bright one. If implemented appropriately, maglev presents the opportunity to break the frustrating cycle in which modest infrastructure improvements produce only a minimal ridership increase that results in disappointing financial performance and a call for additional incremental funding. Successful implementation of just one U.S. maglev project should open the door to an alternative to the cycle of frustration. Government should be an active partner in this process.

❖

Donald M. Rote (don@anl.gov) is a senior researcher and Larry R. Johnson (johnson@anl.gov) is director at the Transportation Technology R&D Center at Argonne National Laboratory.

Cars: Enriching Our Lives, Our Economy and Our Future

"Cleaner air, a healing planet and friendly futuristic cars"

By Jim Lentz,
Vital Speeches of the Day, February 2010

Address by Jim Lentz, President, Toyota Motor Sales, U.S.A. Delivered at the Commonwealth Club, San Francisco, Calif., Nov. 17, 2009

Thank you . . . and good evening everyone.

Let's imagine for a moment that a very strange thing happens tonight.

While we're fast asleep . . . all the cars on earth completely disappear.

Unaware, you come out in the morning to get in your car and it's gone . . . there's nothing there . . . and no sign that it ever existed.

And you're not alone. Your neighbors experience the same thing . . . and you find out from the news that the same thing has happened to every car and truck . . . all over the world.

What would you do? . . .

How would you get to work? . . .

How would you get the kids to school? . . .

How would you go grocery shopping . . . or get rushed to the hospital . . . ?

Suddenly . . . the American Way of life you enjoy . . . is completely gone.

And what if there was no quick solution?

Imagine the changes you'd have to make . . . the strain it would put on your relationships . . . your pocketbook . . . your future plans . . . your teenagers trying to get to the mall? . . .

And you wouldn't be alone.

Society . . . as we know it . . . would be challenged to the max.

Travel would be extremely difficult . . . commerce strained . . . and limited options would become a way of life.

In short, our world would be turned upside down.

***

OK . . . let's snap out of this imaginary nightmare now . . . and come back to the present were everything is just fine.

When we're finished here tonight, your reliable car will start . . . keep you warm . . . and take you home to your loved ones.

I tell you this story because it vividly illustrates the *crucial* role the automobile plays in our lives.

No other product in American life does so much for us. It's the key connection to our lifestyle . . . and to our world.

And since we can't live without it, we need to figure out a way to live with it . . . in harmony with our environment and our planet.

And that's what I want to talk about tonight . . . the vital impact cars make on our lives . . . the economy . . . and our future. And what we . . . as automakers . . . are doing to make sure they're a benefit . . . and not a burden . . . to society.

***

First . . . let me just say that I'm honored to speak to the Commonwealth Club of California . . . the first and biggest . . . public affairs forum in the United States.

In this world of rushed communication and sound bites, the Commonwealth Club is an oasis of sanity, clarity and understanding. You provide a public service by showing us the value of face-to-face communications.

And, you are a heck of a lot of fun, too.

I mean . . . where else can you come hear the director of the CIA . . . or discuss "Freakanomics" . . . or learn how to reinvent your body from Deepak Chopra?

And that's just a few of your speakers . . . last month!

You help to make the Bay Area one of the foremost places for progressive thinking in the world.

I know, because I used to live here. I managed Toyota's regional sales office here from 1995 to 2000 . . . and it was a marvelous experience for me, my wife and our two sons.

Ahhh . . . life in San Francisco . . . I remember that finding a downtown parking space . . . near your destination . . . could move you to tears . . .

In addition, I love this area because it is the "Hybrid Car Capital of the World."

And more hybrids are sold here than anywhere else.

In fact, the Bay Area accounts for more than 1 out of every 10 hybrids bought in this country. And, 3 out of the top 10 Prius dealers are based here, including nearby San Francisco Toyota.

So thank you for that!

You're showing the rest of the world that cars can . . . and are . . . changing for the better and living more in harmony with the environment.

***

I began tonight by making the case that cars play a crucial role in our lives everyday . . . but it goes much deeper than that.

A few years back, a poll found that Americans love their cars so much that they: talk to them . . . name them . . . adorn them with trinkets . . . and involve them in life's most significant events.

In fact, 90% of respondents admitted singing in their cars . . . more than half said they talk to their cars . . . and 1 in 4 give their cars nicknames.

And that love affair between people and their cars continues.

Recently, Roper Reports conducted a poll with Americans on what they were willing to give up during the recession.

And guess what?

People said they were less willing to give up the convenience of their cars than their televisions, cell phones, Blackberries or vacations.

Why that kind of reaction?

Well, I think it's because the automobile is one of the most liberating inventions of all time. A car gives us the means and freedom to go anywhere . . . any time . . . for any reason.

In short, cars enrich our lives.

Or . . . as the Army says . . . cars allow you to "Be All That You Can Be."

***

Cars not only make an enormous impact on our personal lives, they make a huge impact on the economy.

America's auto industry is the engine that drives the economy.

No other single industry supports U.S. manufacturing as much or generates more retail sales or employment.

Nearly 4% of the U.S. domestic product is auto related . . . and auto suppliers operate in all 30 states to produce some of the 3,000 parts used in cars today.

And the auto industry is responsible for 1 out of every 10 U.S. jobs . . . They're good-paying jobs, with workers receiving $333 billion per year in compensation. Let's put that in perspective.

That's more than the total market value of the world's most profitable company . . . Exxon Mobil.

And that's not all. Automakers and suppliers are among the largest purchasers of steel . . . aluminum . . . rubber . . . textiles . . . and computer chips in the world.

In fact, with 25 to 70 microchip control units in today's cars, the auto industry rivals the computer industry in the use of computer chips.

In Toyota's case, the breadth of our presence here and our economic impact on the American economy surprises a lot of people.

We are celebrating our 52nd year in the U.S. and now operate 14 manufacturing plants in North America . . . a design studio in California . . . a state-of-the-art test track in Arizona . . . and an R&D center in Michigan that we recently expanded to accommodate 1,000 engineers.

A few years back, a poll found that Americans love their cars so much that they: talk to them ... name them ... adorn them with trinkets ... and involve them in life's most significant events.

Today, Toyota's total investment in the United States stands at $18.2 billion . . . and we directly employ nearly 34,000 Americans . . . more than General Mills . . . Texas Instruments . . . or Mattel.

And when you add dealer, supplier and "spin off" jobs . . . the Michigan-based Center for Automotive Research says Toyota contributes more than 380,000 American jobs . . . equal to a city the size of Miami.

***

Let me take a moment here to acknowledge that Toyota realizes the upcoming closure of the NUMMI auto plant in nearby Fremont is a blow to this area.

We didn't want to stop ordering products from there . . . we've had a good 23-year relationship with the union . . . Bay area workers . . . and local communities.

Unfortunately, when General Motors abruptly pulled out of the joint venture in August, it severely undermined the economic viability of the plant and precipitated this situation. To their credit, state and Bay Area agencies went out of their way to offer help, but the numbers still didn't add up.

So it was an extremely tough decision . . . and we've taken some lumps for it.

However, we believe in doing our part.

So although NUMMI is an independent company, Toyota *will* work cooperatively with the plant and local agencies where appropriate and where it can to help NUMMI provide transition support to team members, suppliers and the community.

And while NUMMI may be closing, Toyota remains *heavily* invested in California, with sales and production facilities up and down the state. In total, Toyota has invested more than $2.3 billion in the Golden State . . . and along with our dealers . . . we employ 28,000 people here.

And our contributions to this state and country go way beyond employment numbers.

Our highly regarded Toyota Production System . . . which we openly share with anyone who asks . . . has been widely adopted by hospitals, airports and even churches so they can operate more efficiently.

And our sales associates here in America contribute their own money generously to various charities as part of an annual corporate campaign. Results just came in from this year's campaign . . . and during a very difficult time financially . . . our associates, along with company matching donations, raised more than $2.8 million to help others in need.

And our team members at our manufacturing facilities are also generous. For example, our production employees at our big Kentucky plant typically join with the company to contribute $1 million per year to the local United Way.

Our employees also volunteer generously of their personal time to help many worthwhile non-profit groups. In fact, we estimate that Toyota associates across the country volunteer more than 116,000 hours each year to charity.

So . . . when you add it all up . . . there are very few industries in this world that pack the economic punch and nontangible benefits the auto industry does.

And we aren't the only nation to recognize that.

Great Britain . . . Germany . . . Italy . . . and Japan . . . all rose to economic prominence by fostering a strong automotive industry.

That's why Brazil, Russia, India and China . . . the so-called BRIC countries . . . are plowing money into their fledgling auto industries.

These nations know that the auto industry is a powerful economic driver that provides mobility for people and commerce *and* creates long-term prosperity.

And it's a smart bet.

A recent Booz & Company report notes that when per capita income rises in developing countries, rates of car ownership increase, thus improving personal income and stimulating further economic development.

And Brazil, Russia, India and China may soon have company.

The Booz study says Argentina, Indonesia, Mexico, Thailand and Turkey are also on the verge of much greater car ownership.

So there's lots of opportunity for auto industry growth in the future.

But that expansion creates a dilemma for us as a society.

How do we provide mobility that will free people to be more successful *without* permanently damaging the planet we all love?

Well, that leads me to my third key point of the night . . . that cars will play a vital role in our future.

We know we won't give them up, but we also know we can't continue on the same automotive path we've followed for the past century.

The first 100 years of the auto industry were about expansion and exploration . . . the second century is about innovation and harmony.

Since we can't live with cars in their current form . . . and we can't live without the benefits they bring . . . we have to find a better way.

And that's what Toyota and other major automakers are doing today . . . developing better cars and other creative mobility solutions.

To do that, we're concentrating on two critical areas . . . increasing fuel economy and reducing emissions that harm our planet.

On air pollution, we're making great progress. Using various technologies and cleaner fuels, cars today are 99% cleaner than those from the 1970s.

Yes . . . you heard right . . . 99%!

But what about CO_2 and other greenhouse gases?

Well, let's talk about that for a minute.

Some people believe that automobiles are the worst offenders on CO_2 . . . but that's not the case.

In the United States, autos account for about 17% of all man-made carbon dioxide emissions, or less than one-fifth of the total.

That's not low enough, but it is important to understand that . . . although cars and trucks are one of the most visible sources of greenhouse gases in America . . . they are *not* the major contributor.

Toyota has long supported global, economy-wide reductions of greenhouse gases, and we are committed to working with the U.S. and other governments to achieve these reductions in every market where we operate.

And our industry, as a whole, recently made a strong commitment to cut greenhouse gases by committing to achieve higher federal mileage standards.

We'll do that by burning less gas because CO_2 emissions are directly related to fuel consumption. Higher mileage means less carbon dioxide coming out of tail-pipes. How much less?

Our industry is committed to 30% reduction by 2020 . . . nearly one-third less than today's emissions. Think about that for a minute.

That's equivalent to closing 50 mid-sized coal-fired power plants . . . 50!

Now, before I get any letters from the coal industry, let me acknowledge that they are working hard on clean-burning technology.

In any event, the auto industry is making a sizable commitment that will make it a leader in the reduction of CO_2.

And we're not stopping there.

The auto industry spends $86 billion per year on Research and Development . . . more than any other manufacturing industry. And I'm proud to note that Toyota is ranked by Booz & Company as the No. 1 corporation in R&D, spending $9 billion a year . . . or an average of more than $1 million per hour.

Even better, our industry's massive research is starting to pay off.

According to the Alliance of Automobile Manufacturers, there are more than 50 technologies available this year . . . 2009 . . . that reduce emissions. . . . increase mileage . . . or allow vehicles to run on clean fuels.

They range from variable valve timing and stratified charge combustion to superchargers . . . direct injection . . . and sophisticated gas/electric hybrids found in vehicles like our Prius.

In fact, . . . according to the recently released federal Fuel Economy Guide . . . in 2010, consumers can select from more than 193 cars and trucks that achieve 30 miles per gallon or greater on the highway . . . a 47% increase over 2009!

* * *

So where do we go from here?

Well, one of our first assignments as an industry is to keep refining the internal combustion engine to make it as efficient as possible. Right now, automotive engineers in labs around the world are tinkering with refinements that will help gas engines eke out even more mileage than today's super-efficient models.

Beyond that, the auto industry will introduce dozens of new gas/electric hybrids and advanced diesels over the next few years. Those will save even more fuel and further reduce harmful emissions.

I've talked about how clean today's cars are compared to those of the '70s. But, did you know that the Prius emits 70% fewer smog-forming emissions than the average new vehicle on the road today?

It's true . . . so imagine what can be done when all major automakers start selling more hybrids. And you know that day is coming because Porsche, Lamborghini and Ferrari are all reportedly building hybrid models.

After that, you'll see plug-in hybrids. . . . pure electric cars . . . and eventually hydrogen fuel cell vehicles.

Yes, we still need to work out some difficult issues with all those power trains in terms of technical hurdles . . . cost . . . range . . . and fuel and charging stations . . . but the potential is very real.

In fact, Toyota will launch a lithium-ion battery Prius plug-in program early next year.

And I'm proud to announce tonight that some of the 150 plug-in hybrids we'll bring to the United States will go to work . . . right here . . . in the Bay Area.

We know this area supports environmentally advanced vehicles and we need your help to perfect our product for consumer use down the road.

The auto industry is also making great progress on hydrogen fuel cell vehicles that create electricity from hydrogen and oxygen without generating any harmful emissions.

The industry is exploring all these technological fronts because there is no one solution for future mobility needs, but the need for many.

After all, what's good for the Bay Area, may not be the best for Shanghai, or Sydney, or Sao Paulo.

* * *

Now, along with developing better products, Toyota and other automakers are taking a more holistic approach to future mobility.

We know it's not just about the car anymore, but how the car can work in harmony with diverse modes of transportation ranging from single-person pods to high speed, magnetic levitation trains.

To do that, Toyota is addressing four key areas that will help us achieve sustainable mobility.

First . . . we must address the vehicles themselves . . . and I've talked a lot tonight about the progress we've been making on this front.

Second . . . we must address the urban environment where these new technologies will live. In the future, we foresee "mixed mobility" combining intelligent highways and mass transit . . . bike and walking paths . . . shared vehicles . . . recharging kiosks . . . and hydrogen fuel stations.

Third, we must address the need to develop public/private partnerships that will include energy and transportation companies along with universities and government agencies working together to help bring new technologies to market.

For example, Toyota recently joined the SmartGridCity Project . . . a public/private partnership in Boulder, Colorado . . . the first . . . fully functioning . . . smart-grid city in the world.

This large-scale effort is using improvements in electrical generation and real-time communications to help homes and businesses use electricity more efficiently. And that includes the charging of 10 Prius plug-in hybrids we're providing to the project.

By working in partnership with Xcel Energy . . . the federal National Renewable Energy Lab . . . and the University of Colorado, we'll be able to determine vehicle charging patterns . . . how the vehicles interact with the electrical grid . . . and customer expectations that will help us develop future plug-ins and pure electric vehicles.

The Boulder project will also help us tackle the fourth key area of sustainable mobility . . . addressing the energy that will power advanced-technology vehicles.

Here, there are a lot of questions to be answered.

Is the electrical grid we use powered by fossil fuels or renewable sources?

Is it strong enough to charge many vehicles at once . . . and will people have access to charging stations while at work or on the road?

What's the future of bio fuels?

Can a hydrogen re-fueling system be created?

We must address all these areas as we develop tomorrow's transportation systems.

And the answers won't come easy.

Good answers never do.

But where there is a will . . . there is a way.

So tonight, I'm asking you to join with us to help cocreate a future where people, cars and the earth live and work in greater harmony.

A future where transportation allows people to reach their potential without destroying our planet.

A future that includes better cars . . . more fuel efficient trucks . . . hybrids and electric cars . . . fuel cells and light rail . . . shared rides and other modes of transportation we haven't even invented yet.

And a future filled not with the pain of oil dependence, air pollution and global warming . . . but with cleaner air, a healing planet and friendly futuristic cars.

It's not a dream . . . it's possible . . . it really is possible. So . . . let's work together . . . let's keep moving forward . . . and let's create a better future for ourselves, our families and society.

Thank you.

Bilbliography

❖

The following books and articles provide additional information on this subject. Most of the noted articles are available on EBSCOhost databases.

Akers, Becky. "Railroading Passengers." *New American* 26.12 (2010): 33–37. Print.

Brooks, Davis. "The Paralysis of the State." *New York Times* 12 Oct. 2010: A31. Print.

Brown, Stuart F. "Revolutionary RAIL." *Scientific American* May 2010: 54–59. Print.

Budiansky, Stephen. "The Physics of Gridlock." *Atlantic Monthly* Dec. 2000: 20–24. Print.

Caldwell, Stephen L. "Protecting Energy on the Water." *Journal of International Peace Operations* 7.3 (2011): 12–16. Print.

Caruso, Lisa. "Asleep at the Switch on Aviation Reform?" *National Journal* 5 June 2010: 1. Print.

———. "Pushback on Air Auctions." *National Journal* 3 May 2008: 13. Print.

Cary, Mary Kate. "Feds Should Get Out of the Way on Air Travel." *US News Digital Weekly* 15 July 2011: 14. Print.

"Cities Should Embrace Power of the Pedal." *USA Today Magazine* 1 Aug. 2010: 15. Print.

Fitch, Stephane, and Joann Muller. "The Troll Under the Bridge." *Forbes* 15 Nov. 2004. Print.

Goldberger, Paul. "Situation Terminal." *New Yorker* 21 Apr. 2008: 132–34. Print.

Kingsbury, Alex. "Mass Transit Systems Have a Hard Time Paying the Bills." *US News & World Report* 4 Apr. 2008: 25–26. Print.

Leinberger, Christopher B. "Here Comes the Neighborhood." *Atlantic Monthly* June 2010: 58–61. Print.

"Life in the Slow Lane." *Economist* 30 Apr. 2011: 29–31. Print.

Longman, Phillip. "Back on Tracks." *Washington Monthly* Jan./Feb. 2009: 24–30. Print.

Mau, Bruce. "Urbanity, Revised." *World Policy Journal* 27.4 (2010): 17–22. Print.

Murray, Charles J. "The Biggest Thing in Safety." *Design News* 2 June 2008: 58–62. Print.

O'Toole, Randal. "The Real Threat to America's Infrastructure." *Liberty* 1 June 2009. Print.

Pacella, Rena Marie. "The System of the World." *Popular Science* Aug. 2011: 58–65. Print.

Pike, John. "Black Hole of Boston." *Insight on the News* 10 Dec. 2002: 18. Print.

Rendell, Ed. "Honorable Ed Rendell." *Congressional Digest* Apr. 2011: 120–26. Print.

Reutter, Mark. "Bullet Trains for America?" *Wilson Quarterly* 33.4 (2009): 26–33. Print.

Ripley, Amanda. "We've Come Undone." *Time* 20 Aug. 2007: 38–39. Print.

Rivera, Liliana. "Shipping on the Panama Canal." *Americas Quarterly* 5.2 (2011). Print.

Savage, Luiza Ch. "Third World America." *Maclean's* 20 Sept. 2010: 30–34. Print.

Sullivan, Will. "Road Warriors." *US News & World Report* 7 May 2007: 42–49. Print.

Utt, Ronald. "Heritage Foundation." *Congressional Digest* Apr. 2011: 117–27. Print

Wilson, Bill. "Holes in the System." *Roads & Bridges* Apr. 2008: 20–29. Print.

———. "The Spirit of Bridge Building." *Roads & Bridges* Nov. 2001: 26. Print.

Web Sites

❖

United States Department of Transportation
http://www.dot.gov/

The U.S. Department of Transportation is the federal office in charge of overseeing all federal transportation programs. It was founded in 1966 and has a requested budget of $74 billion for fiscal year 2013.

Transportation for America
http://t4america.org/

Transportation for America is a network of political, business, state, and local advocates who work together to promote transportation plans for communities, states, and the nation. Its primary focus is on maintaining and repairing roads and bridges that are structurally deficient or functionally obsolete.

American Public Transportation Association
http://www.apta.com/Pages/default.aspx

APTA is an advocacy group focused on improving access to public transportation around the United States. It is composed of public organizations that operate buses, light rail services, commuter rails, and other public transportation systems.

The Brookings Institution
http://www.brookings.edu/topics/transportation.aspx

The Brookings Institution is a nonprofit think tank that conducts research on a wide range of public policy–related subjects. Its research related to transportation infrastructure is consistently ranked as the most frequently quoted and most influential in the United States among all nonprofit organizations.

Economic Policy Institute
http://www.epi.org/research/public-investment/

The Economic Policy Institute (EPI) is a nonprofit think tank that primarily focuses on issues related to those who earn a below-average income. Its research related to transportation and public investments frequently advocates for policies that will benefit the poor.

The Heritage Foundation

http://www.heritage.org/issues/transportation

The Heritage Foundation is a research institution that publishes a wide range of reports, fact sheets, and commentaries. Its publications related to transportation generally support increased state and local control over infrastructure projects rather than top-down projects from the federal government.

The Reason Foundation

http://reason.org/areas/topic/transportation

The Reason Foundation, a libertarian think tank, publishes materials ranging from popular magazines to scholarly reports, as well as its own internet television channel. Its publications related to transportation frequently discuss city planning problems and budget-related solutions.

Index

About the Editor

❖

Tyler Weidler was born and raised in Pennsylvania, graduated from Pennsylvania State University, and currently resides in Gettysburg. He has worked for EBSCO Publishing since 2008 and edits the Points of View Reference Center databases for the United States, Canada, Australia, and New Zealand. These databases focus on current issues and events relevant to each country and provide useful reference information for debate clubs.